TEEN EDITION

PREVAIL

TEEN EDITION

PREVAIL

365 DAYS OF GROWING IN GOD'S LOVE AND STRENGTH

SUSIE LARSON

WITH **CARRA CARR**

BETHANYHOUSE

a division of Baker Publishing Group
Minneapolis, Minnesota

© 2020, 2024 by Susie Larson

Published by Bethany House Publishers
Minneapolis, Minnesota
BethanyHouse.com

Bethany House Publishers is a division of
Baker Publishing Group, Grand Rapids, Michigan

Printed in China

ISBN 9780764243356 (cloth)
ISBN 9780764243950 (ebook)

Library of Congress Control Number: 2023053579

Cover design by Megan Kilgore

Susie Larson is represented by The Steve Laube Agency.

Baker Publishing Group publications use paper produced from sustainable forestry practices and postconsumer waste whenever possible.

24   25   26   27   28   29   30   7   6   5   4   3   2   1

Dedicated to my longtime friend
and pillar in the publishing industry,
Andy McGuire.
I have no words to express how much
I respect and appreciate you, Andy.
You've profoundly impacted my life.
And this book was one of your many great ideas.
May it grow wings and ignite a revival
in the hearts of many young people.
I know that's your heart,
and it's most certainly my prayer.
Thank you, my friend.

Table of Contents
by Subject

A healthy thought life

Day 16 • Day 236 • Day 300

Amazing grace

Day 34 • Day 104 • Day 110 • Day 133 •
Day 175 • Day 211

Be grateful

Day 13 • Day 92

Be strong and courageous

Day 37 • Day 135 • Day 145

Believe for more

Day 28 • Day 146 • Day 197 • Day 243

Deal with fear

Day 14 • Day 27 • Day 33 • Day 101 •
Day 137 • Day 166 • Day 307 • Day 316 •
Day 352

Deal with sin

Day 6 • Day 32 • Day 36 • Day 39 •
Day 119 • Day 128 • Day 149 • Day 173 •
Day 184 • Day 225 • Day 233 • Day 262 •
Day 276 • Day 325 • Day 337

Delivered from sin

Day 299

Discernment

Day 31 • Day 124 • Day 148 • Day 155 •
Day 249 • Day 252 • Day 312

Faith amid opposition

Day 25 • Day 26 • Day 44 • Day 113 •
Day 191

Forget competition

Day 23 • Day 157 • Day 320 • Day 335

Free from people's opinions

Day 29 • Day 53 • Day 54 • Day 64 •
Day 65 • Day 87 • Day 232 • Day 235 •
Day 247 • Day 274 • Day 283

Future glory

Day 45 • Day 207 • Day 309 • Day 347 •
Day 358 • Day 362

Future reward

Day 50 • Day 51 • Day 143 • Day 228 •
Day 278 • Day 306 • 350 • Day 364

God delights in you

Day 18 • Day 59 • Day 136 • Day 147 •
Day 177 • Day 215 • Day 254 • Day 287 •
Day 292 • Day 348 • Day 357

God is faithful

Day 12 • Day 35 • day 126 • Day 142 •
Day 169 • Day 248 • Day 331

God provides

Day 34 • Day 48 • Day 49 • Day 74 •
Day 111 • Day 222 • Day 230 • Day 259 •
Day 273 • Day 284

God-given assignment

Day 5 • Day 30 • Day 60 • Day 108 •
Day 109 • Day 181 • Day 216 • Day 340

God's favor and power

Day 41 • Day 150 • Day 176 • Day 217 •
Day 257 • Day 289 • Day 310 • Day 318 •
Day 323 • Day 334

God's power to deliver

Day 11 • Day 14 • Day 69 • Day 127 •
Day 188 • Day 189 • Day 342 • Day 351

God's power to heal

Day 83 • Day 152 • Day 161 • Day 267 •
Day 277 • Day 288 • Day 328

God's power to restore

Day 47 • Day 86 • Day 131 • Day 178 •
Day 186 • Day 297

God's untamable power

Day 15 • Day 90 • Day 218 • Day 256 •
Day 271 • Day 353 • Day 358

Guard your heart

Day 2 • Day 33 • Day 56 • Day 93 •
Day 130 • Day 164 • Day 174 • Day 183 •
Day 266 • Day 319 • Day 324 • Day 361

His coming kingdom

Day 98 • Day 227 • Day 301 • Day 362 •
Day 363 • Day 365

How God grows us (maturity)

Day 55 • Day 58 • Day 64 • 148 • Day 180 •
Day 182 • Day 345 • Day 354

Judge your judgments

Day 59 • Day 61 • Day 122 • Day 159 •
Day 242 • Day 343 • Day 351

Leadership

Day 43 • Day 91 • Day 114

Let Him lead

Day 1 • Day 97 • Day 105 • Day 123 • Day 154 • Day 176 • Day 295

Love your enemies

Day 8 • Day 268

Powerful prayers

Day 19 • Day 75 • Day 88 • Day 193 • Day 258 • Day 311 • Day 313

Prophetic insight

Day 73 • Day 102 • Day 199 • Day 201 • Day 212

Protection from the enemy

Day 94 • Day 95 • Day 120 • Day 144 • Day 336 • Day 352

Provision and promotion

Day 49 • Day 62 • Day 67 • Day 134 • Day 190 • Day 192 • Day 226

Rest and replenishment

Day 7 • Day 20 • Day 22 • Day 116 • Day 160 • Day 326

Second chances

Day 153 • Day 205

Sharing your faith

Day 10 • Day 34 • Day 115 • 200 • Day 231 • Day 290 • Day 321

Shining in the darkness

Day 9 • Day 11 • Day 213 • Day 298 • Day 344

Spiritual practices and priorities

Day 13 • Day 26 • Day 72 • Day 121 • Day 282 • Day 308 • Day 327 • Day 360

Spiritual warfare

Day 25 • Day 57 • Day 132 • Day 296

Stay in awe

Day 38 • Day 52 • Day 71 • Day 78 • Day 138 • Day 208 • Day 263

Stay the course

Day 10 • Day 16 • Day 68 • Day 76 • Day 103 • Day 107 • Day 315 • Day 330 • Day 346

The peace of God

Day 85 • Day 168 • Day 172 • Day 198 • Day 210 • Day 219 • Day 303

The power of humility

Day 23 • Day 24 • Day 29 • Day 40 • Day 125 • Day 339 • Day 341

The power of perseverance

Day 17 • Day 139 • Day 229 • Day 317 • Day 338

The power of prayer

Day 24 • Day 76 • Day 81 • Day 96 • Day 214 • Day 329 • Day 349 • Day 355 • Day 359

The power of the gospel

Day 167 • 171 • Day 221 • Day 240 • Day 246 • Day 255 • Day 359

The promises of God

Day 3 • Day 80 • Day 220 • Day 264 • Day 327

There is freedom

Day 42 • Day 63 • Day 162 • Day 162 • Day 224 • Day 247 • Day 250 • Day 253 • Day 280 • Day 293 • Day 337 • Day 346

Time for reflection

Day 4 • Day 100 • Day 129 • Day 158 • Day 165 • Day 275 • Day 314

Unbelief

Day 269

When you're stuck

Day 15 • Day 77 • Day 81 • Day 106 • Day 270 • Day 304

When your self-life shows (anger, jealousy, competition, apathy)

Day 30 • Day 32 • Day 46 • Day 79 • Day 151 • Day 202 • Day 203 • Day 206 • Day 260 • Day 356

When God corrects

Day 187 • Day 204 • Day 209 • Day 238 • Day 251 • Day 328 • Day 332

Whom God uses

Day 10 • Day 21 • Day 84 • Day 156 • Day 194 • Day 223 • Day 237 • Day 241 • Day 272 • Day 279 • Day 311 • Day 322 • Day 363

Wilderness seasons

Day 14 • Day 82 • Day 170 • Day 185 • Day 196 • Day 269 • Day 331

Wisdom

Day 70 • Day 112 • Day 179 • Day 295 • Day 314 • Day 333

Worry

Day 140 • Day 245

You are called

Day 1 • Day 99 • Day 117 • Day 291 • Day 294 • Day 305 • Day 344

You be you (a work in progress)

Day 66 • Day 141 • Day 195 • Day 239 • Day 261 • Day 265 • Day 281 • Day 286 • Day 302

Your authority in Christ

Day 89 • Day 118 • Day 234 • Day 244 • Day 285 • Day 336 • Day 349

Introduction

Have you ever been to an amusement park or fair with rides? Most of the bigger, more mature rides have a sign that says, "You Must Be This Tall to Ride" with a line indicating a certain height. To drive, you must be sixteen years old. To vote or join the armed forces, you have to be eighteen. Maybe your parents have set age or grade requirements for getting your ears pierced, dating, playing sports, or getting a job. Everywhere you turn, it seems like your age, your size, your grades determine what you get to do.

God doesn't have an age requirement. When you accept Him as Savior and bow to Him as King, His promises are as true for you at five years old as they are at fifteen and fifty. He doesn't have a grade or size requirement— He's not waiting until you're sixteen, eighteen, or twenty-five to use you. He's not waiting for you to be a star performer or straight-A student. After all, He created you just as you are, and He has a purpose and plan for you right now.

The enemy of our souls doesn't have an age requirement either. He is pure evil, prowling like a ravenous lion—and no one is off limits. If anything, it seems he strategically attacks teens and kids. You see this in the heartbreaking rise of bullying, drug use, and global sex-trafficking of youth. Why target you? Why kids your age? Because if he can steal your joy, kill your hope, and destroy your influence now, then he won't have to worry about you in the future.

Yet this isn't a reason to fear. Jesus came to destroy the work of the devil. And He wants you to prevail—to prove you're more powerful than our enemy. He wants you to overcome every battle with increasing courage and strength.

As you'll see in the pages to come, God uses teens—like Samuel, David, and Mary—not only to defeat the enemy, but to become powerful forces for the kingdom. He wants this for you too.

But how do we prevail? We align our mind, our actions, and our heart with God's. When we know, deep in our souls, who we are—and Whose we are—we will stay anchored in any storm. We will flourish in any drought. We will prevail in any battle.

This book is devotional. But it's also a tool to help you practically live out your faith every day—right as you are, and where you are, now. Each day you'll be invited to align your life—every part of it—with His Word and His ways. And each day you'll be invited to mature and grow in freedom, wholeness, victory, and redemption you never dreamed possible.

No matter what you're facing, Jesus beckons us to follow Him and, in the process, we become more like Him. Use this book in a way that best suits you. If you want to follow the arc of Scripture and read passages from every book of the Bible, start with Day 1 and read chronologically from Genesis to Revelation. If you'd prefer to read devotions based on topics, check out the topical index at the beginning of the book. Either way, know that I'm praying for you as you work your way through these pages. I'm so very honored to get to spend this time with you.

Affectionately His,

Susie Larson

Build an Altar

Then the LORD appeared to Abram and said, "I will give this land to your descendants." And Abram built an altar there and dedicated it to the LORD, who had appeared to him.

Genesis 12:7

We all have photos of special moments in our lives. The day you were born. The day you graduated from kindergarten. The time your team won a tournament or you performed on stage. These pictures mark these big events, and they help us remember where we've been and what we've done. In a similar way, the Old Testament is full of stories of people building altars to God. Why? So they—and future generations—could remember the incredible moments and the special places where God moved. Abram was a wandering, childless shepherd when God spoke to him and promised him not just a child, but nations. Not just a home, but an entire land. And so Abram built an altar to worship and remember before he ventured into the unknown with God. Like Abram, God has a promise over your life—and the land ahead is good land. But before you take another step, remember His faithfulness. Remember His goodness. It'll strengthen you for the road ahead.

ALIGN YOUR MIND Read Genesis 12:1–9.

ALIGN YOUR ACTIONS Take some time today to build an altar of remembrance with God. Make note of this sacred time and place where you are now. God is in this place. How would you describe the holy ground beneath your feet? What treasures will you take with you to your next place?

ALIGN YOUR HEART

Lord, I'm pausing to remember Your presence in my life. Please bring to mind all the ways You've worked on my behalf. Thank You, Lord, for Your gracious provision.

Release and Trust

"The whole countryside is open to you. Take your choice of any section of the land you want, and we will separate. If you want the land to the left, then I'll take the land on the right. If you prefer the land on the right, then I'll go to the left."

Genesis 13:9

We can go through life one of two ways: We can do whatever it takes to stay on top, stay ahead, and maintain control; or we can live wholly submitted to God, trusting Him with every step. In our reading today, both Abram and Lot acquired great wealth. But when their herdsmen began to bicker, the two men parted ways. Abram gave Lot first choice of the land. Though Lot had benefited greatly from Abram's constant generosity, he still grabbed for himself the best share of land, even though it meant he'd live among the ungodly. His story didn't end well. Both scarcity and abundance reveal the condition of our hearts. If we grab for ourselves in difficult times, we'll grab for ourselves when there's more than enough to go around. But God doesn't bless our greedy grabbing, and He won't pour provision into clenched fists. As Christ-followers, we can refuse selfishness and open our hands, release control and receive His abundance. We can trust God.

ALIGN YOUR MIND ➤ Read Genesis 13.

ALIGN YOUR ACTIONS ➤ No matter what's going on around you, determine to release your grip on anything you're holding too tight. Breathe in faith. Exhale fear. God does His best work through His surrendered saints.

ALIGN YOUR HEART

You come to me with open-handed provision, so I come to You with open-handed trust. You've always provided, so I have nothing to fear. I trust You, Lord. Amen.

Close the Gap

Then Abraham bowed down to the ground, but he laughed to himself in disbelief. "How could I become a father at the age of 100?" he thought. "And how can Sarah have a baby when she is ninety years old?"

Genesis 17:17

God promised Abraham that the generations would come through Abraham and Sarah. His response? He bowed low. *But he laughed on the inside*. How often do we do the same? We sing about God's faithfulness, but do we *really* believe He'll do the impossible in our situation? When we don't believe, a gap appears and widens between our outward "Christian" actions and our inward beliefs. Our faith and actions are disconnected, often because we're weary of waiting for an answer or tired from battle. But we must not allow the gap to linger within us. Today is the day to reconnect what you believe with how you act. God can do in a moment what takes us a lifetime to accomplish. And when faith awakens your heart *and* inspires your actions? Well, that's the stuff of miracles.

ALIGN YOUR MIND   Read Genesis 17:15–17.

ALIGN YOUR ACTIONS   It's time to close the gap. God is better than we know and He's kinder than we can fathom! Your faith is so very precious to Him. Remind your soul today that NOTHING is impossible with Him! Wrestle with God and meditate on His promises until you live like you believe again.

ALIGN YOUR HEART

> *Precious Lord, show me the gaps that exist between what I do and what I truly believe, and then fill in those empty spaces with more of You. Awaken my heart as I renew my faith. Do the impossible in my life. In Your name, I pray. Amen.*

When Our Unbelief Speaks

So Abraham said to God, "May Ishmael live under your special blessing!"
Genesis 17:18

Often, when we've waited a long time to see an answer to prayer or the fulfillment of a promise, our hearts grow faint. Unless we regularly take the time to strengthen ourselves in the Lord and remind ourselves of His faithfulness, unbelief and even resentment will settle into our souls. In due time our own words, which reflect the condition of our hearts, will diminish our own faith. Abraham and Sarah had waited long for their promise. When the time finally came, they laughed in unbelief. Instead of waiting on God, Abraham tried to edit God's promise by doing things his own way, then telling God to bless the outcome of his faithless actions. Pay attention to how you talk about the longings of your heart. What do they reveal? Your faith is precious to Him. There are no time constraints on God's ability to do what He will do. If He's making you wait, it's because He's making you ready. May God bless you with a fresh and hopeful expectancy today. May your words inspire hope and reflect your actively engaged faith!

 ALIGN YOUR MIND ▶ Read Genesis 18:1–14.

 ALIGN YOUR ACTIONS ▶ Has unbelief or resentment settled into your soul? Remember and rehearse the things God has promised you. Talk or write about them. Sing about them. Remember them.

 ALIGN YOUR HEART ▶

> *Lord, I believe; help my unbelief! Help me remember the promises You've made to me. Help me remember in the darkness what You told me in the light. I know Your voice. I know what I heard. I know what Your Word says. Fan the flame of faith within me today. I choose to trust You. Amen.*

God's Wisdom and Revelation

"Should I hide my plan from Abraham?" the LORD asked. "For Abraham will certainly become a great and mighty nation, and all the nations of the earth will be blessed through him."

Genesis 18:17–18

Was God talking to himself here? Wondering out loud? We know this: God knows the end from the beginning. Our days are established before Him. He knows the plans He has for us and they are good plans. He also knows what troubles lie ahead for us, and He intends to be intimately near during such times. In and through His wisdom, God reveals what we need to know. Scripture also tells us that He confides in (tells secrets to) those who fear Him. Eventually God told Abraham about His plan. Interestingly, that occurred *just after* Abraham radically trusted God with his future. Could there be a connection between us walking in obedience and faith and God revealing His secret plans for our lives? Absolutely. As we walk closely with Him, He shows us His heart and His ways. God has some great plans and good gifts up His sovereign sleeve, and they're assigned to you!

ALIGN YOUR MIND ➤ Read Genesis 22:1–18.

ALIGN YOUR ACTIONS ➤ God wants to give you insight into your story and your future. He wants to fill you with hope. He wants you to persevere. Do you believe Him enough to trust Him? What would obedience look like for you today? Don't delay. Trust and obey.

ALIGN YOUR HEART

Jesus, nobody modeled trust, obedience, and faith like You. And Your life was marked by wisdom, power, and revelation. Give me a heart to do Your will. Please reveal Your heart and Your ways to me. In Your name I pray. Amen.

How to Lose Your Credibility

So Lot rushed out to tell his daughters' fiancés, "Quick, get out of the city! The LORD is about to destroy it." But the young men thought he was only joking.

Genesis 19:14

Abraham prayed and interceded for the city of Sodom because God was about to destroy it. He begged God to promise not to destroy the city if He could find even a small remnant of righteous people still there— perhaps fifty people, or forty, or even ten. But Sodom's sins had piled so high, there weren't even *ten* individuals who feared God within its borders. Imagine! God sent angels to warn Lot about the coming destruction. But when Lot tried to warn his family, they thought he was joking. They didn't take him seriously. Lot had camped among the ungodly for so long, he lost his credibility. Because Lot didn't live any differently than his sinful neighbors, his words didn't carry much weight. Most compromise happens subtly. We want to fit in with those around us, so we change, give in, a little bit at a time until we are far from the safety of God's shore. May God pull you back in and recapture your heart today.

ALIGN YOUR MIND ▶ Read Genesis 19.

ALIGN YOUR ACTIONS ▶ Ask God to show you if you've blended in with ungodly actions, beliefs, or people around you. Ask Him for forgiveness. Reset your course and ask God to fill you with the convicting yet comforting work of the Holy Spirit.

ALIGN YOUR HEART

Precious Jesus, show me how my little compromises have affected my relationship with You. I'm sorry I've diminished Your life-giving power in my life. Call me up higher with You. In Your name, I pray. Amen.

Your Birthright for a Bowl of Soup

"Look, I'm dying of starvation!" said Esau. "What good is my birthright to me now?"

Genesis 25:32

God never asks us to push ourselves to the point of exhaustion. Yet this is exactly what we do when we try to do it all or be the best. Such a life wears us out, increasing our chances of taking foolish shortcuts and making bad decisions. And worse yet, we lose sight of our inheritance in Christ—a life of abundance and peace and power. Esau was so wrapped up in his immediate need for food that he lost sight of his inheritance. We must not go through life reacting to our immediate needs or desires at the expense of the greater story God is writing in our lives. Though God graciously gives us all good things to enjoy, not everything is good for us. If you've pursued your ambitions or desires in a way that leaves you exhausted or empty, now would be a great time for a sacred fast—a time to step away, seek God, and reset your ways. Whenever we say yes, we say no. And what we say yes and no to today will impact the lives of many tomorrow. Our story matters that much.

ALIGN YOUR MIND Read Genesis 25:27–34.

ALIGN YOUR ACTIONS Reevaluate your goals or desires, adjust your task list, or give yourself time and space to be restored so you can think and see clearly again. Your choices today deeply impact your tomorrows.

ALIGN YOUR HEART

Lord, I'm so quick to forget who I am and Whose I am. Forgive me for chasing my own desires and for being surprised when they don't satisfy. I want more of You in me! Amen.

No Hindrance, No Harm

"You know how hard I have worked for your father, but he has cheated me, changing my wages ten times. But God has not allowed him to do me any harm."

Genesis 31:6–7

Laban was a manipulative, passive-aggressive man. He changed Jacob's wages ten times. He tricked him and cheated him, seemingly bent on controlling Jacob's future. But God observed everything, and He refused to let Laban stand in the way of His promise to Jacob. Laban was in a position of power and authority, yet ultimately, he'd have no power to actually hinder Jacob or keep him from prospering. Let Jacob's story encourage you today. You may have people in your life who are impossible to deal with. They may seem to slow your progress or dictate your path. But when you're in Christ, there's no enemy scheme or man-made manipulation that can keep you from all God has for you. Christians experience only *temporary* setbacks. God's purposes will ultimately prevail. Psalm 62 tells us that the powerful aren't what they appear to be. Nobody has more power to advance you than God himself. He will use difficult people to chisel your rough edges and to make you more like Christ even as He directs your path.

ALIGN YOUR MIND Read Genesis 31:1–16.

ALIGN YOUR ACTIONS Today, adjust your attitude and rejoice that no person can hinder what God has appointed. Praise!

ALIGN YOUR HEART

> *You are all that I need. Forgive me for giving people power that belongs to You alone. Give me savvy wisdom to navigate difficult relationships. Grant me the calm assurance to know in the face of frustration that all will be well because You are with me. I trust You, Lord. Amen.*

Perspective before the Breakthrough

When Joseph saw them the next morning, he noticed that they both looked upset. "Why do you look so worried today?" he asked them.

Genesis 40:6–7

When Joseph was a young man, God put a dream in his heart. Yet the journey getting there involved painful betrayal, injustice, and false accusation. One day while in prison, Joseph noticed two fellow prisoners who looked distressed—and asked them why. *What?* They were in prison; who *wouldn't* be distressed? And who would even care if they were? Yet Joseph had found such joy and perspective that even there he could minister to others while he waited for his own breakthrough. God used heartbreak to prepare Joseph for greatness. And at every turn, Joseph rose to the top of his game in attitude, performance, and perspective. May you wrestle for a right attitude and perspective. May you see those who are hurting and need what you possess. And may you believe, with all your heart, that God will move you on when the time is right.

ALIGN YOUR MIND Read Genesis 40.

ALIGN YOUR ACTIONS You may not be where you want to be, but God has you here for a reason. Find the high place of joy today. Look for those God has given you to encourage. Forgive your offenders and believe with all your heart that no person, no scheme, and no devil can thwart God's purposes for you!

ALIGN YOUR HEART

Father, show me my heart so I can find You here. Whom do I need to forgive? How should I pray? Help me to steward my life in this place while I wait for You to move me to my next place. I trust You, Lord. Amen.

May God Remind Them, and You

Finally, the king's chief cup-bearer spoke up. "Today I have been reminded of my failure," he told Pharaoh.

Genesis 41:9

Joseph honored God and guarded his heart against despair and bitterness through every painful, unjust circumstance he endured. One day while in prison, God used Joseph to interpret dreams for the cup-bearer and the baker. Interesting how the man with a dream helped others to interpret their dreams. Joseph asked the cup-bearer to remember him when God restored him to his position. But he forgot all about Joseph until a later time. You've no doubt crossed paths with those who've witnessed and confirmed God's gifts in you. Maybe they promised they'd help you and open doors for you. Yet you've heard nothing. Pray for those people today. Ask God to remind them of their words to you. And trust God's perfect time and grace in your life. He is faithful. Though people sometimes forget, He never will. Remember too that Jesus consistently called greatness out of others. He saw them not for where they'd been but for who they could be if they followed Him. May you do the same for others. You have a position of influence.

ALIGN YOUR MIND 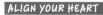 Read Genesis 41:8–13.

ALIGN YOUR ACTIONS Who can you encourage today? Move them forward in their God-given calling. Trust that God will remind your cup-bearers of your God-given gifts at just the right time.

ALIGN YOUR HEART

> *Lord, I seem to fall into one of two extremes: I either forget to dream because I'm consumed by my problems, or I'm so consumed with my dreams, I forget to help others achieve theirs. Use me to help others. And remind others to remember me when the time is right. Amen.*

You Sold Me; God Sent Me*

"But don't be upset, and don't be angry with yourselves for selling me to this place. It was God who sent me here ahead of you to preserve your lives."

Genesis 45:5

How do you endure betrayal and injustice with such honor that you actually feel compassion for your enemies? How do you get to a place where you trust God so much that you know others' hurtful actions against you can never interrupt His purposes for you? When God called Joseph from the prison to the palace, he was ready for it. How do we know he was ready? By looking at his heart for those who hurt him most. The work of forgiveness is painful and messy, and it calls so much out of us. But as Christ-followers, it's our only option. Not that we automatically trust again. But if we, like Joseph, truly believe God can redeem any situation, we will trust Him with those who've hurt us most. A heart like Joseph's is renewed over time, not overnight. Do you believe that God is ultimately in control and cares about your story? Then do the work of forgiveness, fight for a redeemed perspective, and put your trust in the One who will vindicate you.

ALIGN YOUR MIND Read Genesis 45:1–15.

ALIGN YOUR ACTIONS It's for our good and for His glory to forgive as we've been forgiven. Ask God to bring to mind someone you can forgive today.

ALIGN YOUR HEART

Father, refresh my perspective. Help me to see my "enemies" the way that You do. You are ultimately in control. Help me to trust You with my whole heart, and lift my eyes above my problems to the greater purpose You have for me. Amen.

* This line came from pastor and author Steven Furtick.

It's about Who He Is

But Moses protested to God, "Who am I to appear before Pharaoh? Who
am I to lead the people of Israel out of Egypt?" God answered, "I will be with
you."

Exodus 3:11–12

God had prepared Moses throughout his whole life for his purpose and
destiny. But when the Lord finally called Moses, the task still felt too big
for him. Moses asked, "But who am I?" Notice that God doesn't affirm Moses'
giftedness; nor is He bothered by Moses' weaknesses. God simply said, "I will
be with you." *God's nearness* was all the assurance Moses needed. When
the Lord calls you to attempt something that's far beyond you, your instinct
(and your enemy) will compel you to count your weaknesses. But the Lord
God Almighty charges you to rely on His strength. Most of the angst in our
souls comes from focusing on our circumstances and our own limitations.
Yet neither of these things is an issue or an obstacle for God. The truth is, if
God is for us, if His promises are true, what problem will overcome us? The
God who calls you is the same God who moves the mountains and parts the
waters. You are tethered to a good and strong God.

 ALIGN YOUR MIND Read Exodus 3:1–15.

 ALIGN YOUR ACTIONS Write down any limitations you've allowed to define
or confine you. Prayerfully lay them at Jesus' feet, asking for His forgiveness
and a tangible sense of His nearness.

ALIGN YOUR HEART

> *Lord, nothing is too difficult for You! Help me focus on You and rely on
> Your power, not my own. No matter what You ask, give me the courage
> to follow through. Do the impossible in and through me. Amen.*

Not the Shortest Route, the Best Route

> When Pharaoh finally let the people go, God did not lead them along the main road . . . even though that was the shortest route to the Promised Land. God said, "If the people are faced with a battle, they might change their minds and return to Egypt."
>
> Exodus 13:17–18

Though Christ paid a full ransom for our freedom, it sometimes takes a while to get the captivity mindset out of us. On our way to our promised land, God will lead us on a long and winding path that doesn't always make sense. Our feet will get tired, our patience will be tried, and our attitude will be tested. Why? Because when we hit our limits, we learn to seek our limitless God. Our desires are always far inferior to God's desires for us. We want comfort. God wants to conform us to His image. We want convenience. God loves to provide in a way that completely alters our history, which takes time. We want immediate relief. God wants total redemption of our story. So cast aside entitlement and impatience, and embrace a heart of humility and wonder. You follow the star-breathing God. His way might take longer, but it's the best way for you. Go with God. He's most certainly with you.

ALIGN YOUR MIND ▶ Read Exodus 13:17–22.

ALIGN YOUR ACTIONS ▶ Today, replace grumbling with gratitude. Smile and laugh hard. It's healthy for your brain, good for your soul, and wonderful for your spirit.

ALIGN YOUR HEART

Forgive me for being so shortsighted at times. You are faithfully leading me in the way that I should go. Transform me from the inside out. Make me promotable. Write a beautiful story with my life. Amen.

What's Better?

"Didn't we tell you this would happen while we were still in Egypt? We said, 'Leave us alone! Let us be slaves to the Egyptians. It's better to be a slave in Egypt than a corpse in the wilderness!'"

Exodus 14:12

The Israelites predicted their failure before they ever started on their journey because captivity was embedded in the core of who they were. If God promised to deliver them, wouldn't He? Is it really *better* to be held captive than to face your fears of the unknown? My friend once said to me, "The devil can't attack a corpse. Die to your fears and you'll walk free." Lots of things need to die in the wilderness: our love of control, our performance-based identity, our fears, our impatience, and our sense of entitlement. Is it *better* to stay captive than to have your comfort challenged? No. It's better to follow Jesus through your wilderness, trusting wholeheartedly that He brought you here not to dismiss you but to deliver you. Remind yourself of those promises. Say them, pray them, and then march forward unafraid. Some things will die in this wilderness, but you're not one of them. God will purify and preserve you. He's set His affection upon you.

 ALIGN YOUR MIND Read Exodus 14:10–14.

 ALIGN YOUR ACTIONS What plans and fears do you need to let go of? Write down anything that comes to mind and ask God to replace it with fresh promises from His Word.

ALIGN YOUR HEART

Father, I place my hand in Yours; I trust You with my life. Cleanse me from my hidden faults and everyday sins—may they never control me! I want to walk purely and blamelessly before You. Make me ready for my next place of promise. Amen.

He's the Way-Maker

But the people of Israel had walked through the middle of the sea on dry ground, as the water stood up like a wall on both sides.

Exodus 14:29

et's push pause and then watch this scene unfold in slow motion. The people of Israel—who identified more with their captivity than with their Maker—walked through the middle of the sea, *on dry ground*. And the deep waters *stood up like walls* on both sides. *This happened!* This is the God we serve. He takes feeble, weak-kneed saints and reveals His power and good-ness to them time and again. What's your Red Sea—the do-or-die thing that threatens to swallow you whole? Will God part your waters because you are good, or because He is? Dare to believe that though the odds may be against you, they're really irrelevant when God comes on the scene. Today, remember the great things God has done with seemingly no effort: He spoke, and the heavens came to be. He put the stars in their place and calls them each by name. And He knows and loves *you*. He'll intervene at the right time because He is God and He is good. It's time to believe for your miracle.

ALIGN YOUR MIND Read Exodus 14:21–29.

ALIGN YOUR ACTIONS Think about His greatness and nearness today. What do they look like in your life? Trust that He will make a way for you.

ALIGN YOUR HEART

Lord, I invite You into my impossible situation. You are the God who parted the Red Sea, and You will make a way for me! I declare Your good-ness over every area of my life. I refuse to be defined by my troubles. I'm already claimed by heaven! Thank You, Lord. Amen.

Finding Fault, Finding Favor

> Then Moses added, "The LORD will give you meat to eat in the evening and bread to satisfy you in the morning, for he has heard all your complaints against him. What have we done? Yes, your complaints are against the LORD, not against us."
>
> Exodus 16:8

One of the great temptations of the wilderness is to complain, fingerpoint, and blame. We don't like our circumstance and so we look for someone to pin it on. And while sometimes we suffer because of someone else's sin or painful actions, it's no excuse to complain or become bitter, like the Israelites did. No matter what happens, every trial is ultimately a test of our hearts and a challenge to our belief systems. Is God good? And can we trust Him? Our circumstances won't hinder us as much as we think they will, but our attitudes will. An earthbound heart is always looking for someone to blame. A heaven-bound heart knows that we're passing through our valleys to a better place. In Christ Jesus we are surrounded by the favor and the provision of God. What He allows, He will redeem. May we believe it, receive it, and walk in it today.

 ALIGN YOUR MIND ➤ Read Exodus 16:2–18.

ALIGN YOUR ACTIONS ➤ Ask God to bring to mind ways He's been good to you before. Write them down and thank Him. Look above your circumstances and know that He'll be good again.

ALIGN YOUR HEART

Lord, forgive me for giving too much power to people and circumstances. I have every reason for hope because I have You! Help me live with a heaven-bound heart. You will guide, provide, correct, and direct as I need it. Thank You, Lord. Amen.

Your Part in the Epic Story

As long as Moses held up the staff in his hand, the Israelites had the advantage. But whenever he dropped his hand, the Amalekites gained the advantage. Moses' arms soon became so tired he could no longer hold them up. So Aaron and Hur found a stone for him to sit on. Then they stood on each side of Moses, holding up his hands. So his hands held steady until sunset.

Exodus 17:11–12

Why did God insist that Moses keep his arms in the air? Could He have established a victory without Moses? Absolutely. He was able to. He just didn't want to. God loves to involve His children when He intervenes on the earth. Even when we're tired? When it's a battle? Yes and yes. Without faith, how would we change? If we don't persevere, how will we grow? Joshua led the troops into battle and needed Moses to stand in that place of intercession. Moses needed Aaron and Hur to hold up his arms when he lost strength. Together, they won the battle. The victory belonged to all of them! What does faith look like for you today? Who are you helping? Who's helping you? You're part of a grander story than you can imagine.

ALIGN YOUR MIND ▶ Read Exodus 17:8–15.

ALIGN YOUR ACTIONS ▶ Ask God to show you one person you can help today. Let your friends and family know how eternally grateful you are for them.

ALIGN YOUR HEART ▶

Father, give me faith to believe You for the great things You want to do in and through me. Show me those You've put in my life to help me, and open my eyes to those who need my help. May we stand firm together. Amen.

Face to Face, as with a Friend

Inside the Tent of Meeting, the LORD would speak to Moses face to face, as one speaks to a friend.

Exodus 33:11

Once Moses entered the Tent of Meeting, a pillar of cloud hovered over the entrance. Imagine. The people stood back and watched, amazed. God's nearness to Moses caused the Israelites to bow down in front of their own tents. As you read the passage below, notice Moses' humble yet bold appeal to God. And God engaged with him! God distances himself from the proud, but He draws near to the humble. And He loves faith. Jesus is all powerful and intimately near. Jesus invites each of us into such an intimate, thriving relationship with Him. He longs for us to know Him, not just as a star-breathing God, not just as a Savior (though salvation is everything), but also as a trusted and faithful friend. What if your interactions with God were so sweet that your very relationship with Him compelled others to bow before their Maker? Know this: He speaks tenderly to His friends with a heart of love and strength. The Maker of the universe knows your name—and wants to do life with you.

 ALIGN YOUR MIND Read Exodus 33:11–18.

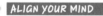 **ALIGN YOUR ACTIONS** What is one thing you long to talk with God about? Tell Him right now! Then sit still, push aside your busy thoughts, and ask to hear Him. He promised we will hear and know His voice.

 ALIGN YOUR HEART

> *Jesus, You've granted me access to Your presence, and You're glad to see me every single time I meet with You! Thank You for Your goodness to me. Speak to me as a close friend. My soul waits for You, Lord. Amen.*

The Power of Intercession

Moses immediately threw himself to the ground and worshiped. And he said, "O Lord, if it is true that I have found favor with you, then please travel with us. Yes, this is a stubborn and rebellious people, but please forgive our iniquity and our sins. Claim us as your own special possession."

Exodus 34:8–9

Dr. Warren Wiersbe writes, "The people of Israel had no idea what Moses had experienced on that mountain and how close they had come to being rejected by God and destroyed. Never underestimate the spiritual power of a dedicated man or woman who knows how to intercede with God. One of our greatest needs today is for intercessors who can lay hold of God's promises and trust God to work in mighty power."* Moses stepped between God and a rebellious people, praying, "Forgive *us* for *our* sins." Even if it doesn't feel natural to you, do the same. Pray for fellow students, teachers, and leaders who leave you annoyed or angry. What would happen in your school or town if Christians humbly stood in the gap, bowed low, and asked for God's mercy? A revival might break out.

ALIGN YOUR MIND ▶ Read Exodus 34:1–11.

ALIGN YOUR ACTIONS ▶ Every time someone annoys or angers you today, pray and intercede for them. Do for others what Jesus does for you every day.

ALIGN YOUR HEART ▶

> *Lord, help me to see Your image in the ones I struggle to love. Give me a glimpse into their story so that Your compassion rises up within me. Forgive me for missing Your heart for Your wayward children. Make me a praying saint, O Lord. Amen.*

* Dr. Warren Wiersbe, *The Wiersbe Bible Commentary* (Colorado Springs: David C. Cook, 2007), 203.

Rest as a Gift

"Keep my Sabbath days of rest and show reverence toward my sanctuary. I am the LORD."

Leviticus 19:30

Messages often get lost in translation when we misunderstand or don't fully know the messenger. Yes, the call to honor the Sabbath—to set aside one special day of rest and worship each week—was a law. But God created it as a gift for people who possessed very real limits, who needed regular reminders that life wasn't about busy work, performing, achieving. To help reset their hearts on Him. Yet the religious radicals found a way to twist this gift, using the day to parade their "holiness" for all to see—and to absolve themselves from literally lifting a finger to help someone in need. Then Jesus came. He offered *real* rest to the weary. He restored the Sabbath to its rightful place—and we still need it today. Our hearts need mending, our souls need healing, and our bodies need rest. And we still need regular reminders that God carries the weight of the world, so we don't have to. We're our best selves when our hearts learn to rest in His provision and rely on His love.

ALIGN YOUR MIND Read Leviticus 19:1–30.

ALIGN YOUR ACTIONS Ask the Lord how He'd like you to start a true Sabbath in your life. What stresses will you set aside? What will you do that nourishes your soul and resets your heart?

ALIGN YOUR HEART

Father, thank You for Your amazing gift of rest, and forgive me for so often refusing it. I want to set aside my busyness and discover heaven's provision and perspective. Show me what a true Sabbath looks like. Help me rest in You, Lord. Amen.

Honor Your Elders

"Stand up in the presence of the elderly and show respect for the aged. Fear your God. I am the Lord."

Leviticus 19:32

I love this command. I've been saying it for years: Honor those who've gone before you. If there's a silver-haired saint in your midst who still has a twinkle in her eye and humility in her heart, know that it's not because she's never endured anything hard. On the contrary, she has weathered the storms of life with her faith intact and her love for Jesus evident. Celebrate her! Stand when she enters the room! Oh, that such honor would make a comeback, especially toward those who've served so faithfully through the years. It's no small thing to finish the race strong. We live in a culture where elders are dismissed and youth are idolized. Yet we need to acknowledge every generation for the Body of Christ to function in a healthy way. Pray for the unborn. Pour into those younger than you. And learn from those who've gone before you. Their hard-fought wisdom is worth more than gold. Find a wise person to honor today! Honor is the equity of the kingdom. Honor means something to God. When you give honor, you actually reveal the honor within you.

ALIGN YOUR MIND ▶ Read Leviticus 19:31–37.

ALIGN YOUR ACTIONS ▶ Thank the seasoned saints in your life—your parents, grandparents, teachers, coaches, pastors. They impact you more than you probably realize.

ALIGN YOUR HEART

Dear Lord, thank You for being so honor-worthy! You call me to honor my leaders and my elders. Raise up a new standard within me. May the way that I honor others, greatly honor You. Amen.

Pay Attention

"As long as the land lies in ruins, it will enjoy the rest you never allowed it to take every seventh year while you lived in it."

Leviticus 26:35

This is a sobering passage. God warned His people that if they refused to acknowledge Him by ignoring the Sabbath, they would endure unimaginable hardship and suffer great loss. We're not the only ones who pay when we grind our gears to the point of exhaustion. Our friends and families pay. Our relationships are strained. Our resources are drained. We're not meant to live in a constant state of motion. God issues a warning to us, but if we blow right past it, He will allow us to suffer the consequences. One way or another, He will get our attention. Is there any area of your life that needs a reset? You'll do your best when you put Him first. He's more concerned with the condition of our souls and the perspective of our hearts than social media likes, good grades, accolades, or expensive clothes and cars. Pay attention to the warning signals God places in your life. He knows what's best for you, and His plans for you are good.

 ALIGN YOUR MIND Read Leviticus 26:18–20, 33–35.

 ALIGN YOUR ACTIONS Are you tired, stressed out, or feeling tension in your relationships? These can be signals you're ignoring God's rest. Examine your activity level and reset your course—and heart—today.

 ALIGN YOUR HEART

I humble myself before You, Lord, and acknowledge my habit of forgetting Your Word and Your ways. Forgive me, Lord. Show me where I've fallen out of balance. Open my eyes to the ways I've stopped honoring You. You are my God, and I will follow You forever. Amen.

Humility and the Lord's Favor

But Moses replied, "Are you jealous for my sake? I wish that all the LORD's people were prophets and that the LORD would put his Spirit upon them all!"

Numbers 11:29

Moses was so humbly confident in God that nobody could steal his thunder (because he had no thunder to steal). He reveled in a rich and personal relationship with God. They were good friends. They talked intimately and often. Clearly, the favor on Moses' public life came as a result of his faithful private life. Something beautiful happens when we're secure in God's love and sure of our place in the kingdom story. We cease to be threatened by the giftedness of others. In fact, we celebrate how God works in and through His people! And we continually remember that God's story is always bigger than ours. This reality inspires holy confidence and humble dependence. See yourself as part of the bigger story. No one can steal your thunder. It's God's thunder that ignites and empowers you!

ALIGN YOUR MIND ▶ Read Numbers 11:16–29.

ALIGN YOUR ACTIONS ▶ Consider the places in your life where you're prone to being jealous, insecure, controlling, and defensive. Imagine these areas of your life as plots of land. Picture yourself kneeling down on the land and offering it back up to the Lord.

ALIGN YOUR HEART ▶

> Lord, fill me afresh with the knowledge of Your love. Assure me once again of my place in the greater kingdom story. May there be no shred of cattiness or insecurity in me! I'm made for bigger things. Do a mighty work in me. Amen.

Humility and the Fear of the Lord

> They said, "Has the LORD spoken only through Moses? Hasn't he spoken through us, too?" But the LORD heard them. (Now Moses was very humble—more humble than any other person on earth.)
>
> Numbers 12:2–3

Since Eden, the devil has sown doubt in believers' hearts. His tactic? *"Did God really say . . . ?"* When we question God's motives or character, we fall down in battle. The enemy uses this same tactic to get us to attack seasoned leaders. He tempts us to question their motives and character. Our distrust and disdain compel us to look for fault (and we usually find it). And before you know it, we're out of rank and in full rebellion—all while thinking we actually represent God's heart in the situation! Someone once said that there's enough flesh in every one of us to singlehandedly destroy any thriving work of God. That should put the fear of God in us. If you want to avoid being used by the enemy to cause conflict and division, stay humble and pray for your leaders; you don't know what their call costs them. The measure that you use will be used on you.

 ALIGN YOUR MIND ▸ Read Numbers 12:1–8.

 ALIGN YOUR ACTIONS ▸ Pray for the leaders you're tempted to criticize. With your words and actions, sow grace, faith, encouragement, and support, and you'll reap those things.

 ALIGN YOUR HEART

Lord, forgive me for my flippant, jealous, or judgmental opinions about others, especially leaders. Help me remember that You hear every word and every thought. I long to live with honor. I will pray for those ahead of me, knowing they're a part of Your bigger plan. Thank You, Lord. Amen.

Obstacles and Opposition

This was their report to Moses: "We entered the land you sent us to explore, and it is indeed a bountiful country—a land flowing with milk and honey. Here is the kind of fruit it produces. But the people living there are powerful, and their towns are large and fortified."

Numbers 13:27–28

God told Moses to send out men to explore the land that He had designated for them. So Moses sent twelve men to get a look at the land God commanded them to possess. It was just as God described—and better than they'd imagined, flowing with provision. Yet they would encounter obstacles, enemies, and battles up ahead. Ten of the men lost their nerve because the threat of battle eclipsed the promise of blessing. Over and over again the Lord has whispered in my ear, *I'm not going to let you lose, but I have to let you fight.* Do you shy away from battle when your promised land depends upon it? Every place of provision God calls us to possess will come with opposition. But the blessing will always far outweigh the battle.

ALIGN YOUR MIND ▶ Read Numbers 13:1–30.

ALIGN YOUR ACTIONS ▶ Spend some time in prayer asking for a fresh revelation of God's love for you and a new understanding of all He's promised you. You'll have the courage to stand in battle when you remember that God is with you.

ALIGN YOUR HEART

> *God of angel armies, open my eyes to see the promised land ahead of me! Help me not to shrink back in fear or self-preservation. I belong to You. Give me faith for every step until I'm standing in the land You promised me. In Your mighty name, I pray. Amen.*

Look above It

> But Caleb tried to quiet the people as they stood before Moses. "Let's go at once to take the land," he said. "We can certainly conquer it!"
>
> Numbers 13:30

God called the twelve spies to scope out the land so they'd better understand the journey before them. Yet ten lost heart once they glimpsed the challenges ahead. Perhaps this is why God, in His wisdom, reveals only so much to us even though we constantly beg Him for more information! Still two spies, Joshua and Caleb, saw what God wanted them to see: possibility, potential, and the reality of God's promise coming to pass in their lives. Yet the other ten were so vocal about their doubts that unbelief spread through the entire camp like a plague. Think of your words and perspective not only as critical food for your own soul, but as fuel for others' faith (or doubt). If the devil can convince you to look down, he'll get you to turn back—and take others with you. Maybe today is a good day to look above your troubles to the One who promised to empower you every step of the way.

ALIGN YOUR MIND Read Numbers 13:30–33.

 ALIGN YOUR ACTIONS Today, when you run into an obstacle, declare your faith in God's goodness and ask for His eyes to see the possibilities and potential instead of a dead end. Spread hope, not discouragement.

ALIGN YOUR HEART

Precious Lord, open the eyes of my heart today! Tilt my chin upward today until I see You—only You. Fill my heart with a fresh perspective and my mouth with words of faith. And then use me to fuel faith in others. You deserve our trust and our praise.

Rebellious Fears

"Why is the Lord taking us to this country only to have us die in battle? . . .
Wouldn't it be better for us to return to Egypt?" Then they plotted among
themselves, "Let's choose a new leader and go back to Egypt!"

Numbers 14:3–4

Our fears skew our perspective, making us miss what God is saying to us in the moment. Scholars describe the Israelites' fears as downright rebellious. They *chose* to feed their fears over feeding their faith in God—to the point that they refused His promises and defied Moses, the godly, humble man who led them out of captivity to a land of freedom. Learn from their error. God's promises are greater than you can imagine, and His intentions for you can never be shaken. Determine not to rebel against the Lord because of your fears. Yes, you'll need courage and grit to walk out His purposes for you. But your faith is a treasure to Him and He's highly protective of you. He aches when you're afraid, and He will bring peace to your heart and deliver you from all your fears.

ALIGN YOUR MIND ▸ Read Numbers 14:1–9.

ALIGN YOUR ACTIONS ▸ We all have faith in something—whether it's our fears or God. Which one are your words and actions feeding today?

ALIGN YOUR HEART

Dear Jesus, thank You for Your patience with me! I repent of and renounce the fears that have held me back up until now. I refuse to allow the enemy to bully me into rebellion. Instead, I submit my will to You. I will obey You. I will trust You. Show me what to do; my eyes are on You. Amen.

Faith Possesses Its Share

"But my servant Caleb has a different attitude than the others have. He has remained loyal to me, so I will bring him into the land he explored. His descendants will possess their full share of that land."

Numbers 14:24

At the edge of the Promised Land, scholars estimate the Israelites—men, women, and children—numbered over one million people. Yet God knew who had faith and who didn't. The lines weren't blurry to Him. We, who've also been promised His presence and His provision, have a decision to make—the same one Israel had: Will we trust Him, or won't we? Yes, He will love us either way. But it's faith that possesses the promise. Our faith shows God that we trust Him. We don't have to do it perfectly; in fact, we never will. What He does ask is for us to follow in obedience if we believe His words are true. Hundreds of thousands of Israelites never made it to their promised place, even though God had offered it to them! How many good gifts has God offered us that have been left untouched because of unbelief? Make no mistake about it: believing God's promises and obeying His commands are the keys to stepping into all God has for you.

ALIGN YOUR MIND Read Numbers 14:10–25.

ALIGN YOUR ACTIONS Today, spend some time asking God to show you where you still struggle with unbelief or obedience. Ask Him to show you your next steps of faith.

ALIGN YOUR HEART

Father in heaven, I want to possess all You have for me! Awaken fresh faith in my heart. Show me where unbelief hides in me. Remove every hindrance to my faith. I want all You've promised me. Amen.

How to Deal with Criticism

When Moses heard what they were saying, he fell face down on the ground.

Numbers 16:4

What do you do when people talk bad about you? Most of us instinctively say harsh things back or come to our own defense. But not Moses. He fell facedown to the ground. When he sought God for direction, interceding for ungrateful, sinful people, he bowed low. And when those very people rose up against him, he went facedown again. But then he rose up and, in so many words, said, "Let's stand before God and see who He defends." When you walk in humble reverence before the Lord and you follow Him wholeheartedly, you can always count on Him to defend and deliver you. It's no small thing to God when someone comes against one of His very own. Keep your heart pure and watch Him defend you. If you find yourself rehearsing your defense in your mind, lay it down. Pick up one of His promises and rehearse that instead. Remember His goodness. Rely on His love. Recall His history with His people. It's precious and powerful. Remember, He knows what's true and what's false. He's meticulous, and miraculous, and He cares about justice. He'll deal with your accusers and will heal and restore your soul.

ALIGN YOUR MIND   Read Numbers 16:1–7.

ALIGN YOUR ACTIONS   Today, stop rehearsing your defenses, complaints against others, or daydreams of getting even. Find a promise in God's Word to rehearse instead.

ALIGN YOUR HEART

> *Father, You are the God who defends and delivers me! I entrust myself once again to You. Deal with my accusers. Vindicate me at the proper time, and protect me when I'm vulnerable. I'm counting on You to save me. Thank You, Lord. Amen.*

Embrace Your Own Territory

Then Moses spoke again to Korah: "Now listen, you Levites! Does it seem insignificant to you that the God of Israel has chosen you from among all the community of Israel to be near him so you can serve in the LORD's Tabernacle and stand before the people to minister to them?"

Numbers 16:8–9

When we minimize the importance of God's unique path and purpose for us because we're jealous of someone else, we set ourselves up for a fall. God has given you this place and this time to train you, to give you a vision of something bigger, and to experience His provision. This is your personal training ground, perfectly fitted to His plans for you. Wishing it away exposes what's truly in our hearts. "Korah had significant, worthwhile abilities and responsibilities of his own. In the end, however, his ambition for more caused him to lose everything. *Inappropriate ambition is greed in disguise.* Concentrate on finding the special purpose God has for you instead of wishing you were in someone else's shoes."* Selfish ambition will always produce jealousy, greed, and disobedience. Holy ambition calls for humility, teachability, patience, and trust. And when you're ready, God will promote you. You can count on it.

ALIGN YOUR MIND Read Numbers 16:8–11.

ALIGN YOUR ACTIONS What do the blessings of others reveal about your own heart? Repent of any selfish ambition today, and ask God to prepare you and use you in miraculous ways.

ALIGN YOUR HEART

Father, forgive me for ungodly ambition. I renounce it from my life. Fill me with faith and holy ambition that I might accomplish great things for Your name's sake! Amen.

---

* *Life Application Study Bible* (Carol Stream, IL: Tyndale, 2007), 302, emphasis mine.

Is It Time to Move On?

> "When we were at Mount Sinai, the LORD our God said to us, 'You have
> stayed at this mountain long enough. It is time to break camp and move on.'"
>
> Deuteronomy 1:6–7

There's a time to pause before the Lord, to seek His face, and to wait for His timing and direction. And then there's a time to get moving. How do you know what obedience looks like for you right now? Should you hold your ground or head out? Before you answer, ask yourself these questions: *When I think of leaving, do I feel the peace of God? How about when I think of staying?* And, *Do I need more faith to stay or leave?* Oftentimes, we want to go so we can feel relief. And we want to stay so we can remain comfortable. But God's highest ways defy our selfish desires. He will always lead us on the best path for us if we will trust Him. You may not have all the answers—He may not offer a full map to your destination—but He promises His presence. Search for His peace. Go in faith. God will faithfully lead you, one step at a time.

ALIGN YOUR MIND ▸ Read Deuteronomy 1:6–8.

ALIGN YOUR ACTIONS ▸ When you think of your current circumstances, what does your flesh want to do: seek comfort, save face, make a hasty change? Pause, open your hands, and listen for His voice. What is He saying to you?

ALIGN YOUR HEART

Father, I bow before You once again. You are all I need. I know Your will for me is my best-case scenario. Let me hear Your voice. Give me courage to do what You say. In Your great name, I pray. Amen.

Here's Where You Trust Him

"And you saw how the LORD your God cared for you all along the way as you traveled through the wilderness, just as a father cares for his child. Now he has brought you to this place."

Deuteronomy 1:31

Imagine the entire nation of Israel, millions of souls, gathered at the edge of the wilderness listening to Moses recount their journey. As they listened to all the miracles, provision, and divine direction they received, I wonder if they winced over how often they doubted and rebelled against God? In our passage today, Moses is reminding the people of their accusations against God, shouting things like, "The Lord must hate us!" It seems ridiculous to us that they did this, and yet how often do we blame God for our own self-induced misery (usually created from selfish decisions because we failed to trust God)? And yet the Lord remains steady and faithful. No matter how many times you've rebelled against God, today is a fresh day to trust Him fully. What He did for the Israelites, He'll do for you: He goes before you. He'll fight for you. He'll care for you. And like the good Father He is, He'll lead you safely to your promised land.

ALIGN YOUR MIND ▶ Read Deuteronomy 1:19–33.

ALIGN YOUR ACTIONS ▶ Think about any entitled attitudes that surfaced this week. Impatience? Grumbling? Ingratitude? Defiant unbelief? Acknowledge and repent of them, and ask God to refresh your soul.*

ALIGN YOUR HEART ▶

> Dear Jesus, You've been so, so good to me. You deserve my trust, my praise, and my gratitude. I will remember Your goodness. I will remember Your Word. And I will trust You on a deeper level, starting today. Amen.

* See Acts 3:19–20.

Motivated by Faith, Not Fear

"I will give the land to your little ones—your innocent children. You were afraid they would be captured, but they will be the ones who occupy it."

Deuteronomy 1:39

Some of my greatest regrets are the times I allowed fear to drive my perspective and my decisions. I didn't cower in constant, gripping fear, but doubts and worry certainly impacted the things I did—or didn't—do. I've since confessed and repented, and our compassionate Lord has always responded with forgiveness and graciousness. The Israelites were deeply motivated by fear as well as by their love of comfort and convenience. Can you see how these sabotage the great things God wants to do in and through us? The most pampered and coddled people tend to have the least amount of substance in their character. Your muscles need resistance to get stronger. Diamonds are created through immense pressure. Storms cause tree roots to grow down deeper. God uses challenges to make you stronger, refine you, and give you depth. May He put faith in your heart where there's fear. May He give you the courage to face any challenge. And may you inherit—and embrace—the land that your fears have kept you out of.

ALIGN YOUR MIND ▸ Read Deuteronomy 1:32–45.

ALIGN YOUR ACTIONS ▸ Delayed obedience is disobedience. Has God asked something of you that you're putting off? You're safest in the center of God's will. Where He guides, He will provide. Obey quickly and trust Him fully.

ALIGN YOUR HEART

Lord, forgive me for the countless times I've let fear (and my love of comfort) dictate my decisions. I want to take risks, enjoy the journey, and occupy the land You have for me. Lead me on, Good Shepherd. Amen.

Tools of Generosity

"If you need food to eat or water to drink, pay them for it. For the LORD your God has blessed you in everything you have done."

Deuteronomy 2:6–7

How much of what you own—clothes, phone, even the food you eat—did you pay for? Most likely your parents paid for what you have. Maybe you have a job to buy what they won't. All of it—whether you bought it or not—is actually a gift from the Creator of the universe. And He cares about how you treat it. If you read through the parables, you'll see how often Jesus speaks of our managing well all He's entrusted to us. Often, we tend to either neglect (like leaving clothes in heaps on the floor) or hoard (not sharing) our belongings. But stewardship isn't just saving money or cleaning our rooms. It's also how we treat others with what we've been given—all our things are tools of generosity. We share the love of Christ when we share our time and talents. When we encourage someone. When we leave a big tip, loan someone a favorite book, or give away clothes we don't need. As Christians, we have the freedom to be generous because our God is faithful and provides all we need—and more! And He replenishes the storehouses of the generous.

 ALIGN YOUR MIND Read Luke 6:38.

 ALIGN YOUR ACTIONS Think of all you have. How can you use these things to be generous this week?

 ALIGN YOUR HEART

Father, You've been so good to me. I lack nothing. Help me to remember that the next time I have an opportunity to offer more than is required of me. In Your mighty name, I pray. Amen.

Remember Not to Forget

"But watch out! Be careful never to forget what you yourself have seen. Do not let these memories escape from your mind as long as you live! And be sure to pass them on to your children and grandchildren."

Deuteronomy 4:9

Though the Israelites seemed to have short-term memory issues (they consistently forgot the ways God loved and cared for them), God instructed them to work on their long-term memory—to remember what they'd seen, to keep those experiences in the forefront of their minds, and to tell others about them. *Why do we forget some of our most important experiences with God?* Because we so often do what the Israelites did: We zero in on our current lack, inconvenience, hardship, or discomfort. Yet we are made for more. We can endure setbacks, hardships, and even lack because the Lord Almighty is with us. He gives us strategies to navigate difficult situations as we focus on how He's come through before—and *not* our current circumstances. He's a breakthrough God, and when the time is right, He'll come through for us. Your history with God reminds you that you also have a future with Him. So focus your heart on His faithfulness today.

ALIGN YOUR MIND Read Deuteronomy 4:1–10.

ALIGN YOUR ACTIONS Today, tell someone a God-story of how He came through for you in the past. Active faith will strengthen your soul in the present and give you hope for the future.

ALIGN YOUR HEART

Dear Lord, I pause today and remember Your kindness to me. Thank You for all You've provided, all You've prevented, and all You've empowered me to do. Remind me of the times You've come through for me. Give me boldness to pass on these stories. Amen.

The First Thing

"And now, Israel, what does the LORD your God require of you? He requires only that you fear the LORD your God, and live in a way that pleases him, and love him and serve him with all your heart and soul."

Deuteronomy 10:12

John Ortberg joined me on my radio show to talk about what it means to truly follow Christ. He said, "What if, on my wedding night, I had asked Nancy this question: 'What's the least I must do for you in order to stay married to you?' If I dared to ask such a ridiculous question, I'd probably be without a wife today." Yet, we reduce our relationship with Jesus to a similar mindset. We want to secure our eternity, but we're not willing to give our whole lives to God. Why does He even ask such a thing of us? John Calvin once said that our hearts are idolmaking factories. We idolize the latest, trendiest, or most glittering things, destroying our hearts and dishonoring God. Our hearts are most full, healed, and whole when they're set on the One who made them. God knows this—He created us to be our best and truest selves when we fully follow Him.

ALIGN YOUR MIND Read Deuteronomy 10:12–22.

ALIGN YOUR ACTIONS Ask Jesus to show you if your heart has wandered or drifted in any way. Smash your idols and live wholeheartedly for the One who made you.

ALIGN YOUR HEART

Lord Jesus, I humble myself before You. Search my heart; show me what I need to see. Though You love me whether I wander or not, I'm my best self when I'm found in You. You deserve my highest honor and praise. Draw me near, O God. Amen.

Find Strength and Courage

"This is my command—be strong and courageous! Do not be afraid or discouraged. For the LORD your God is with you wherever you go."

Joshua 1:9

Fear weakens us. Discouragement derails us. Yet our fears are real. And in seasons of continuous difficulty, it seems we're constantly just moments away from our greatest fears coming to life. Maybe that's why God's voice thunders when He charges us to be strong and full of courage. Our feet tend to follow our gaze, and when our gaze is skewed, we lose our way. Yet Jesus' voice continually beckons us back to the path of faith. The reason Jesus charges us not to fear or to let discouragement win the day is that He knows what it'll do to our souls, to our hearts. And what He asks of us, He also gives to us. When He asks us to be brave, He also gives us courage. Amazingly, He gives us faith and is at the same time pleased by our faith. He has entrusted to us every blessing, every promise, complete access to His presence, abundant wisdom for every situation. You can do this, friend. Just take another step.

ALIGN YOUR MIND ▶ Read Joshua 1:6–9.

ALIGN YOUR ACTIONS ▶ Have you let fear slip in or lost a bit of your fight? Rise up, brave one, and tell your heart to be strong and courageous! For the Lord your God is with you today!

ALIGN YOUR HEART ▶

> *Precious Lord, thank You for making me an heir to Your promises. You've provided for my every need and equipped me for every battle. You've never left me alone and never will. Rise up within me once again, Lord. I am strong in You! Amen.*

The Living God Is with You

"Come and listen to what the LORD your God says. Today you will know that the living God is among you."

Joshua 3:9–10

Joshua was about to lead this new generation of Israelites into the Promised Land. They'd need two very important things in order to successfully make this trip: ears to hear and a heart to know God's mighty power and ability to intervene. We need these too. Pause here for a moment and consider the rogue thoughts and the daily stresses cluttering your brain right now. Take a few deep breaths. Think about God's nearness. Now put on your favorite worship song and sing along, thinking about God's goodness and faithfulness and not your stresses. Lean in and listen to what the Lord your God is saying to you. Do you hear Him? Stay in this moment with Him. Though He sometimes seems slow to intervene, do you still believe that His power is matchless and His strength endless? Do you believe He's able to rearrange circumstances and intervene in ways that defy the gravity of your situation? Your presence with Him matters. He has things to say to you. He intends to display His power in your life. The Almighty God is with you.

ALIGN YOUR MIND Read Joshua 3:5–17

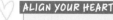

ALIGN YOUR ACTIONS Today, listen for His voice throughout your day. Know He's with you. Write down what He says to you. Add the date so you'll remember it later.

ALIGN YOUR HEART

> *Mighty God of heaven, You are all that I need. Forgive me for racing through my days feeling more stressed than blessed. I want to flourish in my soul. I want to trust You more. I'm listening, Lord. Speak to me. Amen.*

On the Lord's Side

When Joshua was near the town of Jericho, he looked up and saw a man standing in front of him with sword in hand. Joshua went up to him and demanded, "Are you friend or foe?"

"Neither one," he replied. "I am the commander of the LORD's army."

Joshua 5:13–14

God just told Joshua to be strong and courageous, not to fear or fret. Why? Because the Lord was on Joshua's side! If God is for you, who can stand against you? So why didn't this commander also tell Joshua, "I'm a friend. I'm on your side"? It's one thing to put your unwavering trust in the Lord; it's another to presume upon God. Though Joshua's heart was all in, the Israelites still had wandering hearts. The angel reminded Joshua that though God is with us, *we* are the ones on God's side. He sets the terms, He guides our way, and He gets the say. When we fail, He loves us still. When we're unfaithful, He remains faithful. But sometimes we need a spiritual reset—a reminder of just who it is that we serve. He's the God of Angel Armies and we should take Him seriously.

ALIGN YOUR MIND ▶ Read Joshua 5:13–15; 7:1–13.

ALIGN YOUR ACTIONS ▶ Do you take God seriously? Why or why not? Do your actions reflect your choice to wholeheartedly follow Him? Ask God for forgiveness where you fall short—and for a fresh wonder at His love for you.

ALIGN YOUR HEART

God of Angel Armies, forgive me for taking Your grace for granted and acting in selfish ways. You are for me—help me to be for You! Give me a heart to love and honor You all of my days! Amen.

Humility Precedes Honor

Joshua fell with his face to the ground in reverence. "I am at your command," Joshua said. "What do you want your servant to do?"

The commander of the Lord's army replied, "Take off your sandals, for the place where you are standing is holy." And Joshua did as he was told.

Joshua 5:14–15

God charged Joshua to lead His chosen people into the Promised Land. He exhorted Joshua not to fear or get discouraged. Then He sent an angel to remind Joshua of His majesty and honor. Before Joshua could rise up in victory, he first had to bow low in humility. Can you see the progression? The Lord guards and guides our steps the same way. He knows what you need in order to face the battles ahead. He knows what victories He's assigned to you. He knows when you need a word of encouragement and when it's time for you to bow low in reverence. All of these are for your good and for His glory. God never humiliates those who fear Him, but He does humble us. And He meets us intimately in that sacred place and shows us things we'd never otherwise know.

ALIGN YOUR MIND ▶ Read Joshua 5:13–15; 6:1–5.

ALIGN YOUR ACTIONS ▶ Try praying and reading Scripture on your knees. Bow your face to the ground and tell God how wonderful He is. Ask God to show you His heart for you. Give Him your will and ask for His.

ALIGN YOUR HEART

Precious Lord, You modeled humility in the most beautiful way. I will follow Your lead. Open my eyes to see what I cannot see. Grant me a fresh revelation of Your love and majesty. It's in Your matchless name I pray. Amen.

Put the Enemy to Flight

"Each one of you will put to flight a thousand of the enemy, for the Lord your God fights for you, just as he has promised."

Joshua 23:10

When we give God His rightful place in our lives, the enemy will be defeated, his evil schemes against us will eventually fall apart, and his attempts to derail our destiny will end up working in our favor. Whenever they were out of step with God, the Israelites got into trouble and were soundly defeated by their enemies. Whenever they griped and grumbled, lived entitled, disobeyed God's direct commands, and underestimated their enemy, they fell flat on their faces. However, when they obeyed His commands, walked in reverence for the Lord, and trusted Him wholeheartedly, they saw the miraculous unfold before their very eyes. He's the same God today. He deserves our trust, our reverence, and our swift obedience. And He will intervene in ways we never dreamed of as we take our stand and watch what He will do. On your own, you're no match for that enemy of yours—you will fall flat. But with God—through your obedience and faith-filled prayers—you can change the world.

ALIGN YOUR MIND ▶ Read Joshua 23:1–10.

ALIGN YOUR ACTIONS ▶ Dream a little for a moment. If you could live a miraculous life, what would that look like for you?

ALIGN YOUR HEART ▶

> *Father, teach me to walk in Your way! Do the miraculous, the impossible through me! I don't want the enemy to put me to flight; I want to put him to flight! Show me how to stand in battle so my enemy flees and You win the victory through me. Change the world through me. Amen.*

All In

"So fear the LORD and serve him wholeheartedly. Put away forever the idols your ancestors worshiped. . . . Serve the LORD alone. . . . Choose today whom you will serve. . . . But as for me and my family, we will serve the LORD."

Joshua 24:14–15

It's been said that part-time Christians are some of the most miserable people on the planet. With half their hearts pursuing the Lord and the other half pursuing the things of this world, they have no sense of belonging, no sense of identity or purpose, and a constant, plaguing sense that they're missing out, failing, or falling short in every area. And they are. Yet what joy and peace await us when we trust wholeheartedly in Him! His plans for us are our best-case scenario! Nothing the world offers compares to the power, presence, and very personal love the Savior has for *you*. Are you all in? If not, today is a good day to pursue the Lord with all your heart, soul, mind, and strength. May you experience the clarity of purpose, the joy of belonging, and the profound sense of identity that come from going all in and serving the Lord with your whole heart.

ALIGN YOUR MIND Read Joshua 24:11–24.

ALIGN YOUR ACTIONS Are you all in for God? If not, what's holding you back? If so, how can you go deeper? Today, ask God to show you His heart for you in a very real way.

ALIGN YOUR HEART

Lord, forgive me for splitting my attention and my heart between You and this world. Give me a heart to be all in for You. Help me to love You with all my heart, soul, mind, and strength—today and every day. Amen.

Rise Up and Take Your Place!

There were few people left in the villages of Israel—
until Deborah arose as a mother for Israel.

Judges 5:7

From your friends to your classes to the teams or organizations you're a part of to your school and wider community, where there's a void of Christian influence, there's a vacuum for the enemy to fill. And God is looking for willing and humble hearts to step up. In the Old Testament, women leaders weren't exactly commonplace at the time of the judges, yet God called Deborah to rise up, to lead, and to help care for His people. Where's the need in your midst? What stirs up passion in your soul? How might God use you to impact your world because of what Christ has done in you? Don't wait for someone else to do the work—rise up! God has gifts He's called you to use for His glory and lives He's appointed you to touch. May the passion and the purposes of God stir your heart to bow low as you step up to the place of influence He's created you for.

ALIGN YOUR MIND Read Judges 4:4–23; 5:6–7.

ALIGN YOUR ACTIONS Ask God what He's calling you to do in this season. Write it down and put it where you'll see it every day. Each time you see the note, pray for the strength, focus, and grit to rise up into what He has for you.

ALIGN YOUR HEART

King Jesus, I bow before You. I'll never have authority until I'm under authority. You've created me for influence. Show me my place in the greater kingdom story. Where and how shall I rise up in this day for the sake of Your name? Speak, Lord. Amen.

Mighty Hero, the Lord Is with You!

The angel of the LORD appeared to him and said, "Mighty hero, the LORD is with you!"

Judges 6:12

Ever feel outnumbered, outmatched, or in over your head? Imagine how Gideon must have felt when he was first called by God to rise up and defeat God's enemies. He saw himself as a nobody—he was literally at the bottom of Israel's social structure. And if that weren't challenging enough, God required him to thin his troops, putting him at an even greater disadvantage. What would that look like in your life? Maybe the Lord gave you a yes for a certain task or commitment, so you followed His lead, only to experience a setback or loss after the fact. Maybe you were betrayed by a friend, cut from the team, or lost your phone. God told Gideon to thin the troops, and sometimes He allows the enemy to do the thinning for us—but only because He's setting us up for victory, and himself for greater glory. If you've responded to God's invitation only to suddenly feel overwhelmed, you're in good company. Don't lose heart. Go in the strength you have. It's impossible for Him to fail you. Mighty hero, the Lord is with you!

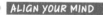 **ALIGN YOUR MIND** Read Judges 6; 7:1–7.

 ALIGN YOUR ACTIONS Today, if you need encouragement, ask for it.

 ALIGN YOUR HEART

Precious Lord, I'm in over my head. Show me a sign of Your favor and goodness, O Lord. Intervene in a way that encourages my soul. I need You every hour. Upward and onward I go. Thank You, Lord. Amen.

Glimpses of Glory

When Gideon heard the dream and its interpretation, he bowed in worship before the Lᴏʀᴅ. Then he returned to the Israelite camp and shouted, "Get up! For the Lᴏʀᴅ has given you victory over the Midianite hordes!"

Judges 7:15

God is so good to grant us glimpses of glory when we need them most. Gideon faced impossible odds. He knew without a doubt God had called him, yet he was still unsure of what the battle might cost him or how the story would play out. If you've walked with the Lord awhile, you know that just because God calls us to do something doesn't mean it'll be easy, without cost, and will turn out exactly as we've pictured it. But He calls us forward in faith with full assurance that if He calls us out, He'll hold us up. His ways are higher, His insights run deeper, and His desires for us *far exceed* our small earthbound desires for ourselves. God knows when we've got the inner strength and courage to move ahead, and when we need a glimpse of His goodness to encourage us to keep going. If you need a peek into His grand plan for you, just ask Him. May a newfound strength rise up within you today! May you be confident of the victory that awaits you on the other side of this battle.

ALIGN YOUR MIND Read Judges 7:9–20.

ALIGN YOUR ACTIONS What do you need from the Lord today? Go ahead and ask Him.

ALIGN YOUR HEART

Father, give me a glimpse into Your perfect plan for me so I will march forward, unafraid and full of faith. I know it's impossible for You to fail me. Help me to know it on a deeper level. Amen.

Focused, Grateful, Humble

> One day when Samson was in Timnah, one of the Philistine women caught his eye. When he returned home, he told his father and mother, "A young Philistine woman in Timnah caught my eye. I want to marry her. Get her for me."
>
> Judges 14:1–2

The Spirit of the Lord rested upon Samson, and yet our first glimpse into his character reveals a heart bent on his own desires. Samson's eyes wandered to things that dishonored God. He spouted demands to his father with a thankless, entitled attitude. Unfocused. Ungrateful. Arrogant. These attributes are the antithesis of God's heart for and through His people. How did Samson get like this? One unfocused, ungrateful, arrogant step at a time. Did his parents spoil him because he was called by God? It seems so. Samson's father didn't *have* to give in to Samson's selfish whim. But he did.* Samson's life is a tragic picture of what it looks like when someone who is anointed, gifted, and clearly called by God refuses to humbly submit *to* God.

ALIGN YOUR MIND Read Judges 14:1–9.

ALIGN YOUR ACTIONS Today, humble yourself when you're tempted to exalt yourself. Look around and thank God for everything you'd miss tomorrow if you woke up without it.

ALIGN YOUR HEART

Father, help me to live humbly and with gratefulness for all You've done for me. Please give me laser-like focus to do what You've called me to. Show me, Lord, where I am arrogant or entitled, and please forgive me. In Your precious name, Amen.

---

* Verse 4 reveals that God worked through Samson's demands to set up His greater purposes, but it doesn't validate Samson's defiant, wandering appetite. God works all things together for the good (Romans 8:28).

When Pain Speaks

"Things are far more bitter for me than for you, because the LORD himself has raised his fist against me."

Ruth 1:13

Naomi had reason to grieve, to lament, and to even wonder where God was in it all. She'd lost her husband and then her two sons. She not only grieved as a widow and as a mother, but as a woman who was now at the mercy of the culture, the elements, and the times. Or so she thought. Truth was, she wasn't at anyone's mercy; she was in the mercies of God. She just didn't know it yet. Even though Elimelech, Naomi's husband, led his family outside the will of God to a land of idol-worshipers, God never left Naomi's side. He'd made a plan to redeem her story long before she ever knew she'd need it. God's always in the process of bringing redemption to our stories. He knows about every enemy scheme, every unfortunate event, and every mess we find ourselves in. Yes, we need to process our pain. Lament is healing to the soul. But consider carefully the great difference between blaming God and crying out to Him. Check your heart today. Your redemption story is already in motion.

ALIGN YOUR MIND Read Ruth 1:1–13.

ALIGN YOUR ACTIONS How have you allowed your pain to speak? Search your heart and ask God to reveal any unresolved grief, hardness, or bitterness hidden in your soul. Ask Him to soften, restore, and heal you.

ALIGN YOUR HEART

> *Precious Jesus, with open hands and a humble heart, I ask You to redeem me from the things I've suffered. Help me sort through my losses in a way that draws me closer to You and heals me from the inside out. Amen.*

When Conviction Speaks

But Ruth replied, "Don't ask me to leave you and turn back. Wherever you go, I will go; wherever you live, I will live. Your people will be my people, and your God will be my God."

Ruth 1:16

Naomi's faith must have impacted Ruth over the years because Ruth—a Moabite—saw through her painful loss and embraced the bigger story God was writing with her life. No one would have blamed her if she'd gone back to her small town and small 'g' gods. But to everyone's surprise, Ruth pulled up her tent stakes to follow God. She knew the travel would be treacherous; she was well aware of what happens to women who don't have men to protect them. She was smart enough to know that even if she made it to Bethlehem, she'd likely be rejected and excluded by the Israelite women because of where she came from. Yet she was still willing to leave what she knew to follow a God she could not see. We know how her story turned out, but at this moment, Ruth had no idea we'd still be talking about her today. Do you believe that your faith matters *just as much*? And that your risks are noted in heaven? Don't choose ease over eternity. Rise up and follow where He leads.

ALIGN YOUR MIND Read Ruth 1:14–22.

ALIGN YOUR ACTIONS What kind of faith risk is before you? What are you waiting for? Today, just take the next step. God will do the rest.

ALIGN YOUR HEART

> *Lord Jesus, give me the courage and conviction to live boldly for You! Forgive me for my tendency to self-preserve and choose comfort over conviction. You deserve my whole heart. Amen.*

Take Action

So Ruth went out to gather grain behind the harvesters. And as it happened, she found herself working in a field that belonged to Boaz, the relative of her father-in-law, Elimelech.

Ruth 2:3

Ruth was a foreigner, new in town, and grieving. However, she was so committed to her heartbroken mother-in-law that she boldly took action and went out among strangers to gather grain. And without realizing it, she ended up working in a field owned by Boaz, a relative of her father-in-law. Boaz noticed Ruth right away and made sure she'd be protected and provided for. He looked past Ruth's ethnicity and social class and saw what God saw: honor, humility, courage, and conviction. (Did you know that it takes honor to notice honor in another?) Ruth took initiative; God took it from there. Isn't it amazing that when we take faith risks to follow God wholeheartedly, He leads us even when we're unaware? He guards and He guides; He protects and provides. One day we'll get to heaven and absolutely marvel at God's intervention in our lives. But for now, we must rest assured that when our hearts are fully set on the Lord, He will be our Good Shepherd every step of the way.

ALIGN YOUR MIND ▶ Read Ruth 2:1–9.

ALIGN YOUR ACTIONS ▶ What does it look like for you to follow Jesus wholeheartedly? Is anything holding you back from taking bold action? Today, take initiative when it's yours to do so. Believe down to your toes that God will determine your steps.

ALIGN YOUR HEART

Father, I trust You. I cannot fathom how many circumstances You've already orchestrated for my good and for Your glory. Help me to take action and follow where You lead. Thank You, Lord. Amen.

Refuge and Reward

"May the LORD, the God of Israel, under whose wings you have come to take refuge, reward you fully for what you have done."

Ruth 2:12

Faith compels us to do what our flesh would rather not. Faith calls us out when we'd rather stay back. Faith charges us to wait when we'd rather run. Ruth's faith compelled her to action. She couldn't know all of the good things God had planned for her. She had faith in a God who was even better than she believed Him to be. *You* have faith in a God who is far better than you know Him to be. Boaz spoke a blessing over Ruth that's meant for you today as well. May God reward you fully for the times you loved when it didn't suit you, for the times you served when no one saw you, for the ways you followed Jesus when it cost you. May the Lord Almighty bless you for finding refuge under His wings. You trusted Him. May you find Him more faithful and kinder than you ever dreamed.

 ALIGN YOUR MIND ▶ Read Ruth 2:10–23.

ALIGN YOUR ACTIONS ▶ What are some ways you can practically take refuge in the Lord? Pause and take time today to do something restful with God.

ALIGN YOUR HEART

> *Precious Lord, thank You for Your kindness to me. You've invited me to take shelter under Your wing. You've put faith in my heart. You've invited me to trust and obey. And then You reward me for doing the very thing I was made to do—follow You. I honor You this day. I know You are good and kind and true. And I am grateful. Amen.*

From Famine to Flourishing

Then the elders and all the people standing in the gate replied, "We are witnesses! May the LORD make this woman who is coming into your home like Rachel and Leah, from whom all the nation of Israel descended! May you prosper in Ephrathah and be famous in Bethlehem."

Ruth 4:11

Widows in Ruth's day had little hope for a flourishing future. Yet somehow God orchestrated events so that this outcast woman of God would marry one of the most honorable men in town. The elders stood at the gate and prophesied a blessing that would surely come to pass. Ruth was no longer a widow; she was a wife. She no longer had to scrape out a living; she was well cared for and provided for. She and Naomi were no longer destitute; they were destined to live out God's sovereign plan for their lives. You may find yourself in the not-yet part of your story. You're still waiting for the breakthrough. I pray Ruth's faith inspires your own. He's the same God yesterday, today, and forever. He loves you as much as He loved Ruth. Don't give up hope. Your story has a wonderful ending. Like my friend Jodi once said to me, "If your story's not good yet, it's because God's not done yet."

ALIGN YOUR MIND Read Ruth 3; 4:1–11.

ALIGN YOUR ACTIONS What parts of your story aren't good yet? Ask God to intervene. Do what He tells you to. And believe that He's up to something good. (Because He is.)

ALIGN YOUR HEART

Lord, I don't want to feel like a havenot. Forgive me for believing I'm less important than Your other children. I know You love me. Help me trust You with my whole story. Amen.

Total Redemption

So Boaz took Ruth into his home, and she became his wife. When he slept with her, the LORD enabled her to become pregnant, and she gave birth to a son.

Ruth 4:13

Ruth—an outcast widow from an enemy nation—married Boaz, son of Rahab, the prostitute. Together, they had a baby boy named Obed, who became the father of Jesse, who became the father of King David. God made it so that these two unlikely yet beautiful people played key roles in the lineage of Christ! A Moabite woman and a son of a prostitute. Aren't the grace and the mercy of God just breathtaking? Like Ruth and Boaz, we've become a part of the family line! Because of Jesus, we have His royal blood flowing through our veins! It doesn't matter where we've come from or what we've done in our past. What matters is our faith in the One who redeemed us. No one and nothing can separate us from His love. Jesus has not only covered our past with mercy and forgiveness, but He's also completely secured our future. Don't let anyone skew your perspective or use your past to derail you: Your story is and will be completely redeemed.

ALIGN YOUR MIND Read Ruth 4:13–22.

ALIGN YOUR ACTIONS Have you let the enemy use your heritage or past against you? When you hear the enemy's lies, stand firm on the promise that you are totally redeemed and secure in the heart of Christ. Raise your hands in praise and thanks today.

ALIGN YOUR HEART

Jesus, what You accomplished for me, I cannot fathom. But I thank You that I'm secure in You! I'm established in You! I possess all the riches of heaven, because of You. Thank You, Jesus. Amen.

Rightly Placed Honor

So Peninnah would taunt Hannah and make fun of her because the Lord had kept her from having children.

1 Samuel 1:6

Hannah was a humble, God-fearing woman who dearly desired children. But for unknown reasons, she wasn't able to conceive. Peninnah was a jealous and petty woman who had lots of kids—and she pridefully took all the credit for her abundance, which was a prized status symbol of the time. More than that, she ridiculed and judged Hannah for her inability to get pregnant. Imagine, day in and day out, being made fun of for your dashed dreams because of something outside your control. It led Hannah to feel cursed. Yet both women misinterpreted their situations. Peninnah honored and elevated herself—and mocked others—when she should have humbly honored God. Neither woman could know that God had kept Hannah from having children because He was waiting for the right time to draw a *whole nation* back to Him. Hannah's future son would become one of the greatest prophets of all time! Do you have an unrealized dream? Don't let the mockers get to you. Their day of discipline is coming. Honor God. He will—in His time—bless you before a watching world.

ALIGN YOUR MIND Read 1 Samuel 1:1–7.

ALIGN YOUR ACTIONS Do you have a God-given dream that seems impossible? Have others been supportive or hurtful? Ask God to show you what's really true.

ALIGN YOUR HEART

Lord of heaven's armies, You are with me. You are for me. Forgive me for putting more weight on my flawed perspective than I do on Your perfect promises. My story fits me perfectly. I trust You. Fill me with faith and perspective this hour. Amen.

Pain Filters
and Passionate Prayers

As she was praying to the LORD, Eli watched her. Seeing her lips moving but hearing no sound, he thought she had been drinking. "Must you come here drunk?" he demanded. "Throw away your wine!"

1 Samuel 1:12–14

Would this dear woman never catch a break? Hannah takes her broken-hearted self to the temple to cry out to God, just as she should. She bows low, humbles herself before almighty God, and asks Him to look upon the sorrow in her heart, only to have the high priest say to her, "Wait . . . are you drunk?" Have mercy! But if you look closer at this story, you'll see that Eli's own sons—who were also priests!—were the ones drinking in the temple. Eli viewed Hannah's heartbreak through his own pain filter. Hurt people hurt people. Thankfully, Hannah was humble enough to respond with truth—but talk about adding insult to injury! Her husband's extra wife taunted her, and the temple priest accused her. Did she make a mistake, running to the temple? Absolutely not. Did Eli misread the situation? Absolutely. Did God redeem her story? One hundred percent yes! Life on earth can be so very messy. But you'll never go wrong running to the arms of your Savior.

 ALIGN YOUR MIND ▶ Read 1 Samuel 1:9–18.

 ALIGN YOUR ACTIONS ▶ Today, be a bit more gracious when it comes to assessing the suffering of another. We don't know what we don't know.

 ALIGN YOUR HEART

> *Jesus, sometimes I allow my wounds and offenses to pull me away from You. But today I take every hurt and every heartbreak, and I bring them before You. People and pain will not have the last say in my life! Amen.*

The Lord Has Made Me Strong!

"My heart rejoices in the LORD!
The LORD has made me strong.
Now I have an answer for my enemies;
I rejoice because you rescued me."

1 Samuel 2:1

The believer's story is one of setbacks and divine setups. The enemy opposes us and God defends us. We lose heart and God strengthens our hearts. We break down and God breaks through. We forget about His goodness and He reminds us once again that He is constantly and continually good. How many nights do you suppose Hannah cried herself to sleep, wondering if she'd done something to chase away God's blessing? How many times did the enemy use that to shoot discouragement into the depths of her soul? Though Hannah struggled through her heartbreak (understandably so), she stayed humble and teachable—and God not only defended her, but He also vindicated her beyond her wildest dreams. Your story has its twists and turns. You have days of ups and downs, and God will be with you every step of the way. But remember this: He cannot strengthen a hard heart, only a humble one. Stay tender and trust Him. He will make you strong and you *will* have an answer for your enemies.

ALIGN YOUR MIND Read 1 Samuel 2:1–11.

ALIGN YOUR ACTIONS Ask God where you are on the journey today. What does it look like to stay tender and teachable even in this place? Can you trust that He's delivering and defending you?

ALIGN YOUR HEART

Jesus, this is my story, and I trust You with it. Intervene where I cannot. Defend and deliver me. Make me strong and steadfast. May Your favor upon my life silence my critics. Amen.

Up or Down?

Eli's sons wouldn't listen to their father, for the LORD was already planning to put them to death. Meanwhile, the boy Samuel grew taller and grew in favor with the LORD and with the people.

1 Samuel 2:25–26

Life is not stationary; it's moving in one way or another. From the outside looking in, both of Eli's sons, as well as Samuel, held places of privilege in the temple. But God sees past our achievements and our social status—or our lack of them. He looks into the depths of our hearts. What you do and the decisions you make, especially when no one is watching, reveal the state of your heart. They show if you're moving toward God—or not. We cannot rest on past laurels or past steps of obedience. The question at hand is this: In which direction are your feet pointing? Where are your most consistent choices taking you? Are you drawing nearer to God, or are you walking away for the sake of acceptance, attention, or accolades? Remember, God's will for you is your bestcase scenario. He intends to take you from strength to strength, glory to glory, shining ever brighter until the full light of day.

ALIGN YOUR MIND ▶ Read 1 Samuel 2:12–26.

ALIGN YOUR ACTIONS ▶ Take time to honestly reflect on your most consistent choices. Are they taking you closer to God or further from Him? Why? What is one thing you can do to point your feet back to Him today?

ALIGN YOUR HEART ▶

Father, I am prone to wander! Keep my heart deeply connected to Yours. Show me where I'm weakest and help me to shore up my life. I want to grow in favor and stature before You, Lord. Draw me closer still. Amen.

Holy Reinforcement

So the Philistines were subdued and didn't invade Israel again for some time. And throughout Samuel's lifetime, the Lord's powerful hand was raised against the Philistines.

1 Samuel 7:13

No one can fathom the power of one life solely dedicated to the Lord Most High. Before Samuel was even born, Hannah dedicated him to the Lord. Samuel lived in the Lord's presence and honored him continually. Because Samuel lived among God's people, their enemies were held at bay. What if we approached our walks of faith in much the same way? When we take seriously our lives before the Lord, He takes very seriously the prayers that come out of our mouths. Imagine, because of your very presence on the earth today, evil plans come to nothing, enemy schemes break down, and God's people are protected in ways they'll never realize this side of heaven. All because you walked closely with the Lord. God has placed you on this earth for such a time as this. History has proven time and time again that one life—wholly dedicated to the Lord—has the power to change the world.

ALIGN YOUR MIND Read 1 Samuel 3:7–14.

ALIGN YOUR ACTIONS What injustices break your heart? What evil in your community stirs you up? Today, while others shake their fists at the darkness, commit yourself more firmly to the Lord. Pray like there's a God in heaven who hears you—because there is, and He does!

ALIGN YOUR HEART

Mighty God, hear my prayer! Foil the plans of the wicked and establish the plans of the righteous! Cut off the strength of the wicked and increase the power of the godly! Break my heart for what breaks Yours. I want my prayers to change the world! Amen.

Insecurity Is Not Humility

> Saul replied, "But I'm only from the tribe of Benjamin, the smallest tribe in Israel, and my family is the least important of all the families of that tribe! Why are you talking like this to me?"
>
> 1 Samuel 9:21

Saul's question sounds a lot like Gideon's, wouldn't you say? But if you watch how their lives play out, you realize that while Gideon may have felt a bit insecure, his weightier attribute was humility, whereas Saul was fueled by his chronic self-sins. Read this powerful study note from my Bible: "Although Saul had been called by God and had a mission in life, he struggled constantly with jealousy, insecurity, arrogance, impulsiveness, and deceit. He did not decide to be wholeheartedly committed to God. *Because Saul would not let God's love give rest to his heart, he never became God's man.*"* When rejection, insecurity, and inferiority remain unchallenged within us, we will repeatedly sabotage our own destiny. We've got to be ruthless with thoughts of insecurity. You and I are called to freedom—humble, bold, courageous freedom. It's the only way we'll live out the amazing call on our lives.

 ALIGN YOUR MIND Read 1 Samuel 9:15–21.

 ALIGN YOUR ACTIONS This takes grit but I dare you to do it anyway: ruthlessly eliminate any hint of insecurity from your thoughts and your speech. Live and walk like you are loved. You are an heir of God and you bear His image!

 ALIGN YOUR HEART

> *Father, forgive me for believing my insecurities more than Your promises. I will stand in faith and believe what You say about me. I am called and I am loved. Lead me on, Lord! Amen.*

---

* *Life Application Study Bible*, 563, emphasis mine.

Are You Not?

And Samuel told him, "Although you may think little of yourself, are you not the leader of the tribes of Israel? The LORD has anointed you king of Israel."

1 Samuel 15:17

When my sons were teenagers, we learned that rules and consequences weren't always enough to motivate our boys to be all they could be through Christ. We needed to cast a vision for what was possible for the one who stays humble, teachable, and faithful. Take Saul, for example. He had a clear call on his life. God confirmed it again and again. Yet Saul was bent on doing things his own way. Then he made excuses, blamed others, and even spiritualized his disobedience in order to justify his actions. Saul never fully grasped what God would have accomplished through him, if only he'd dared to trust Him. Learn from Saul's losses. Ask God to help you see yourself the way He sees you! Ask Him for a vision for your life that makes your heart come alive and for faith to lay hold of it.

ALIGN YOUR MIND ▸ Read 1 Samuel 15:10–23.

ALIGN YOUR ACTIONS ▸ When you're tempted to squander your time or doubt your worth, picture the prophet Samuel grabbing you by the shoulders, looking deep into your eyes, and imploring you, "Are you not absolutely beloved and called by God? Have you forgotten who you are? The Lord has anointed and appointed you!"

ALIGN YOUR HEART

Father, like Saul, I can tend to cut corners, make excuses, and then attempt to strive my way back into Your good graces. But that's not how You operate. I'm already in Your mercy and grace. I humble myself before You. I choose to believe and obey You. Help my unbelief. Amen.

Don't Miss Your Assignment

But Samuel asked, "How can I do that? If Saul hears about it, he will kill me."

1 Samuel 16:2

God anointed and appointed Saul as king. Yet Saul's constant and continual selfish, insecure actions sabotaged his own destiny. If we don't praise God, the rocks will cry out. If we don't step into our God-given assignment with a heart of faith and trust, like Saul, God may choose another to fulfill what He intended for us. I don't want to miss a thing God has for me, do you? While Saul was busy misusing his power, young David was in the wilderness learning how to fight lions and bears. He was both chosen to be, and growing into, God's man to replace Saul. Yet when God told the prophet Samuel that it was time to anoint another king, Samuel froze in fear. Samuel's fear made sense given Saul's irrational, impulsive ways. And yet, the odds, the circumstances, the opposition are all meaningless when the Lord has issued a charge to us. Though it's true that your God-given assignment may involve uncertainty, opposition, and a few giants, don't let your fears keep you from moving forward. Be like Samuel. If God has called you to it, He will see you through it.

ALIGN YOUR MIND Read 1 Samuel 16:1–7.

ALIGN YOUR ACTIONS In what ways have you recently pulled back in fear? That's where God is calling you to engage your faith. What steps of obedience will you take today?

ALIGN YOUR HEART

King Jesus, You are all that I need. So often I forget that if You call me out beyond my natural abilities, You will hold me up. I'm ready to follow You today. I'm all in. Lead me on. Amen.

The Lord Looks at the Heart

"The LORD doesn't see things the way you see them. People judge by outward appearance, but the LORD looks at the heart."

1 Samuel 16:7

When God sent Samuel to anoint the next king, He cautioned the prophet to listen with his spiritual ears so he wouldn't be misled by what he saw with his physical eyes. We so often get it wrong. Our filter is profoundly skewed by our hurts and fears, our culture's trends, and our own judgments. But if our eyes could truly see what God sees, we'd marvel at the things God values, and at what He finds distasteful. We'd see Him ministering to a recovering drug addict humbly repenting after another relapse, while distancing himself from the polished Christian who pridefully lives for man's praise and status. We'd see Him draw near to the humble-yet-messy girl who just cannot keep up with school or work, and watch Him distance himself from the picture-perfect girl who seems to have everything but secretly manipulates and backstabs to get her way. May you discern what God sees when you look at others. And may you be who God is looking for when He's ready to appoint the next influencer.

 ALIGN YOUR MIND ▶ Read 1 Samuel 16:4–13.

 ALIGN YOUR ACTIONS ▶ What you look for, you will find. Start looking for honor, humility, grace, and joy in others. You'll find it.

 ALIGN YOUR HEART ▶

Father, I don't want to live by my assumptions and skewed perspectives. Open up the eyes of my heart so I can see what You see. Help me to discern honor, humility, grace, and joy when I see it. Help me to value those things too. I want to be more like You in every way. Amen.

Promoted Gradually

Saul sent messengers to Jesse to say, "Send me your son David, the shepherd."

1 Samuel 16:19

Samuel went to the house of Jesse and anointed young David to be the next king. Yet it would be years before David actually took the throne. Even so, God was actively working behind the scenes. While the Spirit of the Lord came powerfully upon David, that same Spirit had lifted from Saul. It seemed the king was losing his mind. His men suggested he bring in a young warrior/musician to soothe his fears and anxiety. I wonder if David thought, *Is this the day my call comes to fruition?* This wasn't to be the day, but it was the start of his preparation process. David would go back and forth between his father's house and the palace as he was needed. He learned the ways of the kingdom and how to wait on God's hard-to-understand timing. Often, after receiving a sense of calling from the Lord, we'll experience movement in that direction, only to see it short-lived. Did we hear wrong? Is this all there is? No! You'll go back and forth between the palace and your home until the time is ready for you to take your place. Don't lose heart. Stay humble. Stay ready.

 ALIGN YOUR MIND Read 1 Samuel 16:14–23.

 ALIGN YOUR ACTIONS Do you have a sense of calling from the Lord? If not, ask Him for a vision of it today. As you wait, keep your heart humble and open to learning what each new season brings.

 ALIGN YOUR HEART

Father, I know You make me wait because You're making me ready. Help me to discern Your voice and see Your movement all around me. I'll wait on You. Amen.

What Emerges from Us

When Saul and the Israelites heard [Goliath's rant], they were terrified and deeply shaken.

1 Samuel 17:11

Someone once said that when we get bumped, what's inside spills right out of us. It's true: What's in us emerges from us when we're tested. Saul may have been tall, dark, and handsome, and he may have held the title of king, but when faced with a giant, his inexperience and insecurity surfaced. Saul's perpetual tendency toward self-doubt and self-preservation revealed a consistent thought life focused on himself. David, on the other hand, was a different story. When Saul questioned David's capacity to take on a giant, David rehearsed his victories and reminded everyone listening that God was greater than any giant he'd ever face. David wrote, sang, and spoke of God's continual faithfulness. What emerged from David in the face of battle? Courage, honor, and faith. Every step you take matters, because it's taking you somewhere. Every thought you entertain is shaping you and framing your perspective, which impacts your future choices. You may not realize the importance of your past choices until you face a giant or find yourself in a storm. But your choices matter profoundly because *you* matter. Your life matters.

ALIGN YOUR MIND ▶ Read 1 Samuel 17:1–11.

ALIGN YOUR ACTIONS ▶ When facing a challenge, does faith or your insecurity rise? Write down Psalm 57:10; read this truth over and over each day to train your thoughts on the reach of God's love and faithfulness.

ALIGN YOUR HEART

> *Jesus, show me my heart. Show me all the thoughts that weigh me down and hold me back. Give me a fresh dose of faith so that courage and honor arise when I face a battle. You are mighty in me! Amen.*

A Right Perspective in Battle

David asked the soldiers standing nearby, ". . . Who is this pagan Philistine anyway, that he is allowed to defy the armies of the living God?"

1 Samuel 17:26

When Goliath arrived on the scene, he hurled insults at the warriors of Israel. He exalted himself as a champion, defied God, and mocked Israel's soldiers. He challenged them to battle, then asked why they'd even consider fighting him, a powerful warrior. Do you see how the enemy works? First he baits you into battle, then he diminishes your status by calling you names, hitting you where you're weak, and making it personal. But look at young David. It didn't even occur to him to take things personally (even though his own brothers hurled very personal accusations his way) Because David saw the bigger picture, he asked a faithfilled question: *Who is this Philistine that dares to defy the armies of the living God?* He understood that his battle wasn't personal. It was spiritual. It's the same with you. Don't let your enemy single you out. Stay in step with the Holy Spirit. See the bigger picture. And call on your giant-killer of a God to fight powerfully through you.

ALIGN YOUR MIND ▶ Read 1 Samuel 17:12–27.

ALIGN YOUR ACTIONS ▶ Today, refuse to listen to the voice of the enemy. Just say no. Instead, focus on the Word of God and let Him fill you with courage.

ALIGN YOUR HEART ▶

> *Lord Jesus, teach me how to stand in battle. Help me to raise my shield and stand in faith when the arrows zing my way. I don't have to let things in. I can be unaffected by words and actions that once made me insecure. I am strong in You! Amen.*

When Jealousy Arises

When Eliab, David's oldest brother, heard him speaking with the men, he burned with anger at him and asked, "Why have you come down here? And with whom did you leave those few sheep in the wilderness? I know how conceited you are and how wicked your heart is; you came down only to watch the battle."

1 Samuel 17:28 NIV

Did Eliab know his brother at all? It was David, the younger brother, who, because he saw the bigger story, was more concerned about the reputation of his God and nation than his own safety. Yet his scared big brother—who was passed over by Samuel to be king—accused him of neglecting his duties at home, of being conceited, and of having a wicked heart. When you mature in faith, your heart of conviction will grow; you'll start to care about things like honor, justice, and God's glory. One day you'll step out in faith, and you will spark the jealousies of others. They may accuse you of things they're actually guilty of, and they'll assign motives that don't belong to you. What to do? Pull out your shield of faith and use your capital NO. Don't let their words in—even for a moment. Keep your head up. Stay humble. Stay obedient. He'll deal with your critics.

ALIGN YOUR MIND Read 1 Samuel 17:28–37.

ALIGN YOUR ACTIONS When you hear the critics, hold your head high and focus on God and His Word. Ask to see the bigger picture.

ALIGN YOUR HEART

Lord Jesus, give me Your passion and purpose to do what You would do if You were in my shoes. I entrust my critics to You and I lay hold of Your promises for me. Amen.

Find What Fits You

"I can't go in these," he protested to Saul. "I'm not used to them." So David took them off again.

1 Samuel 17:38–39

David's past battles had prepared him for his present battle. He feared God, knew His voice, and trusted His ways above all else. God trained David well, and He's just as intentional with you. What can we learn from David's example? Follow Jesus wholeheartedly and trust His timing. Don't race ahead, but stay humble and teachable. Do this, and Jesus will lead you forward into your next place of promise. Embrace this mindset as a way of life—always seeking first His kingdom and His righteousness—and your life will bear much fruit. People will start to notice. And they'll have opinions about how you should do things. And while there's wisdom in many counselors, there's also wisdom in discerning whether or not something fits who you are and what God has asked of you. You'll know when something doesn't fit because it'll feel forced and foreign, and even clunky. Wisdom's path is peace. Don't be afraid to be you. Your past battles have prepared you for this moment.

 ALIGN YOUR MIND Read 1 Samuel 17:38–51.

 ALIGN YOUR ACTIONS What have your past battles and struggles taught you? Ask God to show you how to stay humble, teachable, and embrace who He created YOU to be.

 ALIGN YOUR HEART

> Lord, help me to discern when You're calling me to learn new things and when You want me to stay true to what I already know. I am Yours. I want to be like You. Teach and train me, Lord. Amen.

Timing Is Everything

"Now's your opportunity!" David's men whispered to him. "Today the LORD is telling you, 'I will certainly put your enemy into your power, to do with as you wish.'" So David crept forward and cut off a piece of the hem of Saul's robe.

1 Samuel 24:4

David knew he'd be king one day. He also had awe and reverence for God. Saul feared only for himself and tried relentlessly to kill David. In today's passage, David's men assumed God had finally delivered Saul into David's hands. And David could have killed him in self-defense. Thankfully, David had enough conviction and restraint not to kill Saul, but he did cut off a piece of his robe to make a point. But even that gesture ultimately bothered David. He was so given to the Lord's will and timing for his life, he knew that any effort to do it himself would be a faithless one. Oftentimes, on the way to your breakthrough, you'll be faced with opportunities to make things happen yourself and force an outcome, but it will not be God's best timing for you. How do you know what is God's timing and what is your own? You walk intimately with Him. His Spirit will convict you and clarify your steps.

ALIGN YOUR MIND ▶ Read 1 Samuel 24.

ALIGN YOUR ACTIONS ▶ Imagine laying all your dreams and plans in God's open hands. Give thanks for everything He's already done, and let it strengthen your faith that His plans for you are better than you can imagine.

ALIGN YOUR HEART

Lord, help me never to get ahead of You! Awaken my heart to sense Your direction and cherish Your protection. Lead me in power and purity. My soul waits for You. Amen.

Keep Your Heart in It

> In the spring of the year, when kings normally go out to war, David sent Joab and the Israelite army to fight the Ammonites. They destroyed the Ammonite army and laid siege to the city of Rabbah. However, David stayed behind in Jerusalem.
>
> 2 Samuel 11:1

There's a time for engagement and a time for rest. But there's never a time for disengagement. In Old Testament times, spring was the battle season. As king and a warrior, David should have been with his troops. But he chose to stay behind, sending someone else to lead in his place. And from this place of disengagement came David's most infamous sins. When we walk through a battle, all we can think about is getting to the other side, experiencing some kind of relief. Yet it's the battle that teaches us how to fight and stand strong. Our best lessons are taught through our hardships, and we learn to depend on the Lord through the things we suffer. And because God is good, He'll bring us through and give us rest from our trials. However, we're especially vulnerable after an intense battle or a great victory. We forget that we're just as dependent in the good times as we are in the tough times. No doubt, David was weary from battle. But his disengagement made him vulnerable. May you wisely discern the difference between restorative rest and undisciplined disengagement.

 ALIGN YOUR MIND Read 2 Samuel 11.

 ALIGN YOUR ACTIONS Are you disengaging from something because it's hard or overwhelming? Ask God for strength to fight and grace to truly rest.

 ALIGN YOUR HEART

> *Lord, lead me not into temptation and deliver me from evil. For Yours is the kingdom, power, and glory, both now and forever. Amen.*

He Will Come for You

He led me to a place of safety;
he rescued me because he delights in me.
2 Samuel 22:20

David was a man after God's own heart. And because of it, he had a target on his back. The devil hated him, Saul hated him, and David even got himself into some serious trouble on occasion. Yet he knew enough to humbly cry out to the Lord. Humility in our heart activates the mercy in God's heart. He doesn't rescue us because we're good or because we've earned it. He rescues us because we need it. His compassion runs deeper than the deepest sea. His love reaches higher than the highest heaven. He is God. He has no rival. He's all powerful. What in the world would we do if the one true God were anything but good? I can't imagine! But thankfully, He is good. When we cry out to Him, He comes for us. He shrouds himself in darkness and veils His approach before He breaks through. You may not see Him coming, but neither will your enemy. But make no mistake about it. He will come for you.

ALIGN YOUR MIND Read 2 Samuel 22:1–40.

ALIGN YOUR ACTIONS If you're in a desperate situation, cry out to God today, and don't hold back. Shift your thoughts from yourself and your circumstances to His goodness and faithfulness. It'll nourish your heart and ignite your trust.

ALIGN YOUR HEART

Father, I need You to rescue me! I tend to put more trust in my performance than Your goodness. Yet it's only You who saves me. Who rescues me. You're not looking for perfection; You're looking for faith, raw, humble, surrendered faith. So here I am, Lord. Come for me! Amen.

Ask for Wisdom

The LORD was pleased that Solomon had asked for wisdom.

1 Kings 3:10

Solomon could have asked God for anything, yet he asked for wisdom. Why do you suppose that is? Why didn't he ask for relief from his enemies or wealth beyond compare? Solomon had enough wisdom to know that too much ease and too much material comfort would weaken him over time if he didn't also have wisdom to manage those blessings. God's promise of wisdom is one of the best-kept secrets of the Bible. He offers lavish amounts to anyone who asks for it. Why not throw your arms open wide and ask Him for abounding wisdom every single day of your life? What would you do with more wisdom? You'd be less apt to react in fear or insecurity and more likely to respond in love and compassion. You'd spend less time on meaningless things and more time discovering your gifts—and using them to make a real difference. You'd refuse to give in to peer pressure and instead stand firm in who God created you to be. There are certain prayers God loves to answer. Pray for what's on His heart and you'll marvel at how He works in your life.

ALIGN YOUR MIND Read 1 Kings 3:6–14.

ALIGN YOUR ACTIONS Get into the daily habit of boldly asking God for great amounts of wisdom. Then fine-tune your ears and listen for His answer.

ALIGN YOUR HEART

Lord, pour out daily wisdom on me! Fill me with compassion. Break my heart for what breaks Yours. Awaken me to see the value in others. Anoint me to be a light to the lost, the hurting, and the broken. Help me to live a wise, discerning life. Amen.

Stunned by His Presence

> The priests could not continue their service because of the cloud, for the glorious presence of the LORD filled the Temple of the LORD.
>
> 1 Kings 8:11

Experts say that if you don't feel physical hunger at least twice a day, you're eating too much and too often. How much more so with our spiritual life? If we're not hungry because we feed on that which does not nourish—like mindless games on our phones or social media—how will we long for the kingdom of heaven? If we don't hunger for the presence of God, how will be filled with His Spirit—the One who guides us into Truth? What if we stopped numbing ourselves with our fake comforts and paid attention to what surfaces within us? We might feel anxious, irritable, and even uncomfortable. Is God's presence enough to meet us here? Absolutely. Maybe the question to ask ourselves today is this: *What am I trying so hard not to feel?* You have to feel it to heal it. And Jesus is the Great Healer. What parts of our redemptive story are we missing because we're not missing His presence at all? It's in His presence where the fullness of joy is found.

ALIGN YOUR MIND Read 1 Kings 8:10–11, 22–23.

ALIGN YOUR ACTIONS Give up something—like food, your phone, or media—for twenty-four hours this week. Incorporate fasting as part of your regular practice. But don't just fast—pursue the Lord through reading His Word, praying, and worshiping.

ALIGN YOUR HEART

Lord Jesus, I hunger and thirst for You! Forgive me for the countless ways I numb out and miss You. Stir up a passion in my soul. I want to know Your presence, Lord. Amen.

Finish Strong

In Solomon's old age, [his wives] turned his heart to worship other gods instead of being completely faithful to the LORD his God, as his father, David, had been.

1 Kings 11:4

Whether my last breath is tomorrow or twenty years from now, more than anything I want to finish well—to live and die honoring the Lord. You have more years ahead of you than behind you, so finishing well probably hasn't crossed your mind. Yet the choices you make today affect the choices you make tomorrow—and ten, twenty, even fifty years from now. This doesn't mean one bad choice dooms the rest of your life! Our God is good and gracious and abounds in love and forgiveness. But making godly choices today—pointing your feet toward God—gives you a holy momentum, a focused goal, and leads to less heartache and fewer detours on the road ahead. Even though David sinned in profound ways, his heart was *for* God. David was humble, repentant, and deeply in love with the Lord. He finished well. Sadly Solomon, a more successful king than David, stepped away from God in his last days. His choices had enormous consequences, such as the splintering of his nation and the spiritual undoing of his people. Between now and your last breath, your choices matter.

ALIGN YOUR MIND ▸ Read 1 Kings 11:1–13.

ALIGN YOUR ACTIONS ▸ What choices do you need to make today to point your feet back to God and pave the way for a strong finish?

ALIGN YOUR HEART ▸

> *I'm prone to wander, Lord, I feel it! Help me lose my taste for that which distracts me and acquire a taste for that which propels me toward You. Help me to finish well. Amen.*

Discerning God's Voice

> But the old prophet answered, "I am a prophet, too, just as you are. And an angel gave me this command from the LORD: 'Bring him home with you so he can have something to eat and drink.'" But the old man was lying to him.
>
> 1 Kings 13:18

God instructed His prophet to denounce the evil practices taking place at the altar of Bethel and pronounce the coming of King Josiah. This nameless prophet was not to eat or drink anything while he was there. On his way home, a so-called prophet offered him a meal. He declined. Yet this man replied, "Actually, I too heard from God, and you're supposed to eat with me." We live in a day when most anyone will claim they speak for God. What happened during this prophet's mission is happening today. People twist Scripture to justify their sinful choices and claim they heard from God. After all, God wants them to be happy, right? But there's only one true God, and He never contradicts himself or speaks contrary to His Word. God's Word is life to you. May you grow increasingly discerning of the times and sensitive to His voice so you'll not be deceived by the many who claim to speak for Him.

ALIGN YOUR MIND Read 1 Kings 13.

ALIGN YOUR ACTIONS Make it a daily practice to read God's Word. Pray for wisdom and discernment before you read. When you know God's Word, you're better able to know His voice—and what isn't.

ALIGN YOUR HEART

Lord, I want to hear Your voice above all others. Open my eyes to see You and my ears to hear You. Heighten my discernment and give me a fresh love for Your living Word. Amen.

Something Out of Practically Nothing

But she said, "I swear by the LORD your God that I don't have a single piece of bread in the house. And I have only a handful of flour left in the jar and a little cooking oil in the bottom of the jug. I was just gathering a few sticks to cook this last meal, and then my son and I will die."

1 Kings 17:12

God had gone ahead of Elijah and instructed a widow to care for his needs. Let's consider her story for a moment. She had run out of options and resources, and thus was preparing to die. But she didn't know a critical point: Never put a period at the end of a sentence that God is still writing! Her story wasn't over yet. When Elijah asked for help, she knew she had little help to offer. Still, she followed his instructions and experienced a divine miracle in the midst of her impossible situation! God can make something out of nothing. He can take your meager resources and multiply them miraculously. May we never base our perspective solely on our circumstances. If we do, we'll likely despair. But with Jesus on your side, the odds against you are meaningless. All He's asking in return is your faith, trust, and obedience.

ALIGN YOUR MIND ▸ Read 1 Kings 17:8–16.

ALIGN YOUR ACTIONS ▸ When you look at your life, do you have expectancy for what God will do, or do you despair over your circumstances? Today, ask God to breathe fresh faith and vision into your heart.

ALIGN YOUR HEART

> *Jesus, You're always up to something new. Intervene in my life in the most miraculous, impossible ways! Show me Your glory! Amen.*

Answer Me,
So That They Will Know

"O Lord, answer me! Answer me so these people will know that you, O Lord, are God and that you have brought them back to yourself."

1 Kings 18:37

Elijah asked God to show himself strong on Elijah's behalf, both to show that He was the one true God, and to draw people back to himself. Oftentimes when we're in a predicament, we minimize it. We assume that since we're not facing down giants or evil kings, God's intervention on our behalf won't be as significant. But did you know that others are watching your life from a distance? They know you profess Christ, and they want to know how you'll handle things when life pushes up against you. What if you stood back, considered your observers, and dared to pray Elijah's prayer: *Father, this isn't just for me, it's for those who are watching me! I am Your servant. Intervene in my life so that others may see that You are the one true God. Show Yourself strong on my behalf because I belong to You! Draw others to You because of Your very real power in my life.* If you're in step with the Lord and obeying His Word, you're on solid biblical ground to pray such a prayer.

 ALIGN YOUR MIND Read 1 Kings 18:1–40.

ALIGN YOUR ACTIONS Pray big today. And tomorrow. And the next day. The God of heaven knows your name and loves you profoundly. And through you, He wants others to know Him too.

ALIGN YOUR HEART

> *God of heaven, show me how to pray big story prayers! I want my whole life to bear witness to Your redeeming power. Stir up a fresh passion in my soul! Amen.*

A Fist-Sized Cloud

Finally, the seventh time, his servant told him, "I saw a little cloud about the size of a man's hand rising from the sea."

1 Kings 18:44

One morning during my prayer time, the Lord whispered to my heart something that really surprised me. *What have you done with the promises I've made to you? It seems you've set them aside for a season. What happened to your persistence? You've written them down. Go review them, and let's start talking about them again.* So I picked up my journal from the previous year and worked my way through the list of promises I was sure the Lord had made to me. To my surprise, He'd already answered some of them; but since those answers came subtly and not suddenly, I practically missed them. God remembers His promises and He collects our prayers. Yet most answers arrive faintly at first. God not only showed me that He'd been faithful even when I'd forgotten about my prayers, but He also compelled me to reengage and pray these things all the way through to completion. Don't miss the subtle answers to your prayers. They're often a sign of things to come.

ALIGN YOUR MIND Read 1 Kings 18:41–46.

ALIGN YOUR ACTIONS Have you stopped praying about something God has promised you? Have you already experienced a few subtle answers? Celebrate. Thank Him. And reengage and pray them through to completion.

ALIGN YOUR HEART

God, thank You for Your constant and continual faithfulness. Even when I forget, You never do. I'm eternally grateful for Your goodness. Make me into a mighty prayer warrior! Amen.

Remedy for Despair

Then the angel of the LORD came again and touched him and said, "Get up and eat some more, or the journey ahead will be too much for you."

1 Kings 19:7

When we find ourselves in a funk, we tend to let go of healthy, life-giving habits. We make poor food choices (or stop eating altogether), we waste time and don't sleep well, we pull away from community, and we stop seeking God. Elijah was there. He'd just experienced a major victory, but with the triumph came a very real threat on his life. So Elijah ran and hid, curled up in a ball, and asked to die. Yet God's kind and compassionate direction was both practical and spiritual. He provided bread and water and told Elijah to eat and drink. Then, with a full stomach, he put his head down and took another nap. Once again, the angel of the Lord told him to get up and eat some more; otherwise the journey would be too much for him. Elijah still had a purpose. You still have a purpose. When you're worn out and discouraged, get some restorative rest, eat a good meal, and ask God to speak to you. Your story is not over until God says it is.

ALIGN YOUR MIND Read 1 Kings 19:1–8.

ALIGN YOUR ACTIONS What does your soul need today? Do what nourishes it. Take a real rest away from screens. Reinstate a good bedtime. Open your Bible and ask God to meet you in its pages.

ALIGN YOUR HEART

> Jesus, I am both physical and spiritual. Help me to nourish both aspects of who I am. Show me what habits are healthy and lifegiving. Strengthen me once again. Speak, Lord. I'm listening. Amen.

Don't Miss Him in the Subtle

And after the earthquake there was a fire, but the LORD was not in the fire.
And after the fire there was the sound of a gentle whisper.

1 Kings 19:12

Elijah had big, giant faith. He'd seen God move in sensational ways. Yet he felt beat up by the world and worn down by its problems. He needed a fresh revelation from above. God told Elijah to go out and stand on the mountain before the Lord. When the Lord passed by, a fierce windstorm ripped boulders loose from the mountain and crushed them. Imagine! Then there was an earthquake. And then a fire. But the Lord was not in the wind or quake or fire. After the sensational came the subtle. The Lord met and ministered to Elijah through a gentle whisper in a gentle breeze. Some of the most sacred, intimate encounters God has with His people are largely missed by the rest of the world. He meets us in the nooks and crannies of our lives and reveals His hidden secrets to us. How blessed are we? Though God is quite capable of the sensational, we'll often miss Him if we only look for Him there. He's right here. With you. Right now.

 ALIGN YOUR MIND Read 1 Kings 19:10–13.

 ALIGN YOUR ACTIONS Quiet your heart today—turn down the volume on your worries and anxieties. Ask God to send His gentle breeze to revive your soul and speak to your heart.

 ALIGN YOUR HEART

Jesus, forgive me for being so captivated by the big experiences that I miss You in the small, sacred ones. I don't want to miss You. Open my eyes. Touch my heart. I wait for You. Amen.

The Danger of Self-Pity

And a voice said, "What are you doing here, Elijah?"
1 Kings 19:13

We sometimes find ourselves in a predicament through no fault of our own. Oftentimes, while in that place, we make impulsive, reactive choices based on a faulty perspective. Yes, times were tough for God's prophet. But self-pity had set in because he believed he was the only one left who followed God. It's scary how connected self-pity and self-importance are, like two sides of the same coin. While God is patient with our frailties and compassionate about our weaknesses, He doesn't tolerate our self-sins because they'll kill us and diminish our God-given influence. We don't need pity when we have the promises of God! We don't need pity when we have access to the very presence of God! When we find ourselves focusing on our hardships more than the promises of God, we're on a slippery slope. Lament and grief are healthy and an important part of the healing process; ultimately, they point back to God. Pity, on the other hand, points back to yourself and your circumstances. It's a parasite and will suck the passion and life right out of us. Be ruthless with your self-sins. They're not your friend and you don't want them at your party.

ALIGN YOUR MIND Read 1 Kings 19:13–18.

ALIGN YOUR ACTIONS If you've wandered into self-pity or self-importance, repent and reset your course today. Holy confidence and humble dependence are great safeguards for your heart.

ALIGN YOUR HEART

> *Search me, O God, and know my heart. Point out anything in me that offends You; lead me in Your everlasting way. I want nothing in my heart that offends You or hurts me. Revive and renew me, Lord! Amen.*

This Is Easy for the Lord!

"This is what the LORD says: This dry valley will be filled with pools of water!"

2 Kings 3:16

E lisha told the kings who were heading into battle, "Without great fanfare, God will fill this drought-ridden valley with pools of water. You'll have plenty for yourselves and for your livestock. *This is an easy task in the eyes of the Lord.* And He will make you victorious over your enemy!" At every turn, our enemy seeks to steal what's ours, kill what God is growing in us, and destroy what God is doing in our lives. And sometimes he gets away with it. If you're staring at a drought-ridden valley, don't despair. Just whisper a prayer. Jesus came not just to save you, but to destroy the work of the enemy in your life. Picture it. Imagine your valley suddenly filling with water. Imagine splashing your feet in pools of blessing. And don't forget that the Lord intends to put your enemy under your feet. None of this is hard for Him. Remember His strength today. Count on His goodness. Rely on His love. And pray big prayers today.

 ALIGN YOUR MIND ▶ Read 2 Kings 3:1–24.

ALIGN YOUR ACTIONS ▶ If you're in a tough, dry season, remember: droughts and valleys don't last forever in God's economy. Ask Him to fill your valley with blessings and give you hope for the days ahead.

 ALIGN YOUR HEART ▶

> *Mighty God, I call on Your name! Deliver me from the hand of my enemy! Fill my deep valleys with water; offer fresh pools of blessing until I'm overwhelmed once again with Your goodness. Remind me of Your faithfulness. Show me Your strength today. Amen.*

Prepare for Provision

And Elisha said, "Borrow as many empty jars as you can from your friends and neighbors."

2 Kings 4:3

Sometimes the situation in our lives is so desperate, we need to engage the faith and help of our family and friends. The poor widow in this passage not only grieved the loss of her husband, but she also faced the threat of losing her sons to slavery. She cried out to Elisha the prophet. Elisha instructed her to borrow as many jars from friends and neighbors as she could find, which she did. Her husband had served Elisha, which connected her to the family of God. When your circumstances feel like they'll swallow you whole, don't isolate or shrink back. You're part of the family of the living God! Rise up and call your fiercest warriors. Borrow their faith. Ask them to gather on your behalf with open hands and full expectancy that God will move as you seek Him together. Desperate times call for passionate prayer and fierce faith. What if you borrowed faith jars from your parents, friends, mentors, and youth leaders, and you all asked God to fill them on your behalf? Your jars would fill, your hearts would quicken, and you'd experience the clarity and provision you need. Maybe that's your battle strategy today.

ALIGN YOUR MIND Read 2 Kings 4:1–7.

ALIGN YOUR ACTIONS Even if you're not in crisis, plan a prayer meeting with some of your godliest friends or mentors. Seek God together and watch what He will do.

ALIGN YOUR HEART

Precious Father, forgive me for worrying when I have You! I'm asking for a miracle. And I want to participate in a necessary miracle for someone else. Prepare me for Your provision! Amen.

Let Hope Arise

She fell at his feet and bowed before him, overwhelmed with gratitude. Then she took her son in her arms and carried him downstairs.

2 Kings 4:37

This wealthy woman of God recognized that Elisha was a man of God. She and her husband had been so kind and generous to him that Elisha asked what he could do for her. She let him know that her needs were met. It wasn't until Elisha spoke to her about having a child that she fell apart. That desire had long been buried, and it was almost too painful to talk about it now. She replied, "O man of God, don't deceive me and get my hopes up like that." Do you have such a desire buried deep within you? Sometimes it feels easier to live with loss than it does with hope. But is it better? I don't think so. God's promises don't apply to our unrealistic expectations, but they do apply to our impossible situations. What if God wants to breathe fresh life into your hopes? What if He intends to resurrect your long-buried dream? Will you let Him?

 ALIGN YOUR MIND ▶ Read 2 Kings 4:8–37.

 ALIGN YOUR ACTIONS ▶ What is your long-buried dream? Ask God to show you if this is an unrealistic expectation or a God-given—but seemingly impossible—dream. Ask Him for courage to hope again.

 ALIGN YOUR HEART ▶

Father, You know the kind of courage it takes for me to even have this conversation. I don't want to go there—to be disappointed again. But I don't want to miss Your provision either. So here I am. Show me what hope looks like here. What are You up to? I'm listening. Amen.

Detoxifying the Poison

Elisha said, "Bring me some flour." Then he threw it into the pot and said, "Now it's all right; go ahead and eat." And then it did not harm them.

2 Kings 4:41

Elisha detoxified the poisonous stew with some flour. I know a bit about the detox process. I have the genetic inability to process mold, which makes exposure dangerous for me. When I was battling toxic levels of mold, doctors treated my illness with binders that not only bound to the mold spores but pulled them out of my system. When one of my toddler sons tried to drink a bottle of Benadryl, the ER doctors gave him activated charcoal to bind and deactivate the dangerous levels of medicine he'd ingested. Sometimes we're exposed to toxic people and circumstances, and their influence *gets in us*—it deeply impacts us, and we feel poisoned. What will deactivate the toxins in our system? The spoken Word of God! Scripture says that what we bind on earth is bound in heaven and what we loose on earth is loosed in heaven.[*] If you've recently been poisoned by a toxic experience, pray God's Word, say God's Word, and bind the enemy's influence in your life. He *has* to obey.

ALIGN YOUR MIND Read 2 Kings 4:38–43.

ALIGN YOUR ACTIONS Detoxify every day by speaking and praying God's Word over your life. GREATER is He that is in you than any toxins that come against you!

ALIGN YOUR HEART

Jesus, help me to guard my steps so I don't walk into toxic situations. But when I do, give me the firepower to pray boldly and confidently. My heart is bound to You. Poisonous circumstances cannot harm me. Thank You, Lord. Amen.

* See Matthew 18:18 NIV.

Healing the Powerful

One day the girl said to her mistress, "I wish my master would go to see the prophet in Samaria. He would heal him of his leprosy."

2 Kings 5:3

A captive Jewish girl served in the home of a commander of the Syrian army (enemies of the Jews). He was a mighty warrior, but he battled leprosy. This dear girl, though she was taken from her homeland, cared about her master's plight. She pointed him toward healing through the one true God. God used this seemingly insignificant girl to shake things up in the kingdom. Maybe you feel like a captive yourself. You're not valued at home, nor are you in a position of great influence. And yet you can still impact those around you. You have the capacity to speak life, to point the way, and to initiate a healing process. But maybe those in authority over you are prideful and undeserving. Aren't we all sometimes? Naaman went to Elisha for healing and God dealt with his pride as well. God misses nothing. Maybe you're where you are today to speak life into a broken situation. Outcomes are in God's hands. And one day you will see the impact and fruit of your obedience.

ALIGN YOUR MIND Read 2 Kings 5:1–14.

ALIGN YOUR ACTIONS Does the idea of helping someone prideful stir up your own pride or resistance? Humble yourself and repent, thanking God for His grace. Ask Him to show you a difficult situation you can speak life into.

ALIGN YOUR HEART

Jesus, forgive me for my selective grace. I want to be more like the unnamed girl in this story. I want to help whoever You entrust to me! Show me what to do. My eyes are on You. Amen.

Spiritual Eyes to See

"Don't be afraid!" Elisha told him. "For there are more on our side than on theirs!"

2 Kings 6:16

*E*lisha, the prophet of God, walked so closely with God that he knew about the Syrian army's strategy before they took their first steps. As a result, Israel's king was always one step ahead of his enemy. The Syrian forces decided to go after Elisha. They surrounded his city; he seemed to be outnumbered. Elisha's servant was distressed, but not Elisha. In so many words, Elisha prayed, *O Lord, let my servant see what I already know!* So the Lord opened the young servant's eyes, and he saw that the hillside around Elisha was filled with horses and chariots of fire. Our spiritual reality is far more substantial than our physical reality. Things are rarely as they appear in the natural, and God is always nearer than we perceive. Here's what's true: God has assigned angels to care for you and to fight for you. The precious, powerful Holy Spirit resides inside of you. God's promises are true for you. If your spiritual eyes opened up, you'd see that the enemy and your circumstances are no match for the forces that are standing guard on your behalf this very moment. Don't be afraid. Only believe.

ALIGN YOUR MIND ▶ Read 2 Kings 6:8–23.

ALIGN YOUR ACTIONS ▶ What feels too heavy today? Ask God to give you eyes to see His presence and provision in your life. Give thanks every time you notice them.

ALIGN YOUR HEART

Lord, show me how secure I am in You! Help me remember that when I face opposition, I can stand my ground and watch You fight for me. Give me spiritual eyes to see my spiritual reality. Amen.

Expecting the Best
from a Gracious God

> The king got out of bed in the middle of the night and told his officers, "I know what has happened. . . . They are expecting us to leave the city, and then they will take us alive and capture the city."
>
> 2 Kings 7:12

*I*n our passage today, the Lord caused Israel's enemy to hear the sounds of a great army approaching. They panicked, abandoned all of their supplies, and fled for their lives. The Lord delivered an abundance of resources into the hands of the starving Israelites. But Israel's king was more impacted by the famine than by God's voice and miraculous intervention in his life. He assumed this victory was no victory at all, but rather a setup by the enemy. After a long battle, it's almost instinctive to believe the worst, continually pushing down your hope, suspicious of anything good that happens. But that's no way to live. "We must avoid becoming skeptical of God's provision. When our resources are low and our doubts are the strongest, remember God can open the floodgates of heaven."* A weary heart is different from a hardened, skeptical heart. If you're weary, run to Jesus. He'll restore you. If you're skeptical, run to Him too. Repent and receive His grace.

 ALIGN YOUR MIND Read 2 Kings 6:24–7:17.

ALIGN YOUR ACTIONS Give thanks for all the blessings in your life—big or small. When you begin to see all you have is a gift, it's hard to expect the worst.

ALIGN YOUR HEART

> *Lord, forgive me for expecting the worst instead of Your best. Open my eyes to all the good things You've already given me. Revive my heart and perspective today. Amen.*

---

* *Life Application Study Bible*, 768.

Break Free and Believe

There was a man named Jabez who was more honorable than any of his brothers. His mother named him Jabez because his birth had been so painful.

1 Chronicles 4:9

You are not your insecurities. You're not your past mistakes. You're not your family tree. You're not who other people say you are. You're not even the sum of all of your accomplishments. You're something altogether more wonderful than these. Do you believe this to be true? Truth is, most of us need a complete identity overhaul. Jabez's mother had a difficult, painful delivery. I had one too. But I still cannot imagine naming my son after that excruciating experience. Imagine being reminded of the pain you caused every time your mom called your name. Talk about feeling shamed. Yet somehow, Jabez broke free from his given label and lived more honorably than his brothers. Moreover, the God of heaven knew Jabez's name and his heart. And we're still talking about Jabez today. No matter what you've come from, look up, dear one. No matter what words have been spoken over you or what labels have been a reproach to you, break free and believe God anyway. He loves your faith, and He's a miracle-working God.

ALIGN YOUR MIND ▶ Read 1 Chronicles 4:9–10.

ALIGN YOUR ACTIONS ▶ Ask God to show you any negative names, labels, and self-limiting beliefs you're still holding on to. Then refute them one by one with God's Word.

ALIGN YOUR HEART

Father, show me my heart. Show me what negative labels and beliefs I've made a part of my identity. Help me break free so I can be and do everything You've dreamed of for me. In Jesus' name, I pray. Amen.

Do More in and through Me!

(Jabez prayed), "Oh, that you would bless me and expand my territory!
Please be with me in all that I do, and keep me from all trouble and pain!"
And God granted him his request.

1 Chronicles 4:10

I love Bruce Wilkinson's book *The Prayer of Jabez*. Though some find this a selfish prayer, nothing could be further from the truth. Whatever we've experienced of God, it's the equivalent of dipping a tiny Dixie cup into the vastness of the ocean. He is the God of inexhaustible supply, the God of compassions that never fail, the One whose love will never dim, even a little bit. And He's the God who loves our faith. The more deeply we get to know the heart of God, the more profoundly our prayers start to echo His heart for us. The more we pray God's heart, the more His answers change us and change the world through us. Ask God to expand His territory in you and through you, to expand your influence, and to deliver you from evil. Pray prayers that overwhelm you—impossible prayers that only He can answer. Stretch your arms open wide and pray, *Lord Jesus, do the impossible in and through me!* Jealous people will call that selfish. Kingdom people will call it gutsy.

ALIGN YOUR MIND Read 1 Chronicles 4:9–10 (one more time).

ALIGN YOUR ACTIONS You want to change the world? Start praying crazy-big prayers every day and wholeheartedly follow Jesus.

ALIGN YOUR HEART

Jesus, bless me, indeed! Do the impossible through me! Expand my territory, increase my influence, and deliver me from evil. Change the world through me so all will know You're God! Amen.

The Importance of the Impossible

> The Jebusites threatened David, "You shall not pass through these gates."
> Nevertheless David captured the stronghold (Zion), now known as the city
> of David, and made it his capital.
>
> 1 Chronicles 11:5 VOICE

Joshua and his armies never captured the city of Jebus, and it remained in the hands of the Canaanites until David became king.* The enemy told David, "You'll never break through these gates." Nevertheless, David broke through and made it his capital. He not only claimed his God-given territory, but he also renamed the city Jerusalem, which became a hugely significant place—past, present, and future. Jerusalem is where Christ was crucified and rose from the dead. From that city, the gospel has gone out to the ends of the earth.† If you've felt God calling you to a particular place, group, or level of freedom—but it feels like you're running into locked gates—take heart. If the land before you is God-assigned, then no demon in hell can keep you from it. Your story and your breakthroughs are never just about you—they have eternal implications. May God open your eyes to see the significance and importance of the impossible tasks before you. And may the gates open before you.

ALIGN YOUR MIND   Read 1 Chronicles 11:1–9.

ALIGN YOUR ACTIONS   Identify your impossible situation. Why does it feel impossible? Bring each reason to God in prayer today and ask Him for a heart of faith.

ALIGN YOUR HEART

> *Jesus, Your Spirit in me ensures that nothing will be impossible for me! You go before me. I'll follow You. Awaken my faith today. Amen.*

---

* Paraphrase of study note from *Life in the Spirit Study Bible* (Grand Rapids, MI: Zondervan, 2003), 584.
† *Life in the Spirit Study Bible*, 585.

Miracles and Rulings

Search for the LORD and for his strength;
continually seek him.
Remember the wonders he has performed,
his miracles, and the rulings he has given.
1 Chronicles 16:11–12

The ark was finally back home in Jerusalem. David had learned some valuable lessons along the way.* God is not only a miracle-working God and the Creator of the heavens and the earth, He is also the ultimate King and not to be trifled with. When we become too casual about His presence, we operate in our own strength, lean on our own understanding, take credit for the things He's done, and miss what He intends to do. Shout to your soul today, *The God who parted the sea lives inside of me!* Remember His miracles, seek His face, pursue His strength, and rely on His faithfulness. Far too many Christians live underwhelming lives because they've wandered from the beauty of holy expectancy (they've forgotten that He's still moving mountains) and holy fear (they've forgotten that He is God and we are not). Want to reignite your faith? Ask God to increase your capacity to understand what He's capable of. Ask Him for a fresh picture of His majesty and greatness. Believe that His presence in your midst changes everything.

 ALIGN YOUR MIND 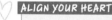 Read 1 Chronicles 15; 16:1–36.

ALIGN YOUR ACTIONS Today, ask God to grow within you a heart of expectancy and reverence. Fill your thoughts and heart with awe of who He is.

ALIGN YOUR HEART

> *Lord, reignite my heart to believe You for great things! Help me better grasp Your majesty and power. I want to live a holy, powerful, reverent life. I bow low and wait for You. Amen.*

---

* Read 1 Chronicles 13 for context.

Counting Your Followers

Satan rose up against Israel and caused David to take a census of the people of Israel.

1 Chronicles 21:1

Our enemy is a legalist. If he finds an opening, he'll take it. David was temptable because a part of him wanted to shift from dependence on God to counting his great accomplishments. And so it goes today. People obsess over numbers, followers, likes, and shares. Yet Jesus never called us to get people to follow us. He called us to follow Him and to feed His sheep. *He calls us to count our blessings, not our followers.* Things in this world are not as they appear. Scripture is clear that some with lots of influence and followers will see their work burn to ashes because they did it all to make a name for themselves, while others, whom the world knows nothing about, will be celebrated and honored for all to see. It matters what we do, but even more so *why we do it*. King David was a man after God's own heart, but in that moment, he tried to validate his own heart. "There is a thin line between feeling confident because you are relying on God's power and becoming proud because you have been used by God for great purposes."* How much can He bless you before you make it about you?

 ALIGN YOUR MIND ▶ Read 1 Chronicles 21:1–17.

 ALIGN YOUR ACTIONS ▶ Forget about the number of your followers. Today, how can you feed His sheep (love those around you)?

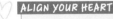 **ALIGN YOUR HEART** ▶

> *Father, forgive me for allowing the wrong things to validate (and invalidate) me. You are all that I need! Help me to be faithful here. I know You'll establish me. Amen.*

* *Life Application Study Bible*, 861.

Everything Comes from You

"Everything we have has come from you, and we give you only what you first gave us!"

1 Chronicles 29:14

King David was nearing the end of his earthly life. He instructed Solomon to follow the Lord wholeheartedly. David gave God credit for his victories and thanked Him for his blessings. Though he certainly had his own regrets, his heart was one with almighty God. David knew the Great Redeemer and could therefore rest in His care. The sooner you come to believe that every good gift comes from God and that you have all you need in Him, the sooner you can live with a heart of freedom, peace, and rest. And the sooner your life will become a pure and beautiful offering to the One who made you and who has entrusted great gifts to you. Don't muddy the waters by grabbing for validation, striving to prove something, or straining to manage others' opinions of you. Open your hands, receive everything God has promised, and then offer it back up to Him. It's the only offering that echoes into eternity, and it's the only way to live.

 ALIGN YOUR MIND Read 1 Chronicles 29.

 ALIGN YOUR ACTIONS Look around and consider every good gift God has given you. What are some new ways you can offer your life back to Him in thanksgiving for all He's done?

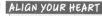 **ALIGN YOUR HEART**

Father, I don't want to waste a moment living out of a lie. Put my heart at ease in Your presence and use every part of my life as an offering to You. Amen.

If We, Then He

"Then if my people who are called by my name will humble themselves and pray and seek my face and turn from their wicked ways, I will hear from heaven and will forgive their sins and restore their land."

2 Chronicles 7:14

When our kids were young, we stood in a circle as a family and held hands. Then I looked at our sons and said, "Your place in this family matters so very much. In fact, whatever you allow in your life, you allow in ours." My husband and I explained that no one lives on an island and nobody's choices stand alone; they affect a whole community. We long for God to move powerfully in our nation, but it needs to start with us. What we allow in our lives, we allow in our community, even if those around us never know. We have a responsibility, especially as believers, to guard not only our hearts, but to also guard the city gate. How do we do that? We walk humbly with our God. We deal quickly with our sin. We pray big-story prayers for our city and our nation. And we ask God to break our hearts for what breaks His. What needs to change in your heart today so God can move in your midst? Your life deeply impacts your community.

ALIGN YOUR MIND ▶ Read 2 Chronicles 7:11–22.

ALIGN YOUR ACTIONS ▶ Set aside time to intentionally pray for your community and nation today. Ask God what needs to change in your life for the sake of those around you.

ALIGN YOUR HEART

> Lord Jesus, I come humbly before You and ask for mercy and blessing upon my nation. Forgive us our sins, cleanse us from unrighteousness, and heal our land. Amen.

Rest from Your Enemies

> They earnestly sought after God, and they found him. And the LORD gave them rest from their enemies on every side.
>
> 2 Chronicles 15:15

Much like the Israelites, many of us have a history of following God, then wandering from Him, building our idols, then smashing them and turning to follow God again. We suffer because of our own wandering ways. And yet every time we seek the face of God, He makes himself available. God's mercies and kindness are breathtaking. King Asa took seriously the Lord's invitation to seek Him earnestly and follow Him wholeheartedly. And as a result, the Lord gave King Asa rest from his enemies. Jesus promised we'd endure hardship, trials, and opposition when we follow Him. But He also promised rest for our souls, restoration, and relief from our enemies. Yet we'll never know such rest if we're continually pulled between two kingdoms. Have you given the enemy access to your life in any way? Shut him down, shut him out, and earnestly seek after God once again. God wants to reveal himself to you in fresh new ways. He wants to restore and strengthen you. May the Lord bring you into a season of rest from battle and relief from your enemy.

 ALIGN YOUR MIND Read 2 Chronicles 15.

 ALIGN YOUR ACTIONS Sometimes we give our enemy access in the subtlest of ways, like an unforgiving heart, a prideful assessment, or an obsession with something other than God. Humbly search your heart today and pray for forgiveness and restoration.

ALIGN YOUR HEART

> Lord, show me my heart. Show me where I've let my guard down. Help me to shore up my life once again. And give me rest from my enemy. Amen.

The Lord Will Fight for You

"This is what the LORD says: Do not be afraid! Don't be discouraged by this mighty army, for the battle is not yours, but God's. . . . You will not even need to fight. Take your positions; then stand still and watch the LORD's victory."

2 Chronicles 20:15–17

The nation of Judah faced total annihilation. Enemy armies marched toward them fully intending to destroy them. King Jehoshaphat earnestly appealed to the Lord for guidance. He ordered everyone in Judah to fast. People from all over sought the Lord's intervention. King Jehoshaphat declared to God His greatness and faithfulness and, on that basis, cried out for His intervention once again. Then the Spirit of the Lord came upon one of their men and he prophesied God's promise to fight for them. The people began to worship *before* the breakthrough came. God inhabits the praises of His people and the devil flees. The enemy soldiers turned on each other and defeated themselves. It took God's people *three days* to collect the spoils of war. God turned their battleground into a valley of blessing. Dare to practice restraint when you want to strike your own defense. Seek God's direction, protection, and intervention. He *will* fight for you.

ALIGN YOUR MIND Read 2 Chronicles 20:1–30.

ALIGN YOUR ACTIONS Today, put on your favorite worship songs, and worship God before the breakthrough comes. Fast and seek His face and His will in prayer. You'll be amazed at what He does for those who wait on Him.

ALIGN YOUR HEART

Lord, You are faithful and true! I don't know what to do, but my eyes are on You. Intervene on my behalf; fight for me and deliver me. My soul waits for You. Amen.

When the Wicked Prosper

When [Athaliah] arrived, she saw the newly crowned king standing in his place of authority by the pillar at the Temple entrance.

2 Chronicles 23:13

After David and Solomon's reigns, much of Israel and Judah's history plays out like an intense political thriller you'd see on TV. Betrayals, power plays, secret alliances, and even assassinations. In our story today, Athaliah, one of the most wicked and ruthless queens to sit the throne, is seeking to kill the rest of the royal family after both her husband and son died brutally. But the wife of a priest hid one of the royal children. The boy stayed hidden until his seventh year, when the priests finally staged a coup and dethroned the woman who'd wreaked havoc in God's kingdom. Because of Israel's disobedience and continual idolatry, God, on occasion, allowed enemies to usurp the throne. But He promised that a descendant of David would sit on that throne, and He *always* comes back to His promises. The wicked queen was removed, and godly leadership was established once again. If you're disheartened by ungodly leadership or by the prosperity of the wicked, don't lose heart. God already has someone in the wings—someone He's hiding and preparing for just the right time. The wicked won't rule forever.

ALIGN YOUR MIND Read 2 Chronicles 22; 23:1–15.

ALIGN YOUR ACTIONS God is always preparing His leaders—maybe He's preparing you to step up! Today, pray for that process and our future leaders.

ALIGN YOUR HEART

Father, You are still on Your throne! You will bring down the wicked and establish godly influence once again. Use me, Lord! Show me how to pray. Show me how to stand. I wait for You. Amen.

Don't Go Through with It

> Amaziah asked the man of God, "But what about all that silver I paid to hire the army of Israel?"
>
> The man of God replied, "The LORD is able to give you much more than this!"
>
> 2 Chronicles 25:9

You've made a plan, you've invested resources, and you've enlisted the help of your friends. But partway through the process, you realize it's the wrong decision. Do you know how many people have gone ahead anyway because they've already spent the money or made the plans—or just don't want to be seen as a coward? King Amaziah was in the process of hiring troops from Israel to form a great army. But a man of God came to him and cautioned him against that decision because the Lord was no longer with Israel. They'd abandoned Him. If Amaziah went into battle with a people under God's discipline, he'd be soundly defeated. He asked the man of God, "What about the money I've already spent?" The prophet assured him that God could restore him and then some! Don't be stubborn about your plans if it's becoming clear that God is not in them. Never mind what you've spent. Honoring God matters most of all. If you honor Him, He'll restore you. And then some!

ALIGN YOUR MIND Read 2 Chronicles 25:1–9.

ALIGN YOUR ACTIONS Are you involved with a person or situation that doesn't honor the Lord? It's not too late to turn back to God. Ask Him for courage to do what's right today.

ALIGN YOUR HEART

Lord Jesus, I want to honor You in all I do. Give me courage to turn back when I'm on the wrong path. Show me the way that I should go. Amen.

He'll Work It Out

This is what King Cyrus of Persia says:

"The LORD, the God of heaven, has given me all the kingdoms of the earth. He has appointed me to build him a Temple at Jerusalem, which is in Judah."

Ezra 1:2

God's purposes will prevail in the end—no matter what. He works through His people. And when necessary, He works through His enemies. The Israelites had so rejected God and His ways that God gave them over to their sinful desires—and they were carried off into captivity. Yet He had a plan to redeem their story long before they understood just how lost they were. After seventy years, He planned to bring His exiled people back to their homeland to rebuild the temple. He prophesied that King Cyrus of Persia—the nation that enslaved them—would issue the decree and guarantee their safe passage home. Imagine that! When Cyrus *happened* to be reading some of the prophetic scripts that had been removed from the temple, he saw his own name! God stirred Cyrus's heart, and he instituted the decree for a remnant of God's people to return home. God is in control; He's always been in control. And while He allows people the freedom to follow Him or disregard Him, He will ultimately bring every detail together and work it out to serve His purposes.

 ALIGN YOUR MIND ▶ Read Ezra 1:1–4.

 ALIGN YOUR ACTIONS ▶ Do you want to be someone through whom God can work with power, authority, and conviction? Today, stop pursuing your own plans and ask Him to show you His.

 ALIGN YOUR HEART ▶

> *Lord, Your patience is breathtaking. Here I am. Use me in powerful ways.*
> *Work out Your greater plan through my life. Amen.*

Remember Your Inheritance

Then God stirred the hearts of the priests and Levites and the leaders of the tribes of Judah and Benjamin to go to Jerusalem to rebuild the Temple of the LORD.

Ezra 1:5

God stirred Cyrus's heart to give all twelve tribes the freedom to leave their captivity and reclaim their inheritance. Yet only two tribes caught the significance of the invitation. The other ten were so fractured—and they'd spent so much time in captivity—that they weren't even sure of their heritage. Because of that, they were unwilling to leave.* And so it goes today. Though much time has passed since God's Word was first written, Jesus hasn't returned yet. As a result, many Christians have lost sight of their eternal homeland. They pursue and identify more with the empty pleasures and accolades of this world—even when those things hold them captive—than they do with the promise of a new heaven and a new earth. But we are on a pilgrimage *now*. You are not made for this world. You're simply passing through. Yet how you live here deeply impacts how you'll live there. Recapture your kingdom identity. Remember your kingdom inheritance.

ALIGN YOUR MIND Read Ezra 1:5–11.

 ALIGN YOUR ACTIONS Have you thought much about heaven—or the new earth? Did you know our lives here, and even the beautiful things of creation, are like shades of gray compared to the vibrance that awaits us? Let yourself imagine what heaven holds for us today.

ALIGN YOUR HEART

> *Jesus, somehow You lived in this world without being captive to it. Help me to do the same. Awaken me once again to the reality of heaven. Amen.*

* *Life Application Study Bible*, 958.

Both Sorrow and Joy

The joyful shouting and weeping mingled together in a loud noise that could be heard far in the distance.

Ezra 3:13

Why was there both joyful shouting and sorrowful weeping at the same celebration? The younger saints rejoiced with glee because they took part in rebuilding the temple. What a testimony to God's faithfulness! The older saints were likely heartbroken over the sin that caused the destruction in the first place. Perhaps they remembered the temple's former glory and wondered if they'd ever be able to capture it again. Or maybe some wept over God's goodness in spite of their own badness. Oftentimes, those who've suffered the most feel things most deeply. If all we ever feel is joy or hype when we come into God's presence, we're missing a significant part of our relationship with almighty God. There's a time for joyful celebration, but there must be a time for sober reflection of our actions and lives—though never with condemnation. And it is always for the sake of moving us to a place of deeper intimacy and appreciation for what God has done for us. There's a time for rejoicing and a time for weeping—and sometimes on the same day! God welcomes your expression and He loves your heart. Enter in, fully engaged, today.

ALIGN YOUR MIND Read Ezra 3.

ALIGN YOUR ACTIONS Do you only come to God with your praises and problems? Today, spend some time talking with Him about the hard and sad things too.

ALIGN YOUR HEART

Father, I raise my hands and praise You with everything in me! You're so good! I honor You for all You've done and all You're about to do. Thank You, thank You, Lord. Amen.

Predictable Enemy Tactics

Then the local residents tried to discourage and frighten the people of
Judah to keep them from their work.

Ezra 4:4

The enemy of our souls is all about counterfeits, deception, and distraction—primarily because he has no new ideas. When the tribes of Judah and Benjamin set out to rebuild the temple, their enemies first sought to distract them by trying to align with them. When that didn't work, they used two age-old tactics that the devil still uses today: fear and discouragement. "Discouragement and fear are two of the greatest obstacles to completing God's work. Most often they come when you least expect them. Discourage-ment eats away at our motivation, and fear paralyzes us so we don't act at all."* Discouragement condemns our present moment. Fear threatens our promised future. Discouragement comes when we compare and then despair, or when we lose heart over where we find ourselves at the moment. Fear goes after the vulnerable or unhealed places in us, or after the truths about God that we're still unsure of. To combat these, we need a higher vision of who God is and what He's up to, and we need a revelation about the enemy's strategy against us. His threat to you is always tied to your threat to him.

ALIGN YOUR MIND Read Ezra 4:1–4.

ALIGN YOUR ACTIONS Today, ask God to show you any source of fear or discouragement in your life. Humbly confess what comes to mind and ask for His healing, strength, and wisdom to combat the enemy's plans.

ALIGN YOUR HEART

Jesus, help me be wise to the enemy's schemes. Grant me fierce faith and divine discernment so I can be and do all You've called me to. Amen.

* *Life Application Study Bible*, 966.

The Prophet in All of Us

And the prophets of God were with them and helped them.

Ezra 5:2

Prophet: *A person regarded as an inspired teacher or proclaimer of the will of God.*

Imagine the journey for the tribes of Benjamin and Judah. They trusted God, left captivity, returned to their homeland, and began to rebuild the temple for His glory. And yet their efforts were met with obstacle, opposition, and accusation—to the point that the work actually came to a halt. It stopped completely. Where was God? Why did He allow the wicked and the liars to prosper? Because obstacles are a normal part of life in a fallen world. The arc of the story of God with His people has always been one of risk, faith, setbacks, and breakthroughs. And it's no different today. The Lord raised up prophets not only to encourage the tribes of Benjamin and Judah, but also to engage with the work at hand. The kingdom needs more people who are so in step with the living God that they can speak words of timely encouragement, see and call out God's best in another person, and accurately discern God's will in any situation. Today, may you step in and help where God invites you to be part of the solution. The world needs your influence.

 ALIGN YOUR MIND Read Ezra 5:1–4.

 ALIGN YOUR ACTIONS Immerse yourself in God's Word and listen for His voice. Then look for ways to encourage and help others today.

 ALIGN YOUR HEART

> *Father, I want to be in the right place at the right time with courage to do or say the right thing. Help me to see what You see and say what You'd say. Amen.*

Holy Vindication

"Do not disturb the construction of the Temple of God. Let it be rebuilt on its original site, and do not hinder the governor of Judah and the elders of the Jews in their work."

Ezra 6:7

The enemies of the Israelites appealed to King Darius to stop the construction of the temple. They used fear, lies, discouragement, threats, and their influence. They even suggested the king search the records to see if there really was a signed decree for the Israelites to move forward with the temple. But they overplayed their hand. Once King Darius found the records, he enforced the will of God. He not only upheld the rebuilding of the temple, but he also decreed that all of its expenses be paid—and that all of the items taken from the temple to Babylon be returned and put back where they belonged. Furthermore, if anyone tried to stand against this decree, their home and lives would be reduced to a pile of rubble. Look at what God did! Vindication. Compensation. Restoration. Divine protection. He's the same yesterday, today, and forever. If you've stepped out to obey God and have encountered one impossible obstacle after another, you're in great company. May you hold your ground, stand in faith, and witness God move mightily on your behalf.

ALIGN YOUR MIND Read Ezra 5:17–6:12.

ALIGN YOUR ACTIONS If events have shaken your faith, return to the promises in God's Word. He's your solid rock, you are secure in Him, and He has a plan for you.

ALIGN YOUR HEART

You are God Almighty, and I trust You! Lord, please shut the mouth of my enemy and restore what's been lost. Part the waters so I can move forward with You again. Amen.

More Than a Moment of Grace

"But now we have been given a brief moment of grace, for the LORD our God has allowed a few of us to survive as a remnant. He has given us security in this holy place. Our God has brightened our eyes and granted us some relief from our slavery."

Ezra 9:8

Ezra fell facedown before the Lord and repented for the continual sins of his people. In light of God's amazing grace, he was overwhelmed with both grief for their actions and gratitude for God's great mercy. The Israelites had been carried off into captivity because of their blatant sin. Yet while their sin was in full motion, God worked out a plan to redeem them. While our sin was in full motion—before we ever knew we needed saving—Christ died for us. While condemnation and consequences were falling into place, Christ took our place. He redeemed us from the law of sin and death, and He redeems us every day with new mercies and grace. In Christ, we're surrounded by more grace than we'll ever need; God made sure of it. Even though we, like the Israelites, wander from God's best ways for us, He still brightens our eyes, grants us relief from suffering, and makes us secure in His presence. This is why we call Him our Redeemer.

ALIGN YOUR MIND Read Ezra 9–10:1.

ALIGN YOUR ACTIONS Picture God's grace as an endless ocean. Ask Him to open your eyes to the ways it surrounds and sustains you each day.

ALIGN YOUR HEART

Father, You've been so good, patient, kind, and true. You knew I'd wander and made a way back for me. You've ransomed and redeemed me. You've always loved me. Thank You, Lord. Amen.

Rebuilding Your Wall

"The God of heaven will help us succeed. We, his servants, will start rebuilding this wall . . ."

Nehemiah 2:20

When God is about to bring renewal in some area of our lives or in the kingdom, He first speaks to us about it privately. Our hearts might start to burn about a particular issue, or we start seeing a situation through new eyes, or we recognize a pattern of answered prayers in our church or community that makes us sit up and take notice. God stirred Nehemiah's heart to rebuild Jerusalem's wall. He'd spoken privately to Nehemiah before Nehemiah went public with his plan. Perhaps God has gotten your attention about a broken-down area in your family, neighborhood, school, or community. Lean in and listen. Pay attention to this newly stirred interest. Don't look for signs; look for God. But rest assured that He can bring you a sign if you need one. If God is calling you to be a part of the solution, it may be in a hidden way through fasting and praying, or more public through speaking up and stepping up. God cares about many things, and He intends to heal some of the world's hurts through you. He'll make sure you have all you need to do what's on His heart.

ALIGN YOUR MIND Read Nehemiah 2.

ALIGN YOUR ACTIONS Ask God to show you which wall in your life He wants you to rebuild. Somebody or something needs your influence.

ALIGN YOUR HEART

> *Lord, use me according to Your will. Open my eyes to how You're moving in my midst. Make a way, stir hearts, and give me faith to do what's on Your heart today. Amen.*

Guard the Low Places

So I placed armed guards behind the lowest parts of the wall in the exposed areas. I stationed the people to stand guard by families, armed with swords, spears, and bows.

Nehemiah 4:13

As God's people worked on the wall, their enemy raged against them. Sanballat and Tobiah stopped at nothing to hinder their progress. But Nehemiah had heard from God and would not be moved. He cried out to God for intervention, and he did the practical thing: stationing armed guards at the lowest, most exposed parts of the wall. We as God's people need to do that for each other. When we dare to move out into the purposes of God, we'll enlist the rage of our enemy. He'll unleash his fury on us, making us feel beat up and worn out. These are the low, exposed places in life for us. This is when we tend to either look inward and wonder if we heard from God or look outward and feel overwhelmed by the impossible task before us—or both. But we need to look upward and cry out to God like Nehemiah did. Then we need to call our warrior friends and ask them to stand guard with us until we're built back up. If you're in a low place, don't isolate like the enemy wants. Call in the guard and stand in faith. You'll get through this.

ALIGN YOUR MIND Read Nehemiah 4:1–13.

ALIGN YOUR ACTIONS Who are your warrior friends? How can you support each other and stand strong? Reach out today if you need help—or see if they do.

ALIGN YOUR HEART

Mighty God, protect me when I'm vulnerable; fight when I am weak. Intervene the way You do. I'm calling on You! Amen.

Don't Fear the Enemy; Remember God

"Don't be afraid of the enemy! Remember the Lord, who is great and glorious, and fight for your brothers, your sons, your daughters, your wives, and your homes!"

Nehemiah 4:14

The enemy is the author of chaos and confusion—and he wields them masterfully to create fear and frenzy in our lives and hearts. But God has not given us a spirit of fear, but of power and love and a sound mind.[*] Nehemiah's enemies intended to surprise the people working on the wall, but God gave them a heads-up; He'll do the same for us. Nehemiah rejected fear and stood in power. He charged the people to battle their fears by remembering God and His greatness. Nehemiah knew the people were tired, but it was time to stand in faith and fight for their inheritance. It's grueling to work hard on the task in front of you *and* endure opposition at the same time. But that's when, if we let him, the enemy gains the most ground against us. So that's when we need to learn how to stand in battle. Don't fear your enemy. Remember the glorious God who fights for you.

 ALIGN YOUR MIND ▶ Read Nehemiah 4:14–20.

 ALIGN YOUR ACTIONS ▶ When you're feeling worn out, remember that God has given you authority over all the power of the enemy.[†] With God, you have the upper hand; fight when He says fight. Rest when He says rest.

 ALIGN YOUR HEART ▶

> *Lord, help me to see through the enemy's chaos and confusion. I will not fear the enemy; I will remember You. You are great and glorious, mighty and true. I stand with You and You stand with me. Thank You, Lord. Amen.*

[*] 2 Timothy 1:7.
[†] Luke 10:19.

Give Generously; God Remembers

Remember, O my God, all that I have done for these people, and bless me for it.

Nehemiah 5:19

The Jewish people returned to their homeland to rebuild their temple and restore their city, only to have some of their wealthy countrymen take advantage of them. They needed loans and assistance to reestablish themselves in a new city, and their wealthy neighbors—fellow Jews!—charged them ridiculous amounts of interest and then took their land when they couldn't make a payment. These poor people traded one form of slavery for another. They complained to Nehemiah, who not only confronted the injustice, but also shared generously from his own resources. Nehemiah worked hard like everyone else, and he earnestly tended to the needs before him. He was a giver, not a taker. Why? Because he feared God and determined to honor Him with every resource entrusted to him. Self-preservation and kingdom life are not compatible. It's tempting to grab what you want and turn a blind eye to those in need, but right now, we're stewards, not owners. One day we'll be owners based on what we did with gifts and resources entrusted to us to use for God's glory. You can't do everything, but you're definitely called to do something. God keeps great records and He cares deeply about those in need. Live and give generously. God remembers. And you'll be changed.

 ALIGN YOUR MIND Read Nehemiah 5.

 ALIGN YOUR ACTIONS Giving isn't just about money. It's about time, energy, your gifts, and your talents—even kindness and listening. Ask God how you can live and give generously today.

 ALIGN YOUR HEART

Lord, forgive me for my tendency to think solely of myself. Show me who to help and what to do. I'm Yours, Lord. Amen.

Discern Distraction

"I am engaged in a great work, so I can't come. Why should I stop working to come and meet with you?"

Nehemiah 6:3

Nehemiah loved and feared God and felt prompted by Him to leave behind a cushy job in the palace to take on a project that seemed impossible from any point of view. Yet he knew God was in it. So he took the great risk, returned to Jerusalem, and began the process of rebuilding. We love shiny new things. It takes grit and grace and vision to take on an old thing and make it new again. Yet that's what Jesus has done for us. He met us in our mess and brokenness, and He made us new again. We are His masterpiece, created anew in Christ Jesus so that we can do the wonderful things He's planned for us.* But if we never grasp the value of our lives, we'll never comprehend the importance of our work. And if we never comprehend the importance of our work, we'll not discern the enemy's attempts to distract us from that work. May you walk so intimately with God that you're intensely, divinely aware of your value and calling. May you be able to say along with Nehemiah, "I'm doing a great work, and I will not be distracted by the enemy of my soul." Not today. Not any day!

ALIGN YOUR MIND Read Nehemiah 6:1–14.

ALIGN YOUR ACTIONS Ask God to show you the value of your life and assignment. Be awakened to their importance and stand strong.

ALIGN YOUR HEART

> Lord, I've lost sight of the value of my soul and calling. Ignite my heart once again! Give me fierce faith and deep conviction to stay the course! Amen.

* Ephesians 2:10.

Celebrate along the Way

And Nehemiah continued, "Go and celebrate with a feast of rich foods and sweet drinks, and share gifts of food with people who have nothing prepared. This is a sacred day before our Lord. Don't be dejected and sad, for the joy of the LORD is your strength!"

Nehemiah 8:10

The people of Israel were as broken as the city walls. Nehemiah knew they needed the word of the Lord. When they heard it, they realized all over again just how far they'd fallen away from Him and His ways—and it grieved them. They were literally weeping as the prophet read aloud even though they'd already repented for their downfall and returned to Him! They were fighting their battles, standing in the strength of the Lord, and persevering in faith. Nehemiah knew this was not a time for them to be dejected; it was a time to celebrate. It's the same with us: when we're worn down, we can feel especially sensitive about our shortcomings. But if you're following Jesus, obeying His ways, and doing your best with the tasks set before you, rejoice. God is not disillusioned with you. He loves you. He'll never have unrealistic expectations of you. And your faith-filled-heart-of-gratitude celebrations mean as much to Him as do your moments of humble repentance.

ALIGN YOUR MIND ▶ Read Nehemiah 8.

 ALIGN YOUR ACTIONS ▶ Take time this week to celebrate and thank God for your progress and His faithfulness. Don't just think about it. Do it.

 ALIGN YOUR HEART

> *Jesus, how far we've come! I rejoice today for the victories won and the lessons learned. I'm not who I was. Thank You, Lord. Onward and upward I go. Amen.*

Provision and Decision

"You gave them bread from heaven when they were hungry and water from the rock when they were thirsty. You commanded them to go and take possession of the land you had sworn to give them."

Nehemiah 9:15

After their celebrations, the Jewish people gathered to confess their sins and recount the ways God had protected and provided for them through the generations. He gave them bread from heaven and water from a rock. And He charged them to take possession of their promised land. But instead of using God's provision to do as He commanded, the people became arrogant and rebelled—they even wanted to go back into slavery! Jesus is our Bread from heaven—our eternal provision who satisfies our deepest hunger. He traded His life for ours, and now we're eternally secure. He's the Rock on which we stand, our place of refuge and strength. And when we believe and follow Him, streams of living water flow through us to a parched and desperate world. Today, you face the same decision as the Israelites: will you become arrogant and complacent, going back to your old ways? Or will you use God's provision and protection to do as He commands, to take hold of the treasure He has in store for you?

ALIGN YOUR MIND Read Nehemiah 9:1–17.

ALIGN YOUR ACTIONS Ask God to remind you of all the ways He's provided for and protected you. Review your list, and trust that His provision and protection will be there for you today.

ALIGN YOUR HEART

> *Father, how easily I forget about the power of Your love and the reality of my inheritance. With awe and humble gratitude, I make the decision to trust You. Amen.*

Humility before Honor

When it was Esther's turn to go to the king, she accepted the advice of Hegai, the eunuch in charge of the harem. She asked for nothing except what he suggested, and she was admired by everyone who saw her.

Esther 2:15

God invites us to approach the throne of grace humbly, but boldly, and audaciously too. He invites us to ask, seek, knock, and believe. However, we will find ourselves in very real, very hard situations that involve ego, competition, and people who do not fear God. At these times, it's wise to be less audacious and a bit more cautious. When it was Esther's turn to see the king, she could have asked for *anything*. This was her one chance to impress him and snag the crown for herself. Yet she humbly accepted advice from a loyal servant and, in so doing, was admired by everyone—especially the king. There's something powerful about a person who entrusts her honor and outcomes not to man, but to God. She doesn't grab for herself or expect too much from others. She's not petty or common. She's uncommon. When she humbles herself, she knows God will lift her up at the proper time, defend her, and deliver her. There's a time to stand and fight, but there's also a time to bow and let God fight for you.

ALIGN YOUR MIND Read Esther 2:1–20.

 ALIGN YOUR ACTIONS Ask God to show you when to move forward in audacious faith—and when to humbly bow and wait.

ALIGN YOUR HEART

> *Lord, I hide myself in You. Give me strength when I need to stand and flexibility when it's time to bow. You will always be my Great Defender. I look to You. Amen.*

When a Leader Abdicates Responsibility

The king said, "The money and the people are both yours to do with as you see fit."

Esther 3:11

King Xerxes, who was out of touch with reality, gave Haman, his second-in-command, way too much power. Leaders are appointed by God and are greatly accountable to God—and yet we live in a fallen world where many leaders don't acknowledge God. While it's a mystery why He allows certain people to remain in position when they do more harm than good, we know He is sovereign in all His ways. Many leaders tend to be a blend of both glaring weaknesses and surprising strengths. (Aren't we all?) And they can either surround themselves with humble, capable, Godfearing associates, or pick eager, scheming yes-men who will use their positions to get their way. It's heartbreaking how many leaders have a second-in-command who misuses his power. Like Xerxes, the guy in charge doesn't really want to know what's going on—and likes it that way—all while good people suffer. The results are heartbreaking. Does God see? Does He care? Absolutely. Will He do something about it? Yes. God always has His saints in the wings. He's preparing them and, when the time is right, will use them to thwart the enemy's plan. When it seems evil has won, it's only because the story isn't over yet.

ALIGN YOUR MIND Read Esther 3.

ALIGN YOUR ACTIONS If you're aware of an unjust situation, fast and pray. Ask God to raise up someone to stand in the gap.

ALIGN YOUR HEART

Great King, intervene like only You can! Humble the proud, promote the humble, and foil the enemy's plan against the innocent. Move, O God! Amen.

When a Facade Won't Do

When Queen Esther's maids and eunuchs came and told her about Morde-cai, she was deeply distressed. She sent clothing to him to replace the bur-lap, but he refused it.

Esther 4:4

Haman had convinced King Xerxes to slaughter all the Jews on the same day. In response to the evil decree, Mordecai donned burlap and ashes and then wailed loudly and wept bitterly outside the palace gate. Word got back to Queen Esther. And this is where the kingdom story turns on its heels. From her place of privilege in the palace, Esther worried Mordecai would get into trouble. Without asking why he was distressed, she sent clothing to clean up his appearance. But a new set of clothes was not the answer. This was no time for self-preservation or for putting on a good face. Mordecai didn't need to step up to the expectations of the privileged. Esther needed to come down to the needs of the oppressed. Like Esther, once we know about oppression and injustice, we must not look the other way. Hiding in our wealth—including our time, talents, possessions, and blessings—is to turn our backs on God. He is for the oppressed. May you lovingly dare to enter into a suffering that's not your own for the greater good of the kingdom.

 ALIGN YOUR MIND Read Esther 4:1–4.

 ALIGN YOUR ACTIONS Ask God to open your eyes to something that breaks His heart—and for the courage to use what you have to do something about it, even if it feels small.

 ALIGN YOUR HEART

> *Father, You've given me everything I have. Please help me use it all with a kingdom mindset—to spread Your love, grace, hope, and redemption to those who need it.*

For Such a Time as This

"If you keep quiet at a time like this, deliverance and relief for the Jews will arise from some other place, but you and your relatives will die. Who knows if perhaps you were made queen for just such a time as this?"

Esther 4:14

Queen Esther's life was on the line. Her fears were real. Her people faced extermination, yet if she dared to appeal to the king on their behalf, she could die and the plan against the Jews could still succeed. She had much to lose. Most of us will never face that kind of pressure. But we *are* called to live boldly right where we are, and that still requires faith, risk, and trust in an unseen God. Picture the people you see every day. In that sea of faces are some who are lost and need to be found. Who are rejected and need to be accepted. Who are broken and need to be restored. You are where you are right now for a reason. Like Esther, you are being called to step out and speak up. And, like her, you have a choice to make: live for earthly success or for eternal impact. Make no mistake about it: God will bring deliverance. He's still a miracle-working God, and His promises are as potent as they've ever been. But the uninvolved will miss the miracle.

ALIGN YOUR MIND Read Esther 4:5–17.

 ALIGN YOUR ACTIONS This week, go out of your way to speak hope and life to someone each day. Compliment a stranger, encourage a friend, thank an adult who's helped you.

ALIGN YOUR HEART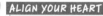

Father, give me boldness, courage, and strength to step into all You've planned for me! I'm available, Lord. Amen.

He Uses the Night Hours

> That night the king had trouble sleeping, so he ordered an attendant to bring the book of the history of his reign so it could be read to him.
>
> Esther 6:1

The king extended his scepter to Esther and invited her into his presence. She asked for a dinner party with the king and Haman. There are varying opinions as to why she didn't tell the king on that first night about Haman's evil plot. My guess is that she felt the inner nudge to push pause. She asked for a second dinner the following night. That evening the king had trouble sleeping, so he read the record books of his reign and remembered afresh how Mordecai had saved his life. God used this delay to add weight to Esther's appeal. Time and again we read how God uses either insomnia or dreams to bring revelation to those who need it. Scripture says that He grants sleep to those He loves,* but He'll also interrupt sleep on occasion to get a message to us. Before you head to bed, ask God to tune your heart to hear Him and claim His protection over your sleep. You belong to Jesus, and He promises that even at night our hearts will instruct us.†

 ALIGN YOUR MIND ▶ Read Esther 6.

 ALIGN YOUR ACTIONS ▶ Start keeping a notepad and pen next to your bed; jot down anything that comes to you at night. In the mornings, ask God for wisdom and discernment about what you wrote.

 ALIGN YOUR HEART ▶

> *Jesus, I claim my night hours for You! I command the enemy to stand down and be silent. I forbid him to speak or interfere with my sleep. My nights belong to You. Amen.*

---

* Psalm 127:2.
† Psalm 16:7.

When God Turns the Tables

And as soon as the king spoke, his attendants covered Haman's face, signaling his doom.

Esther 7:8

Haman was wicked to his core. He ordered the annihilation of an entire people group because one Jewish man dared to honor God above him. For a while, it seemed he'd get away with such a gross mismanagement of power, but then God used a humble Jewish girl turned queen, who dared to trust God and risk her life for her people. God is full of mystery. He spoke the galaxies into place and entrusted His Son to a world that He knew would kill Him. He is a God of justice who will one day set the records straight, but until then, He gives the vilest of sinners a chance to repent *because He loves them*. He knows exactly where and how to bring discipline or deliverance. Nothing gets by Him. He knows what He's doing at all times. Which is why you can take risks and stand in faith against the evil in your day. When the King decides it's time, He'll cover the face of your enemy and signal his doom. He'll turn the tables, dismantle every evil plot, and in a matter of moments, we'll see the redemption of all things. That great day is coming.

 ALIGN YOUR MIND Read Esther 7.

 ALIGN YOUR ACTIONS Today, look for a situation to stand firm in your faith against something unfair or unjust. Ask God to redeem and restore the situation for His glory.

 ALIGN YOUR HEART

> *Lord, You are a God of justice and love. Cut off the strength of the wicked; increase the power of the godly.* I know one day You will redeem all things. Amen.*

* See Psalm 75:10.

Power for a Purpose

Then Mordecai left the king's presence, wearing the royal robe of blue and white, the great crown of gold, and an outer cloak of fine linen and purple. And the people of Susa celebrated the new decree.

Esther 8:15

Haman's wicked plot was exposed, and Mordecai's integrity revealed. In a sudden turn of events, King Xerxes gave Haman's property to Esther and his signet ring—a symbol of authority—to Mordecai. Since the decree against the Jews could not be reversed, the king issued another decree, allowing the Jewish people to defend themselves. Mordecai traded his sackcloth for royal robes. But this wasn't just about vindication; it was about salvation. The enemy army assumed it would overpower God's people, yet the Jews overpowered them! Similarly, the enemy has issued a decree against God's people, to steal, kill, and destroy everything God intends to do in our lives. But God has issued a superior decree, giving us full authority over him. Because we're wrapped in God's robe of righteousness, we have the power to defend ourselves. We wear His signet ring. He's entrusted power and authority to us, but it's not just for us. We're called to contend for those who cannot or don't know how to fight for themselves. You've been given power for a purpose. How will you use it?

 ALIGN YOUR MIND ▸ Read Esther 8–10.

 ALIGN YOUR ACTIONS ▸ Even at your age, you have power. Your words and actions impact those around you. Today, use your power, words, and actions to help and encourage whoever you interact with.

 ALIGN YOUR HEART

Father, show me what You've entrusted to me. Help me to use Your power and authority for the greater good. Amen.

Fear God, Shun Evil

There once was a man named Job who lived in the land of Uz. He was blameless—a man of complete integrity. He feared God and stayed away from evil.

Job 1:1

Proverbs 3:7–8 says, "Don't be impressed with your own wisdom. Instead, fear the Lord and turn away from evil. Then you will have healing for your body and strength for your bones." To be wise in your own eyes is to become either a pagan or a Pharisee. You'll either dabble in things you shouldn't while saying, "I've got this," and find yourself in a ditch, or you'll be impressed with yourself and say, "I already know this," and find yourself in the other ditch. True wisdom starts with knowing and fearing God and mistrusting yourself enough to know that you must turn away from temptation and evil. Job understood his own limits and trusted a God who knew no limits. Despite all he had, he wasn't arrogant but full of integrity. Are you like Job, seeing all you have—your talents, abilities, grades, friends, possessions—as gifts from God? Or are you impressed with yourself, feeling like you deserve all you have—and more? No matter where you fall on the spectrum, humble yourself, acknowledging all you have as gifts from God. Doing so will honor God and bring strength to your soul.

ALIGN YOUR MIND Read Job 1:1–5.

ALIGN YOUR ACTIONS Play the most reverent worship song you know. Listen with your eyes closed and hands and heart open, as if ready to receive something.

ALIGN YOUR HEART

Mighty God, I bow before You. You are matchless, mighty, and true. I have nothing You've not given me. I give all that I am back to You. Amen.

A Wall of Protection

"You have always put a wall of protection around him and his home and his property. You have made him prosper in everything he does. Look how rich he is!"

Job 1:10

The enemy had been patrolling the earth, looking for opportunities to attack. He found no opening in Job's life. The Lord himself called Job the finest man in all the earth.* Satan hated Job and resented the fact that God shielded him. It almost seems like Satan baited God into lifting His protection from Job, but God falls into no one's trap. He's always in control, always knows what He's doing. If anything, Satan fell prey to God's wisdom. We'll explore Job's story over the next few days, but today let's remember that God *does* put a shield around His people. Psalm 125:2 says, "Just as the mountains surround Jerusalem, so the LORD surrounds His people, both now and forever." Psalm 3:3 says, "But you, O LORD, are a shield around me; you are my glory, the one who holds my head high." And Psalm 5:12 says, "For you bless the godly, O LORD; you surround them with your shield of love." Any pain God allows, He redeems. Any trap He allows the enemy to set is meant for the enemy himself. God's on His throne, His heart's set on you, and He's put a wall of protection around you. Believe it.

 ALIGN YOUR MIND Read Job 1:6–12.

 ALIGN YOUR ACTIONS Memorize one of the verses above and pray it every day this week.

 ALIGN YOUR HEART

Lord, You surround me with Your favor as with a shield. Thank You for all You've prevented and all You've provided. Thank You for the countless ways You protect me. Amen.

* See Job 1:8.

Grounded in the Things of God

"The LORD gave me what I had, and the LORD has taken it away.
Praise the name of the LORD!" In all of this, Job did not sin by blaming God.

Job 1:21–22

It's hard to imagine the trauma Job and his wife endured in just a matter of moments. Yet Job's righteousness went so deep that at his worst moment, Job's instinctive response was to bow low and recognize God's sovereignty in his life. He actually fell to the ground to worship. *Worship!* Job had walked so intimately with his heavenly Father that he was more grounded by his spiritual life than he was shaken by his earthly life. That kind of intimacy doesn't happen overnight. Our instinctive responses are born out of a million similar choices—choices we make every day that either acknowledge God or push Him aside. The reason Job didn't sin by blaming God was that he knew everything good about his life came from God. Once we stop acknowledging God and His goodness, we start blaming Him when things don't go our way or we don't get what we want. It's a cycle of sin and shallowness that starts when we drift. If we want to stand strong in the hard times of life, we must stay intimately engaged with God. The world may shake but you don't have to.

ALIGN YOUR MIND Read Job 1:13–22.

ALIGN YOUR ACTIONS Whether life is good or hard right now, make a habit to thank God every time you notice His goodness in your life. It'll transform the way you see everything.

ALIGN YOUR HEART

Father, open my eyes to Your goodness in my life. Take me deeper still. Ground me in You. Amen.

When Silence Is Best

> Then they sat on the ground with him for seven days and nights. No one said a word to Job, for they saw that his suffering was too great for words.
>
> Job 2:13

Job lost his family, wealth, and health. Imagine his grief, torment, and unfathomable physical pain. Yet in all of it, he did *nothing* wrong. Job's friends heard of the tragedy and traveled from their homes to comfort and console him. Now, we know that later in the story, they opened their mouths, which became a problem. But for seven days and nights, they simply sat on the ground with him and said nothing because his suffering was too great for words. Like Job's friends, we have empathy . . . until a certain point. But when the hardships don't let up, we start to assume that the person suffering is actually the problem—and even try to figure out where they went wrong. Is it a lack of faith? Hidden sin? Yet when we do this, we draw lines in the sand, separating ourselves from their suffering. We elevate our own strengths and look down on their weaknesses. Job was righteous and still suffered. We live in a world where evil is real, and it doesn't discriminate in who it hurts. Next time someone you know suffers, simply sit with them. No words. No fixes. No assessment. The world needs more presence and less judgment.

ALIGN YOUR MIND Read Job 2.

ALIGN YOUR ACTIONS Find someone who needs presence more than they need fixes. Do for them what God asks of you.

ALIGN YOUR HEART

Lord, forgive me for my tendency to step back and judge when You call me to step close and serve. Grow Your heart of love within me. Amen.

When the Numbness Wears Off

> "What I always feared has happened to me.
> What I dreaded has come true.
> I have no peace, no quietness.
> I have no rest; only trouble comes."
>
> Job 3:25–26

When someone goes through a major trauma, God often shields them from the brunt of the impact because it would be too much to absorb all at once. People who've walked through unfathomable loss and hardship speak of a supernatural grace and peace that surrounds them immediately after the incident. It's like God carries them along in unseen arms; they don't seem to feel what everyone expects them to feel. Some say it's denial, but more often than not, it's a gift of supernatural grace. In due time, however, the weight of their loss or hardship catches up with them. They're thrust into a season where they feel *everything,* as if their nerves are exposed and highly sensitive. Where onlookers initially wondered about denial, now they assume overreaction. So what's the proper response to someone who's walked through a crisis? Let them be and feel as messy as they are. Then draw near and let them know you're not going anywhere. Withhold judgment. Agree that it's hard. And resist trying to fix it. Grief after loss is not pretty, yet it's a necessary, sacred journey. The Church needs more brave souls to weather the storms with the brokenhearted. Mercy triumphs over judgment.[*]

ALIGN YOUR MIND ▶ Read Job 3.

ALIGN YOUR ACTIONS ▶ Practice compassion by connecting with someone who's hurting. Listen to their story, and don't offer advice or solutions.

ALIGN YOUR HEART

Jesus, Your compassions never fail. Your empathy runs deep. You meet people in their need and weep with them. Make me more like You, Lord. Amen.

* See James 2:13.

Bible Snobs and Christian Bullies

"We have studied life and found all this to be true.
Listen to my counsel, and apply it to yourself."
Job 5:27

Is it possible to be an eloquent speaker and a pompous windbag at the same time? Job's friend Eliphaz fits that description. He mingled beautiful truths about God with flawed opinions about suffering. Yes, there are consequences when we sin and blessings when we obey. But we must *never* use those truths to assess the suffering of another. People thought Jesus suffered because of His own sin, but it was *our sins* He carried.* How do you know if you've encountered a Bible snob or a Christian bully? They use lofty, grandiose-sounding phrases when they talk about God, yet they're quick to pass judgment on others without knowing the full story—or extending grace. They lack brokenness, empathy, accessibility, and humility. They present a demanding God who punishes us as our sins deserve when Scripture actually says that He *doesn't* punish us as our sins deserve.† They're impatient with those who have questions and suspicious of those who see things differently. Just because someone claims to follow God doesn't mean they reflect God's heart. True, seasoned followers of Christ in any denomination will have a twinkle in their eye and humility in their heart, and they will inspire you to walk intimately with Jesus—not run away from Him.

 ALIGN YOUR MIND Read Job 4–5.

 ALIGN YOUR ACTIONS Who is the godliest, humblest person you know? Ask to spend time with them. Listen to their story and soak up their wisdom.

ALIGN YOUR HEART

> *Humble me, Lord. Help me to reflect Your precious, tender heart to a lost and broken world. Amen.*

---

* See Isaiah 53.
† Psalm 103:10.

Dangerous Assumptions

"Does God twist justice?
Does the Almighty twist what is right?
Your children must have sinned against him,
so their punishment was well deserved."

Job 8:3–4

Bildad, Job's second friend to speak, was also annoyed by Job's lament. Job knew in his heart that he hadn't sinned against God. He couldn't figure out why God had made him a target for suffering. Yet in the midst of his pain, his friends insisted there was a reason. They spouted off half-true beliefs that made God seem predictable and explainable, daring to assume they knew why God did what He did. This is dangerous territory. Because the most painful truth about intense suffering is that it's often unexplainable and complicated. Job and his friends wrestled with the age-old question: If God is good, why does He allow so much pain? And like them, we want real-life answers, not uncomfortable mystery. So we cling to half-true beliefs that lead to dangerous assumptions about God's motives. Bildad's false beliefs about God led him to pass false judgment on Job's children. In the end he was wrong, but in the moment, his words inflicted even more pain. When it comes to the goodness of God and the suffering of man, we don't know what we don't know. And it's wise to say so.

ALIGN YOUR MIND   Read Job 6–8.

ALIGN YOUR ACTIONS   When you face a hard situation, focus your mind on trusting God rather than on scrambling for an answer or solution.

ALIGN YOUR HEART

> *Father, I think I know so much. Forgive me, Lord, for assuming answers and passing judgment. I bow low in humility. Fill me with more trust. Amen.*

My Redeemer Lives!

"But as for me, I know that my Redeemer lives,
and he will stand upon the earth at last.
And after my body has decayed,
yet in my body I will see God!"

Job 19:25–26

We often forget that Job declared God's resurrection power while he was still suffering. He had no new answers, no idea why God had seemingly lifted His wall of protection. Yet Job held on to his faith. "Although Job struggled with the idea that God was presently against him, he firmly believed that in the end God would be on his side."* At this point of the story, Job had no idea that the enemy had asked for permission to test Job because he was so righteous, or that God would restore him to an even greater place than before. Some parts of your inheritance are reserved for that great day when you see Jesus face to face, but God still has good things planned for you in the land of the living. He's already planted graces and gifts in every one of your tomorrows. Declare His goodness now, before He gives you what you hope for. One day you'll stand with Him and you'll be glad your heart trusted Him when your eyes couldn't see Him.

ALIGN YOUR MIND ➤ Read Job 19:25–27; 23:10.

ALIGN YOUR ACTIONS ➤ Is there a situation in your life that makes you sad or angry? Hold that in your mind as you say out loud: "Lord, even here Your goodness and faithfulness will triumph. Help me believe it and see it!"

ALIGN YOUR HEART ➤

> *Lord, I will one day see what I can't now. I declare that You are good, and soon my eyes will see it. Amen.*

* *Life Application Study Bible*, 1072.

He's Just and He Knows Me

"But he knows where I am going.
And when he tests me, I will come out as pure as gold."

Job 23:10

Eliphaz condemned Job. He assumed Job's suffering was a result of some hidden sin in Job's life. I picture Job mustering up all of his courage and strength to reply to this toxic accusation. Job's response is also a good one for us: *"I admit I'm walking through a difficult time right now. I acknowledge that God seems painfully silent and hard to find. Though I cannot find Him, I know that He knows where to find me. He knows where I am, and He knows where I'm going. And when He tests me, He'll bring me forth as gold. I'll know Him better and love Him more than I did before."* Job knew in his heart that he wasn't blatantly sinning and trying to cover it up. Yet he also knew God's holiness in a way that made him tremble with holy terror, for who can stand self-assured before the Most Holy God? If you're walking through pain right now or are feeling unfairly assessed, two things are called for: holy confidence and humble dependence. Trust God's opinion far above other people's. And remember, humility is always appropriate when approaching the throne of God. He's a God of justice and knows you intimately. This should assure you and undo you, all at once.

ALIGN YOUR MIND ▶ Read Job 23.

ALIGN YOUR ACTIONS ▶ Holy confidence is fully trusting that God will defend and deliver you—no matter what it looks like now. Make this your mindset this week.

ALIGN YOUR HEART

Father, may it be true that when You test me, You bring me through pure as gold. Thank You, Lord. Amen.

Playing the Performance Card

"Everything I did was honest.
Righteousness covered me like a robe,
and I wore justice like a turban."

Job 29:14

When tragedy hit, Job went facedown to the ground and worshiped. He declared God's goodness in times of both favor and hardship. But as the battle raged on, and his "friends" assessed and accused him, Job lost his footing. He'd had enough. Instead of remembering the majesty and goodness of God, he began recounting the goodness of Job. He's not alone here. When pushed far enough, we all reach for that performance card in our back pocket. We pull it out and ask, "You allow *this* after all I've done for You?" Yet every time we use past accomplishments to defend our case before God, we're actually accusing God of being unjust—we're questioning His sovereignty and goodness. Some storms bring out the worst in us—and God knows how deep your self-reliance goes. In His mercy, He uses the storm to uproot it before the enemy uses it against you, costing you more than what you're going through right now. It's not God's harshness that allows us to endure hardship; it's His goodness. God is not only your Defender; He's your Deliverer. And He will come for you.

 ALIGN YOUR MIND Read Job 29.

 ALIGN YOUR ACTIONS If you catch yourself defending yourself to God by measuring your good deeds, instead offer them up as seeds for His glory. You'll be amazed at the harvest He'll produce in your life.

 ALIGN YOUR HEART

> *Jesus, I stand on Your grace, and Your grace alone. I can't save or deliver myself. Only You can. My soul waits on You. Amen.*

Encountering the Living God

"I had only heard about you before,
but now I have seen you with my own eyes."
Job 42:5

When it was God's turn to speak, He spoke of heavenly storehouses, earthly phenomena, and the ability to put intuition into the heart of man—all far beyond Job's ability to even understand, let alone perform. Job repented, not because his friends were right about him, but because he'd been wrong about God. Still, Job knew God. He even declared God's sovereignty amid his own suffering. But he actually *encountered* God during this exchange. We long for an encounter with God—as we should—but are we prepared for what His presence will reveal to us and in us? Never condemnation, but definitely revelation. We don't know what we don't know, and we can't see what we can't see. When the God of heaven moves in close, our hearts melt, our knees buckle, and we realize we're not nearly as wise as we thought ourselves to be. For God to change us, we need to know *Him*—the Person and His heart. Job found God to be more than enough for him. Beyond anything he'd lost, he'd gained something more of God. The Lord met Job in the ashes of his pain, opened his eyes, and then restored him to even greater honor, wealth, and health than before.

ALIGN YOUR MIND ▶ Read Job 42.

ALIGN YOUR ACTIONS ▶ Tell God He's more than enough for you! Ask Him for fresh revelations of who He is. Trust Him to redeem your pain.

ALIGN YOUR HEART ▶

> *Lord, I want to encounter You in a way that changes me! Open my eyes that I may see You with greater clarity. Show me Your glory. Amen.*

Walk, Stand, Sit

Blessed is the one
> who does not walk in step with the wicked
or stand in the way that sinners take
> or sit in the company of mockers. . . .

Psalm 1:1 NIV

God wants us to flourish. He wants to bless us. Though we're saved and empowered by grace, the choices we make impact the quality of our lives and relationships—and whether or not we flourish in our circumstances. Notice the progression in Psalm 1: *Walk. Stand. Sit.* If we *look* to anything besides Jesus to find our worth and satisfaction, our feet will take us there. Eventually, we'll stand at a crossroads and have a decision to make. If we still don't see the error of our ways, we'll end up sitting with, and eventually acting like, those who have no fear of God. But Jesus calls us to *walk* in His way: with the wise and in a manner worthy of our calling. He reminds us to *stand* in faith with our feet securely on the Rock of our salvation. And He paid a high price for us to *sit* at the table of grace and be *seated with Him* with all of His authority and right standing before the Father. *Profoundly blessed* is the one who walks His way. Why would we walk any other way?

ALIGN YOUR MIND Read Psalm 1.

ALIGN YOUR ACTIONS What are you focused on? School? Sports? Music? Relationships? Money? Today, focus on Jesus first and ask for His direction in all you do—and see how differently your day goes.

ALIGN YOUR HEART

> *Lord, I want to walk in Your way. Help me keep my focus on You and make choices that lead to Your abundant life. Amen.*

But You, O Lord

But you, O LORD, are a shield around me;
you are my glory, the one who holds my head high.

Psalm 3:3

Brokenhearted and weeping, David fled his kingdom. His own son be- trayed him, usurped his authority, and undermined his throne. Armies chased him, people doubted him, and circumstances looked grim for him. Though some of David's troubles were the consequence of his own sin,* he was still a man after God's own heart, and God still listened to his prayers. David knew that God was always on His throne, and if He intended to restore David to his throne, nothing and no one could stop Him. Even so, to be be- trayed, undermined, and tossed aside (especially by someone you trusted) is excruciating. If you stare too long at your circumstances, they'll overwhelm you. That's why David only glanced at his situation and then set a fierce gaze on the One who would deliver and defend him. Never look at your hardships and injustices in isolation. Acknowledge them, yes, but always with this caveat: "But you, O LORD, are a shield about me; you are my glory, the one who holds my head high." Stay humble and hopeful that you will see God—the One who fights for you—intervene on your behalf. Your circumstances may be true, but truer still is God's presence and power in your life.

ALIGN YOUR MIND ▶ Read Psalm 3.

ALIGN YOUR ACTIONS ▶ Write down your greatest worry or fear. Then write Psalm 3:3 underneath it. Pray it until you believe it.

ALIGN YOUR HEART ▶

> *Lord, You're greater than my circumstances and more powerful than my enemies. You're my shield, my glory, and the One who fights for me. Hold my head high. Amen.*

---

* See 2 Samuel 12:11.

He Trains You for Battle

He trains my hands for battle;
he strengthens my arm to draw a bronze bow.

Psalm 18:34

David was able to look back over his life and recount the faithfulness of God. Even when David was a boy watching over sheep, God began training him to become the mighty warrior and king we know. David was your age when his life as a shepherd led him to kill lions and bears. And because he killed those, He defeated Goliath as a teenager. Which led him to command armies and eventually become the greatest king in Israel's history. It didn't happen overnight. No training does. Yet God used everything in David's life to train him for promotion to greater responsibility and victory. And He is doing the same with you. Everything in your life, big and small, is strengthening you, testing you, molding you into the person He's called you to be. He's already training you for your next battle. He's making you spiritually agile, able to walk with holy confidence in uncertain situations. And He's showing you what you're capable of when you're carrying His shield of faith. You may think you're too young to do anything important, but like David, God will use every twist and turn in your story for your good and His glory. Before you know it, you'll be a fierce warrior ready for greater promotion and victory.

 ALIGN YOUR MIND Read Psalm 18.

 ALIGN YOUR ACTIONS When facing a challenging situation, be fierce in your resolve to follow God no matter what, knowing He's training you for greater impact.

 ALIGN YOUR HEART

> *Mighty God, You're making me into a mighty warrior! I trust You! I will not be defeated or discouraged, because You are with me. Thank You, Lord! Amen.*

He Speaks

The heavens proclaim the glory of God.
The skies display his craftsmanship.
Day after day they continue to speak;
night after night they make him known.
Psalm 19:1–2

King David was continually awed by God's greatness and majesty—and how God reveals himself to us through the wonder of creation. David also knew how quickly we lose sight of that majesty, how quickly we grow blind to beauty. Yet the One who spoke the stars into the sky has made himself available to us. *Imagine!* His magnificent creation reveals His lavish love and meticulous attention to detail. His handiwork is all around us—in the glory of sunrises and sunsets. The beauty of a butterfly, the joy of laughter, the sound of a bubbling brook. When we acknowledge His creation, we get a very real sense of His presence. *Every* good gift comes from Him. Those who seek Him, find Him. He speaks through His Word, through others, through the inward nudge of the Holy Spirit within us, through a song, a sense, and even a subtle shift in circumstances. But we'll miss Him if we we're not watching and listening for Him. We must learn to tune both our physical senses and our hearts to the evidence all around us. We must learn, like David, to see everything around us with wonder.

 ALIGN YOUR MIND Read Psalm 19.

ALIGN YOUR ACTIONS Write out a journal prayer thanking God in detail for the parts of creation you're most grateful for today. It honors God and is good for your soul.

ALIGN YOUR HEART

> *Glorious God of heaven, thank You for Your lavish love, the beauty of nature, and the gift of Your presence. I will enjoy all of these today. Amen.*

Honor, Anointing, and a Cup That Overflows

You honor me by anointing my head with oil.
My cup overflows with blessings.

Psalm 23:5

David's younger wilderness seasons prepared him for promotion. He learned to embrace courage and to rely on the Lord's provision. He also learned how to guard what the Lord had entrusted to him when an enemy preyed upon his territory. We must learn these things as well. That's why we have a Shepherd, one who cares for us *always*. He steers us away from evil, to places of rest and restoration. He leads us off the distracting pathways of the world to roads where truth and righteousness remind us who we are to Him. The closer we follow Him, the more we rely on Him until our hearts beat in rhythm with His. Over time, we're transformed into the royal heirs we were always meant to be. In the face of our enemy, He claims us as His own. He stands by us, pours out fresh anointing on us, and equips us for battle. From preparation to promotion, from the valley to the mountain, from the battlefield to the victory table of celebration, we will *always* have all that we need. We, like David, will one day look back over our lives and declare that we never—not for a moment—lacked any good thing because God's goodness and mercy followed us every step of the way.

 ALIGN YOUR MIND Read Psalm 23.

 ALIGN YOUR ACTIONS What do you need at this moment? Look to your Shepherd today. He's leading you even now.

 ALIGN YOUR HEART

> *Precious Shepherd, You've always been faithful. I've never lacked a thing. Even now, I will trust You. I have all that I need. Thank You, Lord. Amen.*

Strength and Resilience

The LORD is my fortress, protecting me from danger,
so why should I tremble?

Psalm 27:1

My husband is a giant of a man. He's solid as an oak, and as righteous as one too. When our sons were teens, they'd overconfidently barrel into their dad and try to knock him over. But he never budged. All of the force they'd muster against him would only reverberate within them as they bounced off him and landed in a heap on the floor. What a picture of sturdiness and strength! King David was as resilient. His many enemies taught him to be strong in the strength of the Lord. You don't have to be mighty in stature to be mighty in battle. You just need to stand in the strength of your God. The more time you spend in the sanctuary of God (constantly and continually acknowledging His presence in your life), the less the offenses and attacks of people will affect you. Imagine them, in their foolishness, mustering up their strength to knock you over, only to land themselves in a heap on the ground. Refuse to be derailed by mere humans. *Be strong in the strength of the Lord.* Don't fear. Don't fret. Expect to see His goodness in the land of the living.

ALIGN YOUR MIND ▶ Read Psalm 27.

ALIGN YOUR ACTIONS ▶ Your strength in the Lord starts in the sanctuary of Lord. Start building it in your life today: ask God to make you constantly aware of His Presence in your life. Then thank Him for it.

ALIGN YOUR HEART

Mighty God, You are my Defender, my Deliverer, my strong tower. I will remain confident in You. Teach me how to trust You for greater things. Amen.

The Eyes of the Lord

But the LORD watches over those who fear him,
those who rely on his unfailing love.

Psalm 33:18

When we rightly honor, fear, and revere the Lord Most High, His eyes are instinctively *drawn* to us. Think about that for a moment. You wake in the morning, open your Bible, and bow your head: God's eyes are drawn to you. You go about your day, whispering a prayer and acknowledging His presence: His eyes are drawn to you. You're facing a choice to walk in His way or your own, and you choose His because you love Him: His eyes are drawn to you with great affection and tenderness. Just imagine! God is aware of everything that goes on in the earth today. He made us so He understands everything we do and why we do it. But He's especially drawn to the sons and daughters who walk this earth with reverence in our hearts. He leans in, breathes fresh life, uses us in His plans, and delivers us from evil. When we fear the Lord, we know enough not to put our trust in lesser things. *He* is our help and our shield. We trust in His holy name. We rely on His love. The beautiful thing about walking intimately with God and reverently honoring Him is that we are continually drawn to Him, and He to us.

ALIGN YOUR MIND Read Psalm 33.

ALIGN YOUR ACTIONS Choose to honor God in your choices today, and smile at the thought of Him fixing His eyes on you.

ALIGN YOUR HEART

Father, I am Yours. I'm more spiritual than I am physical. Help me to walk in Your ways, to rightly honor You, and to remember Your heart for me. Amen.

Delivered from All My Fears

I prayed to the LORD, and he answered me.
He freed me from all my fears.

Psalm 34:4

'd never thought it possible to be delivered from all of my fears. I didn't even think it was possible to be delivered from *most* of my fears. But as I've continually looked away from the roar of my enemy and set my gaze on the Lord, He has—over time—set me free. God wants to do the same for you. He wants to remove your fears and worries and occupy more space in your heart, mind, and life. But how do you cultivate a life of freedom and truth? You taste and see that He is good. Every day, in multiple ways, note the goodness of God all around you. Acknowledge His influence. Believe His truth over the enemy's lies. Open your heart to His peace, and let it calm the angst in your soul. Picture fear, shame, and anxiety shriveling to nothing and falling right off you because your face is radiant with God's all-consuming power and presence. Your fears are real. Your battles will be significant. But there's a *supernatural* power on your side—God himself. Don't wait for heaven to be free. He's here for you right now.

ALIGN YOUR MIND   Read Psalm 34.

ALIGN YOUR ACTIONS   Make it a regular practice to look to God. Picture your fears coming to nothing. Believe it's possible and that He will deliver you.

ALIGN YOUR HEART

Lord, I never want to settle for less than Your best for me! I want freedom! Deliver me from all my fears. May my countenance reflect Yours. Amen.

Your Heart's Desire

Take delight in the LORD,
and he will give you your heart's desires.
Psalm 37:4

When I first read this passage as a new believer, I didn't at all understand the magnitude of this promise. God's not pining away, trying to bait us into an occasional visit or moment of worship. He's the unequaled, untamable, unfathomable, powerful life Source from which everything in creation originated. He needs nothing, holds everything in His hand, and loves us with a passion that cannot be contained. Any gift from His hand pales compared to the treasure of knowing His heart. We pine for gifts, for answers, for change, but we're so temporary—even shallow—in our wishes. *God wants us to more deeply long for His presence.* He's eternal when it comes to His desires for us. The more we delight in His presence, in Him, the less we pine for lesser things. Our souls get filled up with His goodness. Our hearts beat in rhythm with His. Suddenly His desires become our desires, and we find ourselves praying His kingdom right to earth. Nothing compares to the greatness of our God. Nothing we desire on earth compares to Him. Enjoy His presence. Delight in Him. It'll change everything.

 ALIGN YOUR MIND ▶ Read Psalm 37.

ALIGN YOUR ACTIONS ▶ To delight in God is to praise Him, admire His beauty, think about His Word—and more. Today, find a way to engage Him, whether you sing to Him, go outside and enjoy His creation, write your own psalm of praise, or wonder at His love for you.

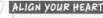 **ALIGN YOUR HEART** ▶

Unstoppable God, I marvel at Your goodness! May You be my biggest delight today and always. Thank You, Lord. I bless Your name. Amen.

Wait Joyfully, Expectantly

He has given me a new song to sing,
a hymn of praise to our God.
Many will see what he has done and be amazed.
They will put their trust in the LORD.

Psalm 40:3

New songs rarely come out of times of ease. They rise up out of the ashes, or settle in during times of Sabbath, or thunder through us in a time of battle. God invites us to sing a new song when circumstances cloud our view of Him. Worship breaks through the overcast sky and connects us once again with the warmth of His presence. Just this morning I battled some discouragement because I've waited a long time for complete healing. I want to be symptom free, but I'm not. Not yet, anyway. The Lord whispered to my heart, *Active waiting produces perseverance, but perseverance won't do the miraculous in you unless it's coupled with joyful expectancy.* We are all waiting for something; but *how* we wait is so important. Are you discouraged or despairing? Instead of counting the days of your waiting period or battle, God calls us to count the promises He's made to us. When we wait actively, we wait with faith, joy, and expectancy. Because God is always up to something new—and soon your eyes will see it. Embrace joyful expectancy—and you will find your new song.

 ALIGN YOUR MIND Read Psalm 40.

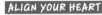 **ALIGN YOUR ACTIONS** Find your song today. Embrace joyful expectancy. God is up to something altogether new in your life. Soon your eyes will see it.

ALIGN YOUR HEART

> *Lord, I thank You by faith that You're coming for me! You're breaking through for me! Help me to persevere with joy. Do the miraculous in me. Amen.*

Be Still and Know

"Be still, and know that I am God!"
Psalm 46:10

How do you know when it's time to double down, hang on, and fight for victory, or when it's time to let go, rest your heart, and let the Lord fight the battle for you? Pay attention to the state of your soul. If restlessness drives you to strive, then you know it's time to *be still and know* that He is God. In other words: let go, sink down, relax, and in some cases, be quiet. When our souls are stressed, our words follow suit. And before we know it, our own declarations defy the goodness and faithfulness of God. Sometimes the most faith-filled thing you can do is to quiet your heart, close your mouth, and let go of the thing that stresses you so. Jesus doesn't drop things, so you can trust Him to hold whatever you give Him. We'll talk another day about discerning when it's time to run to the battle line, but today there are some things God wants you to let go of. He wants to make a trade: your stress for His peace, your burden for His grace, your earthbound perspective for His eternal one. His yoke is easy and His burden is light. May your precious, restful heart of faith honor Him greatly today.

 ALIGN YOUR MIND Read Psalm 46.

 ALIGN YOUR ACTIONS Let go of your stresses and worries, relax, and be still. Today's going to be a great day.

ALIGN YOUR HEART

> *Lord, forgive me for the angst I've allowed in my soul. I'm ready to make a trade: my stress and burdens for Your peace and grace. Give me Your eternal perspective. I love You, Lord. Amen.*

Your Great Unearthing
Is the Devil's Undoing

You crown the year with a bountiful harvest;
even the hard pathways overflow with abundance.
Psalm 65:11

We don't determine the seasons of our lives; God does. We need a faith perspective in every season. Maybe you're walking through a time when you feel undone, exposed, and scattered. Your once well-defined boundaries have been replaced with holes in the ground, dirt mounds, and boulders that have surfaced. You wonder what in the world happened to your tidy life. It's during these seasons that God sets the plow a little deeper into the soil of our hearts because He's about to do a *new* thing. Beneath the surface, you've got buried hurts, embedded lies, and weeds that choke the life right out of you. It's a messy process, and the enemy wastes no time in leveraging his lies to make you feel worse than you already do. But if you could look up and listen for the Lord, you would hear Him say, *"My dear child. This isn't about who you are; it's about who you're becoming. Your great unearthing will soon be the devil's undoing. Hold on. Listen for My voice. And know that this season will not last forever. A time of great flourishing is ahead for you."* Believe it, friend. You will get through this.

ALIGN YOUR MIND Read Psalm 65.

ALIGN YOUR ACTIONS Today, hang on to hope. Prayerfully sort through your losses, buried traumas, and the lies you picked up when life let you down. Ask God to unearth them so His life can grow.

ALIGN YOUR HEART

Precious Lord, meet me here. Give me faith to believe You for greater things! Heal me from the inside out. My soul trusts in You. Amen.

When God Seems Silent

But then I recall all you have done, O LORD;
I remember your wonderful deeds of long ago.

Psalm 77:11

It's easy to stay attentive to God's presence when the heavens seem to be open over us, when things go smoothly and His voice is crystal clear. But how about when He's gone silent—like He's lost our address? This so often happens when we're suffering, and we wonder, *Why now? Now's when I need a word from You!* During such times, we instinctively turn inward. Our self-focused nature emerges when God stops talking. Like Asaph, we sometimes blame God for our suffering, our insomnia, and His lack of involvement in our lives. We accuse Him of forgetting to be himself—kind, compassionate, and loving. Negative accusations and assumptions about God will always be destructive to our soul. So why does God allow the painful, silent season? Because we need to learn to turn on a dime like Asaph did. We won't mature in our faith until we learn to stop in our tracks and redirect our focus, our thoughts, and our words. If you're there today, remember God. Remember His goodness, recall His miracles, and revive your trust in Him. Don't confuse His silence with His absence. He's right here and He's developing gritty faith in you. Rise up, dear one.

ALIGN YOUR MIND Read Psalm 77.

ALIGN YOUR ACTIONS If your thought life is on a track that's taking you downward, stop now and redirect your gaze. Declare God's goodness. Rejoice in His faithfulness.

ALIGN YOUR HEART

> *Lord, it seems like others are flourishing while I'm floundering. And Your silence is hard to understand. But my heart trusts You! You are mighty to save. Do a new thing in me! Amen.*

Your Pilgrimage

What joy for those whose strength comes from the LORD,
who have set their minds on a pilgrimage to Jerusalem.
Psalm 84:5

Our souls were not made for aimless wandering. If we wander too long, we'll wear out, lose heart, and eventually lose our way. The Israelites wandered into trouble time and time again because they relied on their own strength and trusted in their own ability to reason. They forgot about their heritage, which made them forget about their inheritance. Two things will keep you from making the same mistake: dependence on God and vision for where He's taking you. Conversely, if you're in a season when the wind is at your back and all is flourishing, walk wisely, carefully, and stay humbly dependent on the Lord. Remember Who all this is for. And if you're feeling dry, barren, and lifeless, don't worry. That's the perfect atmosphere for God's power to awaken and establish you. He's not done with you. He's got more for you to do. Find your strength in Him. Through every twist and turn in life, remember that your purpose is powerful. Your pilgrimage, sacred. You're just passing through. Keep the vision of eternity before you, and in every season rely humbly and wholeheartedly upon His strength. No good thing will He withhold from those who walk uprightly before Him. Jesus will get you safely home.

ALIGN YOUR MIND Read Psalm 84.

ALIGN YOUR ACTIONS Prayerfully check your course and your heart today. Do you need more dependence or vision? Ask for it.

ALIGN YOUR HEART

I'm prone to wander, Lord, I feel it! Bind my heart to Yours. I'm leaning in hard today, relying on Your strength, counting on Your goodness. Awaken eternity within me. Amen.

Divine Protection

This I declare about the LORD:
He alone is my refuge, my place of safety;
he is my God, and I trust him.

Psalm 91:2

There's a story about a godly young man, held captive in a Nazi prison camp. After he read Psalm 91 and asked the Lord, "Men are dying all around me. Will I die here too, Lord?" the Lord whispered back to his heart, *Rely on what you've just read and walk out of here.* This brave soul approached the inner gates of the prison with his Bible clutched tightly against his chest. The guards aimed their guns at him and spewed, "*What* do you think you're doing?" He replied, "I'm under the protection of the Most High." The soldiers immediately dropped their guns and opened the gates. The same thing happened at the outer gates: The guards shouted with guns drawn, only to stand down and open the gates to his freedom. The man found out after the war that he was the only one to get out of that camp alive. He also learned that Hitler insisted his inner circle refer to him as "Most High." It was God Most High who orchestrated his freedom. And He's done the same for you. No enemy can take you out sooner than God's appointed plan for your life. Walk free. Walk courageously. You're under the protection of the Most High God.

ALIGN YOUR MIND ➤ Read Psalm 91.

 ALIGN YOUR ACTIONS ➤ Read Psalm 91 every day this month. Let the idea of His divine protection sink deep into your heart.

ALIGN YOUR HEART

> *Most High God, help me to walk free, be brave, and live courageously. You're my shelter and protection. My days are anointed and appointed by You! Amen.*

Strong As an Ox; Anointed Too

But you have made me as strong as a wild ox.
You have anointed me with the finest oil.
Psalm 92:10

It's good and important to start out your day giving thanks to God. Before even one thing happens—good or bad—you have reason to celebrate God. He's worth it, He deserves it, and believe it or not, it's good for you. Gratitude profoundly impacts your health. Grateful people have a more optimistic outlook on life than most; they have fewer aches and pains, and they sleep better than ungrateful people.[*] *Proclaim* God's goodness in the morning and His faithfulness at night. When you get into the habit of declaring God's goodness over every situation that you face between sunup and sundown, you will find that God's presence in your life carries more weight than your temporary, fleeting circumstances. Another amazing benefit of keeping your perspective tethered to God's consistent faithfulness is that you'll recognize the countless ways He protects you and honors you in the face of your enemy. He claims you as His own, equips you to win your battle, and *refuses* to let your enemy triumph over you. You are anointed indeed.

ALIGN YOUR MIND Read Psalm 92.

ALIGN YOUR ACTIONS Declare out loud, "You have made me as strong as a wild ox and anointed me with Your finest oil. I'm strong, blessed, called, and equipped!" It might feel silly, but repeat it. It'll shoot adrenaline into your soul.

ALIGN YOUR HEART

Lord, I declare Your goodness over my life. You've been so faithful, kind, and true. I am strong in You, anointed in You, secure in You. Thank You, Lord. Amen.

[*] Amy Morin, "7 Scientifically Proven Benefits of Gratitude," *Psychology Today*, April 3, 2015, www.psychologytoday.com/us/blog/what-mentally-strong-people-dont-do/201504/7-scientifically-proven-benefits-gratitude.

Never Forget His Benefits

Let all that I am praise the Lord;
may I never forget the good things he does for me.
Psalm 103:2

It's impossible to fully fathom the staggering, radical nature of our salvation. Our finite minds cannot grasp what Jesus saved us from and what He has promised us. We are destined for heaven, where every aspect of our life story will be redeemed. His Word is alive in us! His power, available to us! So why are some Christians' lives marked by power, insight, and authority, while others seem as earthbound as the rest of the lost world? A. W. Tozer once asked a similar question, and after much consideration and study, determined that those who rise up and do great things for God and with God possess what he calls spiritual receptivity. They cultivate a lifestyle of listening to God, and when He speaks, they do something about it. What if we did the same? What if we began to speak with precision, pray with power, and obey with the full assurance that God will do what He promises? What if we thanked God by faith for healing, redemption, renewal, and rescue? What if we asked for the impossible? Outcomes are up to Him. But our faith changes us and pleases Him. May we *never* forget all He's promised us.

ALIGN YOUR MIND Read Psalm 103.

ALIGN YOUR ACTIONS When faced with a difficult situation, err on the side of faith. Ask Him for direction and ACT on what you hear. Live expectantly, and leave the results to Him.

ALIGN YOUR HEART

> *Faithful Father, I come to You in faith today. I'm reaching for You and grabbing hold of Your promises. I'm believing You for greater things. Awaken faith in me, Lord! Amen.*

Wonderfully Made

Thank you for making me so wonderfully complex!
Your workmanship is marvelous—how well I know it.
Psalm 139:14

You are God's beautiful, amazing idea. You are not an accident, a side note, or an afterthought. God put intricate thought into every nuance of your personality so that His precious plan for your life would divinely fit you. He determined your birthday and celebrated when you took your first breath. He sings and rejoices over you. Really, *imagine it!* He wired you with passions, convictions, and gifts to reflect His heart to a world in need. You've got some good work to do, battles to fight, and giants to confront. You have some gifts to steward, moments to enjoy, and wisdom to acquire. You were crafted by God's own hand. You may also have genetic predispositions handed down from your family line that may or may not make life tougher for you than most. But do not allow family sins, weaknesses, or tendencies to take precedence over God's promises! Your spiritual inheritance through Christ is more powerful than anything you inherited from your family. The very power that raised Christ from the grave is alive and active in you. You couldn't be more loved, empowered, or secure if you tried. Scripture says it: You are fearfully, beautifully, and wonderfully made.

ALIGN YOUR MIND Read Psalm 139.

ALIGN YOUR ACTIONS Look in the mirror today—really look. You may not like what you see, but God loves what He sees and treasures you beyond your wildest imagination. Picture His fatherly smile when He looks at you.

ALIGN YOUR HEART

Father, it's hard to comprehend the reality of Your fatherly affection for me. Make it real to me. I want to live fully alive, knowing I'm profoundly loved, gifted, and called. Amen.

In All Your Ways, Know Him

Trust in the LORD with all your heart,
and do not lean on your own understanding.
In all your ways acknowledge him,
and he will make straight your paths.

Proverbs 3:5–6 ESV

My middle son, Luke, was a strong-willed little one who challenged us on every front. During one of his childhood meltdowns, he lamented, "How will I know when God is speaking and when the devil is just trying to trick me? I seem to get into trouble a lot." I suppressed a smile as I answered: "Suppose we took a walk in the woods and at first you held my hand and we explored together, but eventually you let go and ran ahead. How easy would it be for someone else to whisper from the shadows and pretend they're me? In the same way, stick close enough to know God and His ways and you'll recognize His voice." The word *acknowledge* in these verses is *yada* in Greek, which means "to know and experience intimately." The word *trust* is to be bold and secure—to be so confident in your relationship with Him that you trust Him more than you trust yourself. So the promise here is that when you live intimately with Him, fully reliant on Him, He'll make every crooked way within you and every crooked path in front of you straight. He will literally straighten out the path before you. What a miracle!

 ALIGN YOUR MIND ▶ Read Proverbs 3.

 ALIGN YOUR ACTIONS ▶ Ask God to show you where you're trusting yourself more than Him.

 ALIGN YOUR HEART

Jesus, revive my relationship with You so I can enjoy You more fully, trust You implicitly, and follow You to new heights. Amen.

What God Loves

There are six things the LORD hates—
no, seven things he detests. . . .
Proverbs 6:16

One Sunday morning I noticed one of my mentors standing in line to receive prayer. Her eyes sparkled; her wrinkles revealed her hard-earned wisdom. Someone in front of her took a sudden step back, causing her to do the same. The young woman behind her was so annoyed that she let out a huff and rolled her eyes. I was appalled. I prayed, *Lord, help me to never be so blind.* There are things God absolutely loves. And there are things He hates. He hates haughty eyes that look down on others, for any reason. He loves *humble eyes that reflect His.* He hates a lying tongue that destroys. He loves a *truthful tongue that sets others free.* He hates hands that kill the innocent. He loves *hands that help the vulnerable.* He hates hearts that plan evil. He loves a *heart that plans good things.* He hates feet that race to do evil. He loves *feet that promote justice* and are quick to help those in need. He hates false accusations and a slandering tongue. He loves those who *courageously yet humbly stand up in truth and love.* He hates it when someone sows discord. He loves the one who *humbly promotes unity in Him.*

ALIGN YOUR MIND ▶ Read Proverbs 6.

ALIGN YOUR ACTIONS ▶ Each day this week, practice honing one of the things God loves: humble eyes, a truthful tongue, hands that serve, a heart that plans good things, feet quick to obey, an advocate of justice, and one who promotes peace and unity.

ALIGN YOUR HEART

Lord, help me love what You love and do what You'd do. Make me more like You. Amen.

Search for God; Find Favor

If you search for good, you will find favor;
but if you search for evil, it will find you!
Proverbs 11:27

What you look for, you will find. In life, you'll experience good and bad, gladness and sadness, feast and famine. But in Christ, you can be sure that there's a redemptive aspect to every element of your life. God issues daily invitations and opportunities to be a blessing to a world in need. Look for the good and you'll find something more: *favor that comes from walking in God's power and reflecting His heart*. Those who relish division and drama, whose bent is gossip, whose hearts beat for idols, well, *evil will find them*. Sobering, yes? One day, we'll live forever with the Lord and enjoy opportunities to serve Him without enemy opposition and the hindrances we face in this life. But our search for good today is producing a beautiful grit in us that goes against the tide of culture and flies in the face of the enemy's intent for us. You are an ambassador of heaven. You have access to joy, peace, perspective, and power. You can change the atmosphere wherever you go when you go in the strength and perspective of the Lord. May you be a force to reckon with and may you enjoy favor wherever life finds you.

ALIGN YOUR MIND Read Proverbs 11.

ALIGN YOUR ACTIONS 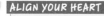 Lean in and look for the good in your life. Ask God for opportunities to serve Him. Be glad about your status in Him. You're highly favored.

ALIGN YOUR HEART

> *Lord, please help me to always search for Your goodness, and open my eyes to see redemptive possibilities all around me! Use me, Lord. I'm available. Amen.*

Fill Your Space; Run Your Race

Thieves are jealous of each other's loot,
but the godly are well rooted and bear their own fruit.

Proverbs 12:12

Thieves are jealous of each other's loot. . . . Yet we as God's people also tend to be jealous of another's fruit. We compare and despair. We wonder why God blesses them and not us. We spend too much time feeling disappointed about, or wrongly assessing, the success or popularity of others. But allowing our hearts to do that is like abandoning our own God-given garden to stare over the fence at another's garden—and resent them for their bounty even as we let what we have die. The truly godly are well rooted in the things of God, which yields fruit in our lives that nourishes others. Jealousy is a huge hindrance to this process of depth, growth, and fruit. In fact, jealousy is the gateway sin to every other sin.* Oh, if we could see the heavenly deed with our name on it! We would not only be content to fill our own space and run our own race, we'd be inspired, encouraged, and empowered to do so! Walk away from the fence and get excited about your own garden—your own life. There are amazing things waiting for you there!

ALIGN YOUR MIND ▶ Read Proverbs 12.

ALIGN YOUR ACTIONS ▶ Whose fence are you staring over? Who has what you want? Today, determine to shut down every hint of jealousy. Ask God to help you love your life and empower you with what He's given you.

ALIGN YOUR HEART

Father, forgive me for losing perspective when I look to others. Help me tend to what You've given me and use it for Your glory! Amen.

* See James 3:16.

A Reliable Messenger Brings Healing

An unreliable messenger stumbles into trouble,
but a reliable messenger brings healing.
Proverbs 13:17

I marvel that God entrusts the kingdom to such broken people. Yet He puts His Spirit in us and works wonders through us, all while we work out our salvation and gradually discover who we are to Him. I shudder to think back on how often His message of love got lost in translation through me because I was too broken, insecure, and self-focused to rightly relay His heart to others. Yet still, He loved me through it all. Because of His unrelenting love, I'm not who I was; I am someone altogether new. And I'm not who I will be. I'm counting on His goodness to continually transform me. The same goes for you. We get to be a work in progress without the condemnation. And yet we must contend for freedom. Far too many Christians stay stuck because they prefer a known captivity to an unknown freedom. *A reliable messenger brings healing.* When we understand who we are to God and who He is to us, we more reliably communicate His message to a lost and broken world. The freer we become, the more clearly His kingdom is communicated through us.

 ALIGN YOUR MIND ▸ Read Proverbs 13.

 ALIGN YOUR ACTIONS ▸ Do your words and actions bring healing, or do they stir up more trouble? Ask God to give you a picture of how His kingdom message can flow through you and bring healing and hope to others.

ALIGN YOUR HEART ▸

Thank You, Lord, for Your patience, steadfast love, and commitment to me. Transform me into someone I never dreamed I could be. Share Your message of love through me to a world in need. Amen.

The Miracle in the Mess

Without oxen a stable stays clean,
but you need a strong ox for a large harvest.
Proverbs 14:4

I once knew a business owner who was all about appearances. He had the nicest building. The nicest equipment. And he lived extravagantly. Yet his employees were discouraged, underpaid, and overworked. He's since gone out of business. When appearances matter more than fruit, we sacrifice our influence and our impact. However, when we're committed to God's people, process, and purposes, we'll find miraculous life change, community impact, and kingdom movement. But it's often messy. People are broken. Relationships are complicated. Conflict is no fun. Sacrifice and serving others—especially those we find hard to love—is *hard*. It's why, short-term, it seems easier and faster to create the flashy image you want without doing the hard, and usually messy, work of growth—growth that takes time and intention. But there is no shortcut to a fruitful life. Don't get discouraged by the messes. It just means you're alive and on the road to redemption like the rest of us. It takes a strong person to stay the course, maintain perspective, and keep hope alive. Don't miss the everyday miracles in the messes of life. Jesus did life this way. He understands. And He's in it with you.

ALIGN YOUR MIND ▶ Read Proverbs 14.

ALIGN YOUR ACTIONS ▶ What parts of your life seem messy? Look for God in them. Pray and watch for a miracle.

ALIGN YOUR HEART ▶

> *Lord, I sometimes want to trade the mess for a perfect-looking life, but there's no life in that! Help me to embrace the real and forsake the fake. Help me to see the beauty and the miracle in the mess. Amen.*

Make Your Plans; Stay Flexible

> We can make our plans,
> but the LORD determines our steps.
> Proverbs 16:9

I remember when I finally mustered up the courage to write the first words of my first book. Up till then, two agendas warred within me—obedience and procrastination. I sensed the inner invitation from God to trust Him and take the first steps toward publishing. At the same time, the self-preservation monster stirred up my fears, compelling me to stop so I'd never have the chance to fail. One day, my giant of a husband hovered over me and my bowl of popcorn and said, "It's time to get writing. You're out of excuses. God's made it clear. Get going." The next morning, I stared at a blank screen and nothing came to me. Except the still, small whisper that I knew was God. *Your neighbor needs you.* So I found myself knocking on her door. She answered with tears in her eyes, and I got to spend some precious, God-ordained time with her. As I headed back home, the Lord reminded me that life with Him always requires flexibility and sensitivity to His Spirit. And after that simple act of obedience, the words poured out onto the page. Life with God is life, indeed. Ask for some God-given dreams. Make your plans. Stay flexible. Be interruptible. Jesus will lead you on a fruitful faith-adventure of a lifetime.

ALIGN YOUR MIND ▸ Read Proverbs 16.

ALIGN YOUR ACTIONS ▸ Are you postponing obedience? Make some plans! Are you flexible? Pay attention to His divine interruptions.

ALIGN YOUR HEART

> *Lord, I don't want anything to stand in the way of Your best for me. Awaken me to the plans You have for me. Help me to respond to Your divine interruptions. Amen.*

A Time for Everything

For everything there is a season,
a time for every activity under heaven.
Ecclesiastes 3:1

I'm not afraid of death. I'm afraid of dying." My dear brother-in-law held my hand as I sat next to his hospital bed. His skin was yellow, his eyes gaunt, his smile weak. I didn't have the heart to tell him he *was* dying—and doing it so very gracefully. Though we believed God still performs miracles today, we sensed this was Donny's time to pass from this life to the next. God decides and determines the seasons. It's ours to discern those seasons. There's a time to fight with everything in you, and a time to let go and let God—a time for pruning and a time for flourishing. There's a time to forge ahead with what little strength you have, and a time to wait on God when it makes no sense at all. There's a time to walk away quietly and allow God to vindicate you, and a time to stand strong in the face of persecution, knowing He'll deliver you. Here's what's true: Obedience to God will always strengthen your soul and sturdy your stance. You don't pick or decide your seasons. You can't force outcomes. And you can't rush through a season that God intends for you to grow from. But as you discern the season, you can embrace it. He's set eternity in your heart—therefore every season is bursting with eternal possibility.

 ALIGN YOUR MIND ▸ Read Ecclesiastes 3.

ALIGN YOUR ACTIONS ▸ Prayerfully discern your current season. What do faith and obedience require of you here?

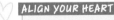 **ALIGN YOUR HEART** ▸

Father, Your ways are higher than mine. Show me what You're up to in this season. Help me to find You here. Amen.

Strong in Battle—Together

A person standing alone can be attacked and defeated, but two can stand back-to-back and conquer. Three are even better, for a triple-braided cord is not easily broken.

Ecclesiastes 4:12

I stared at the woman in front of me, marveling at her calm demeanor but her audacious questions: "Why won't you let me in? Who hurt you so deeply that you've built up such a wall?" She was right. I'd been hurt enough that I'd subconsciously decided I didn't need any new friends. Yet I feared God and recognized His influence enough to know that He was behind her insistence that I open up and trust again. That was twenty years ago. And to this day, that woman is one of my closest, most trusted friends. We've journeyed through life's twists and turns; we've stood back-to-back and conquered our enemy. We've both suffered some pretty horrible storms, but the storms have passed, and our bond is stronger than ever. And our history with God is stronger still. Brady Boyd once said on my radio show, "It takes a long time to make an old friend." Especially a friend who loves and fears God. Those are the best kind. It's been said that the wolves attack the sheep that have wandered from the fold. We wander sometimes because of sin, other times because of pain. Either way, the devil hopes to find us alone. Don't let that happen.

ALIGN YOUR MIND ▶ Read Ecclesiastes 4:7–12.

ALIGN YOUR ACTIONS ▶ Put some time into your most trusted relationships this week. Don't take them for granted.

ALIGN YOUR HEART

> Lord, You've wired me for togetherness. Help me to nurture deep, godly, through-thick-and-thin kinds of friendships. Be the center of them all. Amen.

Laboring from Envy

Then I observed that most people are motivated to success because they
envy their neighbors. But this, too, is meaningless—like chasing the wind.

Ecclesiastes 4:4

Scripture says that a lazy person is as bad as someone who destroys things. Their apathy not only hinders flourishing, it destroys it. Similarly, workaholism that springs out of a drive to outdo, surpass, or compete is also destructive. From the outside, a person may appear a great success. They may have a nicer home and a better reputation than the lazy man, but they'll destroy a few things along the way too. They'll ruin their relationships with those closest to them. They'll destroy their own faith perspective because they're not inspired by faith; they're driven by lust. They'll kill their own capacity to enjoy life because striving born out of envy is not a sustainable way to live. If God has gifted you, embrace those gifts. But enjoy them too. Consider everything you do as an offering back to God. Ask Him to multiply every offering. Believe Him for great things. God is all about harmony, health, wholeness, and flourishing. Deal with even the smallest hint of envy so it won't destroy you or your offering.

ALIGN YOUR MIND Read Ecclesiastes 4:4–6.

ALIGN YOUR ACTIONS Check your motivation for doing what you do. If you find envy or striving behind any of your motivations, humbly repent and reset your focus on God's plans for you.

ALIGN YOUR HEART

Jesus, You paid it all! I have nothing to prove and all of eternity to live for. Help me to steward my gifts with a heart of faith and an assurance of who I already am in You. Help me to enjoy my life. Amen.

Better a Funeral Than a Party

> Better to spend your time at funerals than at parties.
> After all, everyone dies—
> so the living should take this to heart.
>
> Ecclesiastes 7:2

Who prefers a funeral over a party? Almost no one. Still, Scripture says it's *better* to go to a funeral than a party. Why? Parties are fun. They help us forget our troubles so we can enjoy a special occasion. God *calls* us to celebrate, feast, and remember His goodness to us. Celebration is a gift from God. It's good for the heart and healing for the soul. So what could possibly be *better* about a funeral? It's where all of life comes into clear view and we remember what's truly important. It's the place where life is reset for us. We're forced to reckon with all of our running, all of our striving, all of our performing. Who's it for? What's it accomplishing? Who's it helping? Funerals help us see life through an eternal lens. We tend to take our own life for granted until someone loses theirs. Loss is heartbreaking, especially when that person has squandered their life. But their funeral might be the very thing that wakes you up to the significance of your own life. You don't know how many days you have left on this earth. But you have today. Don't wait for someone else's funeral to make your life count.

ALIGN YOUR MIND Read Ecclesiastes 7:1–8.

ALIGN YOUR ACTIONS Make life count today: taste your food, love well, be kind to a stranger, give a gift. Thank Jesus for everything good in your life.

ALIGN YOUR HEART

> *Jesus, You've given me this life, and I want it to count! Awaken my heart to every eternal possibility before me. Amen.*

It's Better to Fear God

Even though a person sins a hundred times and still lives a long time, I know that those who fear God will be better off.

Ecclesiastes 8:12

Scripture is clear: There's a day of disaster coming for the wicked person who refuses to repent. But what about the *believer* who continuously tries to control and manipulate others? Who harbors bitterness and refuses to forgive? Who repeatedly uses others for his own gain? Do you ever wonder why God waits so long to intervene, humble, or discipline His own? Especially when you feel like you can't get away with a thing. You feel the inner wince of conviction and you know you're out of line. So how does that work? *It's all about the fear of the Lord.* To fear God is to hold Him in high regard, with honor and reverence. You can love God from a distance without fearing Him. But you cannot walk intimately with God without reverently honoring Him at the same time. If you're quick to feel conviction over the slightest departures, it's because His light shines brightly in your heart. If you wonder why He's not disciplining another, know this: He will, at exactly the right time.

ALIGN YOUR MIND Read Ecclesiastes 8:9–13.

ALIGN YOUR ACTIONS Who are the impossible people in your life? Who seems to get away with everything? Today, give those people back to God. Turn your eyes away from them and back to Jesus. He'll deal with everything. You fear God.

ALIGN YOUR HEART

> *Lord, forgive me for questioning Your timing and Your dealings with others. I know You don't miss a thing. I entrust _____ to You. Help me to honor You in all that I do. Amen.*

I Recommend Having Fun

> So I recommend having fun, because there is nothing better for people in this world than to eat, drink, and enjoy life. That way they will experience some happiness along with all the hard work God gives them under the sun.
>
> Ecclesiastes 8:15

King Solomon surveyed all of life's outcomes and came to a conclusion: Life isn't fair. It's downright hard sometimes. So what's a person to do? Have fun. Eat, drink, and enjoy life. Make room for happiness amid the hardships of life. Don't forget to laugh—really belly-laugh. Slow down long enough to taste your food—really taste your food. Watch a good movie and enjoy a big bowl of popcorn. Stop at a lemonade stand and bless the child for her noble business venture. Give yourself room to breathe. Put something on your calendar that you're excited about. Plan activities that nourish your soul and breathe life back into you. Every year, millions of earned vacation hours go to waste because employees never take their hard-earned time off. Where's the fun in that? Shouldn't joy and gladness be two of the most defining factors in our lives? Dallas Willard once gave this advice to John Ortberg: "You must arrange your day so that you are experiencing deep contentment, joy, and confidence in your everyday life with God."* Amen.

ALIGN YOUR MIND ▶ Read Ecclesiastes 8:14–16.

ALIGN YOUR ACTIONS ▶ Plan something really fun this month. And next month too.

ALIGN YOUR HEART

Lord, You've provided countless ways for me to add enjoyment to my life. Help me to not only work hard, but to also arrange my days so they reflect Your joyful heart toward me. Amen.

* John Ortberg, *Soul Keeping* (Grand Rapids, MI: Zondervan, 2013), 85.

Dark, yet Lovely

I am dark but beautiful.
Song of Songs 1:5

King Solomon's heart awakened when he saw the Shulamite woman. He pursued her and won her affection. She was both excited about new love and self-conscious about her imperfections. Her brothers forced her to work the vineyards under the hot sun, which darkened her skin. (Pale, delicate skin was the standard for beauty back then.) Do you see the parallel to our lives? The King loves us. Pursues us. Finds us in our hardship. Invites us out of the fields of striving and effort and into His kingdom of grace. As we move toward Him and align with His kingdom ways, we see all of the ways we fall short, how the hardships of life have marred us. The enemy spews from the shadows, "You're darkened with sin! I know where you've been!" How wonderful to become so secure in the Father's love that we can say, "I may be dark, but I am lovely." God wants to bring such inner healing to your soul that you can look at your painful history with a grounded sense of grace. You're enough for God. He's not surprised by or disappointed in you. He sees you through and through and loves you more than you love yourself. Imagine your healed self, whispering back to Him, "I *am* lovely." Let the healing begin.

ALIGN YOUR MIND ▸ Read Song of Songs 1.

ALIGN YOUR ACTIONS ▸ What do you feel shame over? Why? Today, find a verse the speaks truth into your shame. Memorize that verse, and say it until you believe it.

ALIGN YOUR HEART ▸

> *Lord, I want to know that kind of assurance and holy confidence. Bring truth, healing, and wholeness to the deepest places within me. Amen.*

The Season of Singing Birds

"The flowers are springing up,
the season of singing birds has come,
and the cooing of turtledoves fills the air."
Song of Songs 2:12

At the opening of this chapter, the Shulamite woman lapses back into an old mindset. She sees herself as a common, ordinary flower. But her lover tilts her chin upward that she might see herself once again through his eyes. She soon realizes that a new season truly is upon her. And that love, indeed, has found her. The winter is past, the rains are over, and flowers are now in bloom. The season of singing birds has finally come. This exchange reflects our journey toward understanding what Jesus sees when He looks upon us. The thought of being known deeply enough to be truly loved is both terrifying and exhilarating. One moment we find ourselves running toward our Savior, but the next we're tempted to run away. One moment we're drawn to His loving voice as He sings over us, but the next we refute His words with our own earthbound assessments. But to move into the next place of maturity, we must also move with Jesus to a new place of intimacy, where we trust His perspective over our own. Wholeness comes when we see ourselves and the world through His eyes. *To know this love is to be filled with the fullness of God.*[*]

ALIGN YOUR MIND Read Song of Songs 2:1–13.

ALIGN YOUR ACTIONS Ask Jesus to give you a fresh revelation of how He sees you.

ALIGN YOUR HEART

> *Jesus, open my eyes to see what You see in a way that heals and changes me. Help me to trust You more than I trust myself. Amen.*

* See Ephesians 3:19.

Let Me See Your Face

My dove is hiding behind the rocks,
    behind an outcrop on the cliff.
Let me see your face;
    let me hear your voice.
For your voice is pleasant,
    and your face is lovely.

Song of Songs 2:14

After I dared to share a private dream with a woman, her words hit me like a punch to the gut: "You don't have the voice for radio." She had a scowl on her face and zero compassion in her eyes. Later that day I heard God's whisper, *Don't you dare hide. Let me see your face. Your voice is sweet, and you are lovely.* I faintly remembered reading that in Scripture, and my heart fluttered when I found it. I've now worked in radio for over sixteen years, and one thing listeners most often say to me is, "I love your voice. It's so soothing. It puts my heart at ease." The lady was wrong. If I'd listened to her and turned away from the dream that God put in my heart, I would have missed countless opportunities to encourage hundreds of thousands of people over the years. Maybe someone has spoken words over you that are untrue. Don't you dare hide. Listen for Jesus instead. Hear your Shepherd as He calls to you, *"Let me see your face. Your voice is sweet. And you are lovely."*

ALIGN YOUR MIND Read Song of Songs 2:14.

ALIGN YOUR ACTIONS How have negative words impacted your actions? Your dreams? Ask God to replace those words with His. Today, dare to dream big dreams with God again.

ALIGN YOUR HEART

Lord, I don't want people's voices to ring truer than Yours! I want Your dreams in my heart. Give me courage to be done hiding. Amen.

Catch the Foxes

Catch all the foxes,
those little foxes,
before they ruin the vineyard of love,
for the grapevines are blossoming!
Song of Songs 2:15

When God is doing a new thing, the devil hides in the shadows with a plan. He aims to demolish everything God creates. Thankfully, Jesus came to *destroy* the works of the devil.* One of the most important Scripture passages for the believer comes from Proverbs 4:23: "Guard your heart above all else, for it determines the course of your life." The word *guard* in this passage speaks of diligence, protection, and continual attention. How often are we *this* attentive to the condition of our hearts? Especially in a season of flourishing, we're tempted to let our guard down. If the enemy can't dismantle our destiny in big, traumatic ways, then he'll send in the little foxes—harassment, envy, distraction, irritation, temptation, resentment to name a few. We'll make little concessions and think nothing of it. But then one day, a crisis hits. One that could have been prevented had we paid closer attention to our hearts and the work of God in our lives. Study where God is working in your life. Are there any foxes nipping at the vine? Is the enemy picking away at your resolve? Don't put up with it. Guard your heart. Guard your yard. Catch the foxes. And let love grow.

 ALIGN YOUR MIND Read Song of Songs 2:15–17.

 ALIGN YOUR ACTIONS Wherever God grows fruit in your life, the enemy sends in the foxes. Prayerfully find them, and deal with them immediately.

 ALIGN YOUR HEART

Father, heighten my discernment and my awareness of the state of my life. Teach me how to walk wisely and powerfully before You. Amen.

* See 1 John 3:8.

Sober Reflection

"Come now, let's settle this,"
says the LORD.
"Though your sins are like scarlet,
I will make them as white as snow."

Isaiah 1:18

From an earthly point of view, the nation of Judah appeared to be prosperous. But from heaven's point of view, God's people were on the brink of destruction. Their sins? Perverting justice, oppressing the poor, turning from God to idols, and looking for military aid from pagan nations rather than help from God.* They'd so lost their way that God actually *detested* their religious practices! He doesn't want empty worship, meaningless sacrifices, or token gifts. He doesn't need anything from us. He longs for our hearts. Imagine God's heartbreak. His own people had turned their backs on Him. Dr. Warren Wiersbe writes, "Before passing judgment on worshippers in a bygone era, we should confess the sins of the worshipping church today. . . . The average church allocates about 5 percent of its budget for reaching others with the gospel, but 30 percent for buildings and maintenance. At a time when the poor and the aged are pleading for help, churches in America are spending approximately three billion dollars a year on new construction."† Isaiah's call is not an outdated one. Yet God's invitation to return and repent stands just as true today. He'll wash away *every* sin.

ALIGN YOUR MIND Read Isaiah 1.

ALIGN YOUR ACTIONS Does God have your whole heart in all areas of life? If you've wandered in any way, return to Him. Pray for others to do the same.

ALIGN YOUR HEART

Father in heaven, purify my heart! Show me what You see! Awaken my nation for You! Amen.

---

* *Life Application Study Bible*, 1418.
† *Wiersbe Bible Commentary*, 1157.

Don't Fear What They Fear

"Make the LORD of Heaven's Armies holy in your life.
    He is the one you should fear.
He is the one who should make you tremble.
    He will keep you safe."

Isaiah 8:13–14

Fear of invasion was a continual threat for the people of Judah.* They constantly braced for impact. Much like today: war, terrorism, anarchy, and godlessness seem to be the norm. But when we look to the endless streams of social media and news reports for perspective, we'll lose heart and lose faith. Our souls aren't wired to live in a perpetual state of alert. Proverbs 3:7–8 says this: "Don't be impressed with your own wisdom. Instead, fear the LORD and turn away from evil. Then you will have healing for your body and strength for your bones." Fearing the wrong things—whether on a global level or a personal one—puts incredible stress on our health and on our faith perspective. Though evil threats are real, God tells us to *tremble before Him*. He's the One we should fear; He's the One who'll keep us safe. Because when you tremble before Him in awe and reverence, you'll tremble at nothing else. How do you live in this fear-driven world with a grounded sense of faith? Make Him holy in your life.

 ALIGN YOUR MIND Read Isaiah 8:11–22.

 ALIGN YOUR ACTIONS This week, cut back on your social media and news consumption and increase your intake of worship, the Word, and times of reflection.

 ALIGN YOUR HEART

> *Lord, how I think about things impacts me and those around me. Help me to steward my perspective in a way that rightly reflects Your power to intervene in this hour. Amen.*

* *Life Application Study Bible*, 1436.

A Son, Given to Us

For a child is born to us,
a son is given to us.
Isaiah 9:6

A Son was given to us. We sing it, we say it, we pray it. But stop for a moment and consider God's gift. He surrendered His perfect, beautiful, joyful, grateful, obedient, sinless Son for an imperfect, disgruntled, ungrateful, disobedient, sinful people. Why? Because He loves us like He loves His own Son. He envisioned an eternity with us, countless hearts transformed, stories rewritten, lives reclaimed. Though the way would be costly, beyond our comprehension, the result would be breathtaking. Lost people found. Broken people restored. Sick people healed. Sinful people redeemed. Jesus—with a heart full of compassion, abounding in love, and on a mission—came to earth that His light might shine in our hearts and light up the darkness around us. Jesus willingly offered to come to us, to die for us. All for the sake of love. He laid aside His robe and crown and entered our universe through the womb of a poor teenage girl. Much suffering awaited Him, and He knew it. *Yet He came.* God gave Him to us. *Unto us a Son was given.* And He carried the weight of the world on His shoulders. Unfathomable, astonishing grace. Thank You, Lord.

ALIGN YOUR MIND Read Isaiah 9:2–7.

ALIGN YOUR ACTIONS Spend today thinking about the mystery of God's gift. Recapture the awe and wonder of it all. Put on your favorite worship song and go all in!

ALIGN YOUR HEART

Wonderful Counselor, Mighty God, Everlasting Father, Prince of Peace, how is it that You love me so? I bow low and praise You with my whole heart. May my whole life be an offering back to You. Amen.

Perfect Peace

You will keep in perfect peace
all who trust in you,
all whose thoughts are fixed on you!

Isaiah 26:3

What's *perfect* peace? The phrase translates this way: *Shalom*. When our thoughts are fixed on the Lord, He touches our hearts with His peace, tranquility, rest, safety, friendship, prosperity, and well-being. *Wow.* He is the essence of all these things, and He imparts himself to us as we draw closer still. We have everything we could ever possibly need, and then some, in Him. Picture climbing a mountain until you're up in the clouds. Imagine the startling white clouds are saturated with healing elements that settle your nerves, restore your soul, put your heart at ease, and open your eyes to the spiritual reality around you. You suddenly see yourself as the clean vessel of God that you are. You realize as you ponder the miracle of your remaking that absolutely nothing is too difficult for Him. You see the problems of this earth as fleeting while you grasp more firmly that the promises of heaven are sturdier than the mountain under your feet. God's provision is greater still. Scripture says that all of the riches of the heavenly realm belong to you.[*] We don't spend enough time pondering who God is and what He is willing to impart to us. His love changes everything.

ALIGN YOUR MIND Read Isaiah 26:1–19.

ALIGN YOUR ACTIONS Decide today to upgrade your relationship with God. Spend more time with Him. Think about His greatness. Rely on His goodness.

ALIGN YOUR HEART

> *Mighty God of heaven, I raise my hands and worship You. I lay hold of all You've promised me. I set my gaze on You. May Your power change my life. Amen.*

* See Ephesians 1:3.

New Strengths, New Heights

But those who trust in the LORD will find new strength.
They will soar high on wings like eagles.

Isaiah 40:31

My health relapse lasted about three years. During that time, I instinctively rehearsed my symptoms—how I was *feeling*. But when you think too long about how you're feeling, you'll just feel more of the same, and on a deeper level. I longed for God's intervention. I prayed for it too. But in my weaker moments, I followed my feelings right into the ditch. One day as I stood at the base of our stairs, the Lord whispered to me, *Take those stairs! You're not as weak as you feel! In Me, you're stronger than you know.* I sprinted up those stairs with so much strength, it surprised me! But I was still sick and tired. He whispered, *Let the weak say I am strong.* The Lord challenged me that day to engage my faith at all times with everything in me. Waiting on God with hopeful expectancy is not meant to be a hit-and-miss proposition. It's a way of life. We're meant to go about our days with a deep conviction that God is who He says He is, and with a deep expectancy that any day now, He will break through. You want to rise up with new strength and soar to new heights? Actively wait on, hope in, and believe that the Lord is coming *for you*.

ALIGN YOUR MIND Read Isaiah 40:21–31.

ALIGN YOUR ACTIONS How might God want you to lean in and trust Him more?

ALIGN YOUR HEART

> *Father, You give strength to the weak and power to the powerless. My soul actively waits on You. I know You'll come for me! Thank You, Lord. Amen.*

A Pathway through the Wilderness

"For I am about to do something new.
See, I have already begun! Do you not see it?
I will make a pathway through the wilderness.
I will create rivers in the dry wasteland."

Isaiah 43:19

When the way is long and the battle rages on, we tend to identify more with our circumstances than with our royal status in Christ. But Scripture says we're pilgrims, traveling to a most holy city. We're just passing through. No one can snatch us out of His hand. No enemy scheme can keep us from His plan. We're secure in His love and established by His grace. However, we *will* find ourselves in painful seasons, trying circumstances, and situations with no easy way out. We may stop dreaming, forget to look for the *new*. We may feel stuck and thus despair over the sameness of it all. Here's where we must make the distinction between surrendering to our circumstances and surrendering to God in our circumstances. One camps in the valley with no hope for change. The other declares, "This place doesn't define me. God will make a way where there is no way. I'm passing through this valley; I don't live here. I'm a child of God. And He's masterful at bringing beauty out of ashes, rivers in the wasteland, and solutions where I can't see one." He's *already begun* to do something new for you. Soon you'll see it.

 ALIGN YOUR MIND Read Isaiah 43:1–19.

ALIGN YOUR ACTIONS Look for the new thing God is up to in your life. Watch for the subtle shifts in your circumstances. God is up to something good.

ALIGN YOUR HEART

Lord, open my eyes to see what You're up to in and all around me! Amen.

Jesus Paid It All

But he was pierced for our rebellion,
crushed for our sins.
He was beaten so we could be whole.
He was whipped so we could be healed.

Isaiah 53:5

I cannot read Isaiah 53 without tearing up. I think about our suffering Savior, who took on the sin and rebellion of the world—and the world assumed His suffering was *His* fault. He bore the weight of the world, along with our wrong assessments and flippant judgments, to purchase our freedom *from our own rebellion*. From our countless self-serving ways. From the wounds inflicted on us by others. From everything that ails us in our bodies. As He hung on that cross, His blood trickled down to the ground and into the lowest nooks and crannies of the earth. Then the earth shook. The veil tore in two—from the top down. The sky darkened. And a guilt-ridden soldier realized this criminal was actually an innocent man. Our Savior *defeated* sin and death for us! No other religion honors a King who sacrificed for His people. If you are in Christ, *Christ is in you*. His blood flows through your veins. The power that raised Him from the grave is alive and accessible to you. So why do we live such earthbound lives? Maybe because we're still trying to earn our way. Jesus paid it all. May you live from that reality.

ALIGN YOUR MIND ▸ Read Isaiah 53.

ALIGN YOUR ACTIONS ▸ Christ's death and resurrection frees you from earthbound thinking and living. Today, determine to live, love, and dream with His eternal power and perspective.

ALIGN YOUR HEART

Father, open my eyes to what Jesus won for me! Heal me from the inside out. May resurrection power mark my life in every way. Amen.

Beauty for Ashes

To all who mourn in Israel
　　he will give a crown of beauty for ashes,
a joyous blessing instead of mourning,
　　festive praise instead of despair.
In their righteousness, they will be like great oaks
　　that the LORD has planted for his own glory.

Isaiah 61:3

I watched my younger sister walk through the valley of the shadow of death when her husband was diagnosed with pancreatic cancer. He died ten months after his diagnosis. We sat at my kitchen counter and cried together. We laughed too as we remembered moments when Donny was alive. I asked her, "How are you getting through this?" She replied, "I'm sure everyone grieves differently, but for me, here's what I've done: 1) I get out of bed every single day; 2) I've determined that God's goodness *will not* be up for grabs; 3) I tell myself, *You will get through this*; and 4) I tell myself, *You are stronger than you know.*" I'm watching God restore her day by day. If you've walked through loss, hardship, or overwhelming adversity, I pray you've given yourself time to grieve and sort through your losses. For those who mourn, God promises to bring honor and beauty where you've known loss and heartbreak. He will strengthen you once again. Your life may look different than you imagined, but you'll be stronger than you ever dreamed. Jesus came to proclaim good news to those who've lived under the shadow of perpetual bad news. Your Redeemer has come.

ALIGN YOUR MIND ▶ Read Isaiah 61.

ALIGN YOUR ACTIONS ▶ Where are the ashes in your life? Imagine beauty, honor, and praise emerging from that very place.

ALIGN YOUR HEART ▶

Father, thank You for promising redemption in my life. Awaken fresh hope within me once again. Amen.

The Heavens Gasp

"The heavens are shocked at such a thing
and shrink back in horror and dismay,"
says the LORD.

Jeremiah 2:12

I was helping my Bible study host in her kitchen when she leaned in and whispered, "I keep having affairs, and I can't seem to stop." My jaw dropped, and I was at a loss for words. For a second, I thought I'd heard her wrong. Their home was cozy. They were a church-going family. Christian plaques decorated the walls. She hosted a Bible study. Yet she turned away from what was a bubbling brook of life—away from a husband who knew her sins and still fought for her heart—to drink water out of a mud hole. Yet *daily* the heavens gasp because all of our lips are covered with dirt. Every time we turn to our idols to fill us up, we drink muddy water. Every time we shift our dependence or identity onto our possessions, our status, or our abilities, we're lapping up grimy water. God wants us to enjoy life, to flourish in the good gifts He entrusts to us. Yet time and time again, we turn His gifts into idols. I don't want the heavens to gasp; I want them to *rejoice* over my faith. May streams of living water flow through you because of Christ's transformative power within you.

ALIGN YOUR MIND ▸ Read Jeremiah 2:1–13.

ALIGN YOUR ACTIONS ▸ Ask the Lord to show you your idols. Humbly repent and reaffirm your commitment to Him.

ALIGN YOUR HEART ▸

Father, forgive me for the countless ways I look to Your gifts to give me life. You are the Source of life, and all I'll ever need is in You. May I thirst for more of You! Amen.

Take the Ancient Path

This is what the LORD says:
"Stop at the crossroads and look around.
   Ask for the old, godly way, and walk in it.
Travel its path, and you will find rest for your souls.
   But you reply, 'No, that's not the road we want!'"

Jeremiah 6:16

The prophet Jeremiah appealed to the people to come back to God, to do His will, His way. Meanwhile, other so-called prophets promised a false peace without addressing any of the selfish, sinful tendencies of the people. Following Jesus isn't about rigid religion or pious self-denial; it's about understanding and believing God when He says that sin, rebellion, and self-sufficiency are devastating to the soul and in direct conflict to His kingdom ways. Imagine our holy God appealing to these rebellious souls, asking them to return to Him so He could bring rest and restoration to their souls and lives. But they'd have none of it. Every day we face a similar crossroad. Will we go our own way? Lean on our own understanding? Choose an earthbound perspective instead of an eternal one? God's way will ultimately, always, bring life, rest, healing, and wholeness. But it's not a way traveled by the masses. Only those with a keen eye of faith will find it. The saints before us found His ancient, godly path. Now it's our turn.

 ALIGN YOUR MIND Read Jeremiah 6:1–21.

 ALIGN YOUR ACTIONS What crossroads are you at? Stop and look around. Discern God's way and walk in it. You'll be glad you did.

 ALIGN YOUR HEART

Father, help me to discern Your highest and best will for me. Show me the ancient path that You've placed before me. Lead me onward. Amen.

Boast in *This*

"But those who wish to boast
should boast in this alone:
that they truly know me and understand that I am the LORD
who demonstrates unfailing love. . . ."

Jeremiah 9:24

As a new Christian, I understood that I was saved, but I didn't grasp that I was loved. It wasn't until all of my self-striving props were pulled out from under me—and I found myself on a sickbed, in need of help, unable to return countless favors—that I reckoned with the idea of God's unfathomable grace. I knew He was the one true God, that He sent His Son to save sinners. I couldn't fathom, though, how profoundly He *loved* me until He met me in my mess. I found that my greatest treasure was the intimate, personal, active love of God. Suddenly I saw all of my striving and feeble attempts at self-worth for what they were—dirty rags.* If you're in a season where the props have been pulled away, don't panic; see the gift of grace in it all. Here's your opportunity to know and experience God's love like you've never known before. His love is an endless ocean, and we've only dipped our toes in the water. As you experience your Father's love, you'll find that nothing else satisfies, nothing else is worth bragging about. If you're known for anything, be known for knowing Him.

ALIGN YOUR MIND Read Jeremiah 9.

ALIGN YOUR ACTIONS When was the last time you felt proud about yourself or something you did? How about God? Today, look for His love and goodness—and boast about it to a friend.

ALIGN YOUR HEART

Lord, help me to know You so deeply that all I boast about is You and Your love. Amen.

* See Isaiah 64:6.

You Will Speak for Me

"If you return to me, I will restore you
so you can continue to serve me.
If you speak good words rather than worthless ones,
you will be my spokesman.
You must influence them;
do not let them influence you!"

Jeremiah 15:19

Have you noticed that people who deeply fear God don't seem to fear man? They walk, talk, and pray with power. They're the true influencers in every generation. I remember reading about Catherine Booth. She co-founded the Salvation Army with her husband, William. She was a small, somewhat frail woman who battled health issues off and on. And yet she went boldly before the British Parliament, confronting those men for lowering the age of prostitution to thirteen. She challenged those who had daughters to consider the implications of their decision. Another translation of the verse above reads, *"If you extract the precious from the worthless, you will be my spokesman."** We're surrounded by decadent ways, irreverent attitudes, and reasons to react in fear. And yet, if we stay connected to God's power and perspective, we'll be able to extract the precious from the worthless, see what God sees, and speak with precision and power. Oh, the world needs more lionhearted men and women of God! It's time to speak good words, extract the precious from the worthless, and be God's spokesman.

ALIGN YOUR MIND ▶ Read Jeremiah 15:10–21.

ALIGN YOUR ACTIONS ▶ Ask God if there's a treasure, something precious, you can extract from the hard situations you face. Speak words with His precision and power to others today.

ALIGN YOUR HEART

> *Lord, I want to be bold and brave for You. Refine me, heal me, prepare me, and use me! Help me be courageous for You. Use me, Lord. Amen.*

* NASB.

When You've Been Scattered

"But I will gather together the remnant of my flock from the countries where I have driven them. I will bring them back to their own sheepfold, and they will be fruitful and increase in number."

Jeremiah 23:3

The priests and the prophets—who claimed to speak for God—were supposed to care for, lead, and protect the Israelites. But they did the opposite. They misused their positions for their own gain, misled the people by their own poor examples, and allowed good people to be driven off their land because of their sinful and poor leadership. God saw every bit of it, and finally He'd had enough. These things still happen today. Jeremiah prophesied that God would deal with ungodly leaders, and that those who'd been scattered would once again be gathered, drawn back to the land they lost. God promised to appoint faithful, godly shepherds to watch over them. He promised too that they'd be more fruitful and established than before. Maybe you've been hurt by an ungodly leader in your life. Know that God sees it all. He'll restore what the enemy has stolen from you. He'll make you more fruitful than before, more established than you've ever been. God knows the whole story and He's in the process of redeeming it.

ALIGN YOUR MIND ▶ Read Jeremiah 23:1–8.

ALIGN YOUR ACTIONS ▶ Is there a hurt or betrayal you've suffered that it seems God missed? Instead of blaming God for your hurt or His silence, believe He is—right now—working to redeem your story.

ALIGN YOUR HEART

Good Shepherd, thank You for being my advocate, for redeeming, restoring, and opening new doors. Help me get excited about new fruit, new strength, and the new day ahead of me. Amen.

A Future and a Hope

"For I know the plans I have for you," says the Lord. "They are plans for good and not for disaster, to give you a future and a hope."

Jeremiah 29:11

We often picture this beautiful passage on a greeting card or inspirational wall art. But Jeremiah prophesied this word to a people in *captivity*. He told them to plant gardens, have babies, and build houses—in short, to establish this place as home. They were captives of Babylon, but God would, in due time, rescue them and restore them to their land. He said to them, *"Multiply! Do not dwindle away!"* Our tendency during troubled times is to shrink back. When hardships press in, we hunker down. Self-preservation instinctively kicks in. But faith plans for the future in the face of fear. Faith rises above the current circumstances and envisions a new place of promise, a new place to thrive, and a new strength in the Lord. One thing God asked of the Israelites amid their captivity was to return to Him in *all* of their ways; to seek Him wholeheartedly. And He promised to listen to their prayers. If you're hunkering down or shrinking back, rise up today. Dream today. God has purposes and plans for you. Run to Jesus with everything in you and get a vision for where He's taking you.

ALIGN YOUR MIND Read Jeremiah 29:1–14.

ALIGN YOUR ACTIONS Where are you dwindling or shrinking? What does it look like to engage your faith in these places? Grab hold of hope, and take the first step into your future.

ALIGN YOUR HEART

Father, how quickly I forget to trust You! Help me engage my faith, rise up in hope, and dream Your dreams for my future. Amen.

God-Revealed Secrets

"Call to me and I will answer you and tell you great and unsearchable things you do not know."

Jeremiah 33:3 NIVZ

Things are rarely as they appear. And we don't know what we don't know. We see from an earthbound perspective, and what we do perceive, we view as if looking through a dark glass.* Our perspective is skewed by our own experiences, pain, personal opinions, and the media we consume. Thankfully, when we walk with the Lord and spend time in His Word, we gain otherworldly wisdom that flies in the face of how things appear. What a privilege to be acquainted with the Most High God! He actually confides in those who fear Him.† He invites us to call on Him so He can tell us unsearchable things we do not know. The word *call* in this passage is *qara*, which means to shout out, to proclaim, to cry out to get someone's attention. It can also mean to name something. What if you cried out to God with passion and purpose? And what if you named Him for who He is and who you need Him to be? Cry out to God as your Healer, Defender, Deliverer, and Advocate. Then wait expectantly, for He will surely grant you unsearchable wisdom and the revelation you need.

ALIGN YOUR MIND   Read Jeremiah 33:1–16.

ALIGN YOUR ACTIONS   If you've settled for an earthbound perspective in some area of your life, call on God. He'll bring revelation to your soul.

ALIGN YOUR HEART

Holy God, I cry out to You as my Healer, Defender, and Deliverer! Grant me unsearchable wisdom and revelation. Show me what You want me to know and see. I wait for You. Amen.

* See 1 Corinthians 13:12.
† See Psalm 25:14.

Oh, the Mercies of God!

The faithful love of the LORD never ends!
His mercies never cease.
Great is his faithfulness;
his mercies begin afresh each morning.

Lamentations 3:22–23

*I*magine a world where the punishment for every crime is immediate death. Even the tiniest white lie or the merest flicker of a jealous thought costs you your life. This is sin—anything less than holy is a crime against our Holy God—and it deserves our swift and immediate death. And yet here we are. *This is mercy.* Mercy is *not* getting what we deserve. And if God's mercies were anything but inexhaustible, we'd be dead, forsaken forever. But not only does His mercy never cease, it's also new each morning. We get a do-over every morning. And when we fall short, which we will, His mercy is there, pardoning our crime. Again and again and again. Isn't this astounding? Jeremiah looked at a nation and people in ruins—a consequence of their blatant evil actions and disregard for God. He was tempted to be overwhelmed by the destruction before him. But then he *called to mind* the mercies of God. He *dared to remember* the inexhaustible love of God. He *thought about* God's unexplainable compassion. And do you know what rose up within him? *Hope.* Because God's heart beats so compassionately for us, our sins will not have the last say in our lives. His mercies are in motion even now.

 ALIGN YOUR MIND ▶ Read Lamentations 3:17–33.

 ALIGN YOUR ACTIONS ▶ Call to mind the endless mercies and compassion of God toward you. Humble your heart before Him with praise.

 ALIGN YOUR HEART ▶

Precious Father, thank You for Your mercy! I will not be consumed by my sin because I'm already consumed by Your love. Amen.

He's Made You Equal to the Task

"But look, I have made you as obstinate and hard-hearted as they are. I have made your forehead as hard as the hardest rock! So don't be afraid of them or fear their angry looks, even though they are rebels."

Ezekiel 3:8–9

God called Ezekiel the prophet to confront a stubborn, rebellious people given to idolatry and apathy toward God. Yet He also told Ezekiel that the people wouldn't listen. Imagine being commanded to do something outrageous—in front of everyone you know—knowing you would fail. So why the assignment? Because every act of God changes the story on earth. Changes us. When we're tied up with the fear of man, we will look to others' responses for our cues. But when we look to the Lord and remember how He's trained us in our past battles, we'll stand firm in confidence that He is strong in us. If you're facing an impossible assignment or impossible people, dare to consider God's faithfulness in your present and how He's prepared you in the past. You're stronger than you know. And when you face opposition, seeming to gain no ground, trust that something's changing in you and in the greater story. Some of these things we won't see until heaven. But ours is to trust and obey today. Outcomes are in His hands. And you are equal to the God-given task before you.

ALIGN YOUR MIND Read Ezekiel 3:1–9.

ALIGN YOUR ACTIONS What battles have changed and strengthened you? Let your mind linger on these triumphs awhile. Rise up with fresh confidence today.

ALIGN YOUR HEART

Jesus, thank You for Your mighty work in me. You've made me equal to the task before me. I will trust You. Amen.

Listen for Yourself First

Then he added, "Son of man, let all my words sink deep into your own heart first. Listen to them carefully for yourself."

Ezekiel 3:10

How often do we listen to sermons, read books, and take notes *for everybody else*? We hear a good point and we want to remember it for a friend. Or we hear a word of correction and wish so-and-so could hear it. But when we listen for others and not for ourselves, we skim the surface of what God is saying, and we miss the potency of His living, breathing Word to us. It's easy to view the Bible as a content machine from which we get tidbits of wisdom and meme-able verses. Yet He is the living God who *spoke the world into existence*. He gave us His living, active Word to teach us and train us to truly know Him. We need God's consistent voice in our lives like we need oxygen. And He will speak *through* us, but only to the extent that we allow Him to first speak *to* us. Some words will be just for us. Others, God wants to season with time before we share them. And still others, well, they must be shouted from the rooftops. How do we discern the difference? The more secure we are in Him, the easier it'll be to know when to hold our words and when to share them.

 ALIGN YOUR MIND ▶ Read Ezekiel 3:10–11.

 ALIGN YOUR ACTIONS ▶ Develop the habit of listening first for yourself. Trust the Holy Spirit to prompt you to share what He wants, when He wants.

 ALIGN YOUR HEART ▶

> *Speak, Lord. I am listening. I humble my heart and tongue before You. Amen.*

A Time Is Coming

Tell the people, "This is what the Sovereign LORD says: I will put an end to this proverb, and you will soon stop quoting it." Now give them this new proverb to replace the old one: "The time has come for every prophecy to be fulfilled!"

Ezekiel 12:23

When our sons were teens, we packed hot cocoa and snacks and took them to where two rivers collided, forming one raging river. That Thanksgiving morning, the boys tossed sticks into the water and watched them disappear in a matter of seconds. As we wrapped ourselves in our blankets and hugged our steaming mugs close, my husband and I said these words to them—words I want to say to you, too: "We believe we're entering a day of acceleration when destructive choices will take us where we don't want to go faster than we ever imagined. Just as the strong current pulled those sticks downriver, we believe our sinful choices will do the same. It matters deeply that you guard your hearts and walk in the fear of God." Things sped up exponentially in our culture after that day and have continued to do so—and you, dear one, are living in the thick of it. A day is coming when God will deal with the sin, wickedness, apathy, and decadence in our world. He's been patient because He wants none to perish. May we live as if Jesus could return any moment. Because He might.

ALIGN YOUR MIND ▶ Read Ezekiel 12:21–28.

ALIGN YOUR ACTIONS ▶ Recommit yourself and your heart to God. Temptation is all around you; determine not to dabble in things you shouldn't.

ALIGN YOUR HEART ▶

Father, help me to live ready for Your imminent return. Amen.

Sodom's Sins

"Sodom's sins were pride, gluttony, and laziness, while the poor and needy suffered outside her door."

Ezekiel 16:49

zekiel had an impossible job. The book itself is difficult to read through. But we must, since it's the Word of God. Oftentimes when we think of the city of Sodom, we think of her sexual sin, which was blatant, and a huge problem in the sight of God. Yet it's interesting that Scripture notes Sodom's core sins were pride, gluttony, and apathy—and particularly, all while the poor and needy suffered outside her door. That hits closer to home, wouldn't you say? These three sins open the door to greater decadence. Who hasn't elevated their own importance over another? That's pride. *Lord, forgive us.* And who hasn't consumed more than is necessary? That's gluttony. *Lord, forgive us.* And who hasn't shrugged their shoulders at a need or taken an easy road instead of the obedient one? That's laziness. *Lord, forgive us.* Sodom's sins are our sins, and until we're honest about our own tendencies, we will stay captive to them. Sodom was obliterated because of her own prideful blindness. May we live purely and humbly. May we consume only what we need and give generously to others. May we engage in this faith journey with our whole hearts and tend to the needs around us. God empowers us to live differently from the rest of the world. May your life defy the gravity of the times.

 ALIGN YOUR MIND ▶ Read Ezekiel 16:46–63.

 ALIGN YOUR ACTIONS ▶ Spend some time with the Lord. Ask Him to reveal anything buried in your heart that needs to go. Respond accordingly.

 ALIGN YOUR HEART ▶

Lord, forgive and cleanse me. Renew and restore me. I am Yours. Amen.

The Ones Who've Strayed

"I will search for my lost ones who strayed away, and I will bring them safely home again. I will bandage the injured and strengthen the weak."

Ezekiel 34:16

This part of Ezekiel's prophecy came after he confronted the leaders who fed on the fruit of their high position while scattering those they were appointed to care for. The world is filled with Christian misfits who feel dismissed, abandoned, and driven out by leaders who didn't understand, protect them, or care for them. They've walked away from the faith disillusioned and disheartened. I have a son who wandered for a time for this very reason. He still loved Jesus, but he no longer trusted the church. Perhaps someone you love fits this description. Know this: God sees them. He knows the whole story. Jesus himself has determined to go and find them, to bring them back into His fold, and to bind up their wounds. Though we often talk about God's unfathomable love (as we should), we must also consider His anger, which is born out of His fierce love for us. He is furious that His followers have been driven away by poor leadership. He sees and He cares. So don't despair. He loves your loved one more than you do. He won't forget about them.

ALIGN YOUR MIND ▶ Read Ezekiel 34:1–16.

ALIGN YOUR ACTIONS ▶ Pray for every broken wanderer on the earth today. May the Lord bring them back, heal their wounds, and ignite their faith once again.

ALIGN YOUR HEART

> Good Shepherd, You don't miss a thing! Thank You, Lord. Hear my prayer and do what You said You would do. Bring back every wandering heart. Heal and restore them. Use them powerfully in the kingdom today. Amen.

From Ruins to Redemption

"I will make a covenant of peace with my people and drive away the dangerous animals from the land. Then they will be able to camp safely in the wildest places and sleep in the woods without fear."

Ezekiel 34:25

Why did the Israelites perpetually wander? How did they forget about God's love, time and time again? Since God is a loving, wise heavenly Father, He gave them over to their desires and allowed them to experience the consequence of their choices. They were ruined. They were captives. They were without hope if not for the love of God. It's the same with us. Our capacity to ruin our own lives is staggering. Yet God knows the end from the beginning, and He is set on the full redemption of our story. He's made a covenant of peace with us, and one day we will *flourish*. The things we feared will have no power over us. We will be able to move freely in the land He gives us. Our fruit will be bountiful and our hearts will be whole. We'll know in the depths of our soul that we couldn't save ourselves; it was the Lord who broke our chains and set us free. Jesus will replace the broken parts of our story with health, wholeness, and restoration. We'll live with the deep joy of serving in our giftedness without any hindrance, obstacle, or enemy. This is our God.

ALIGN YOUR MIND Read Ezekiel 34:25–31.

ALIGN YOUR ACTIONS What choices have you made that led to pain and heartache? How is God redeeming those even now?

ALIGN YOUR HEART

> *Mighty God, sometimes I forget how wonderful You are. Though my choices could have ruined my life, you are making all things new. Thank You, Lord. Amen.*

A Tender, Responsive Heart

"And I will give you a new heart, and I will put a new spirit in you. I will take out your stony, stubborn heart and give you a tender, responsive heart."

Ezekiel 36:26

Over the years, I've interviewed some notable Christian leaders who were once prodigals. In their wild years, they didn't care who they hurt or how their choices impacted others, especially their own family. Then the Holy Spirit met them in their rebellion and asked questions like, *"Is this how you want your life to go?"* and *"Are you done yet?"* One by one, these world shakers responded to the voice of God, and He radically changed the trajectory of their lives. What's even more amazing is how profoundly God tenderized their hearts. They talk about their past sins with a humble tremble in their voices because they know what God saved them from. They talk about the grace of God through tears because they know they could never earn their way. You don't need to go through rebellion to become a world shaker, but you do need a heart for Him. May your heart beat in rhythm with His and your soul respond to His loving guidance. Nothing changes the world like a person with a tender, responsive heart toward God.

ALIGN YOUR MIND Read Ezekiel 36:22–38.

ALIGN YOUR ACTIONS Take stock of the state of your heart. Is it tender and responsive to God? Stubborn and stony? A little of both? Ask God to give you a new heart for Him today.

ALIGN YOUR HEART

Heavenly Father, tenderize my heart so it beats in rhythm with Yours. Soften the hearts of those around me that they too might respond to You. Amen.

Dry Bones,
Hear the Word of the Lord!

Then he said to me, "Speak a prophetic message to these bones and say,
'Dry bones, listen to the word of the LORD!'"

Ezekiel 37:4

God called Ezekiel to prophesy to a valley of dried-out bones (they'd been dead a long time). Not just any dried, dead bones, but a nation buried in despair and hopelessness. God called it a grave of exile. Yet God can bring life to anything, anytime, anywhere. The wind of the Spirit blew, the valley of old bones reassembled, and they came to life and formed a great army! Note the progression of restoration. First there was the sound of rattling of old bones coming back to life. After the bones came together, muscles formed, and then skin. And then suddenly there was a great army. This is such a picture of God's order of things. First He builds an infrastructure, then He adds the strength. Then He mobilizes us into our God-given purpose. God is a God of order, and He works from the inside out. He first puts lives back together, then He builds strength. After that, He mobilizes us to conquer enemy territory as the army of God. So dare to look at the barren parts of your life and the dead bones scattered in your valley, and speak life. Believe, wait, and watch for God to do the impossible.

ALIGN YOUR MIND Read Ezekiel 37:1–14.

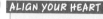

ALIGN YOUR ACTIONS Identify the valley in your life that needs the breath of God. Speak as though you are speaking the very words of God.*

ALIGN YOUR HEART

> *God of heaven, breathe life in and through me! Show me how to speak life into every situation. Amen.*

* See 1 Peter 4:11.

Fasting in Times of Trial

"Please test us for ten days on a diet of vegetables and water," Daniel said.
Daniel 1:12

Daniel and his friends were sent as slaves to a foreign land. God allowed their nation to be conquered as a consequence of its rebellion against God. But even when a nation goes astray, God always has a remnant, a small fragment, of His people who still honor and revere His name. Daniel was one such man. He and his friends were brought to the palace to be trained for royal service. They were ordered to drink wine and eat unclean foods. And who would have blamed them given all they'd lost? Yet Daniel had a conviction to follow God. He wanted to be clearheaded so he could hear the voice of God. We tend toward comfort foods and other indulgences when we've been treated poorly, lost something unjustly, or been overlooked completely. It's natural. But it's *super*natural to go against our flesh and to press in through prayer that we might hear from God in this place. If you've recently been hurt, betrayed, or ignored, don't pamper yourself in a way that's harmful, weakens your resolve, and dulls your hearing. Do the opposite. Engage in a fast. Lean in. He will surely speak to you.

 ALIGN YOUR MIND ▶ Read Daniel 1.

 ALIGN YOUR ACTIONS ▶ This week, practice fasting. Stay off social media, skip one meal each day, forgo anything but worship music. Turn your heart to God as you refrain. This is not just for the sake of giving up something, but to lay hold of something more in Christ Jesus.

ALIGN YOUR HEART ▶

> *Mighty King, give me a Daniel-like heart! Help me to practice self-restraint, high conviction, and courageous faith. Amen.*

Unbound and Unharmed

"Look!" Nebuchadnezzar shouted. "I see four men, unbound, walking around in the fire unharmed! And the fourth looks like a god!"

Daniel 3:25

King Nebuchadnezzar issued a decree that all people must bow and worship his statue. Daniel's three friends loved and feared God and refused to obey. These were just young men, likely around your age. While they were captives, they were more privileged than most because they lived and served in the palace. They had much to lose. This was a test to the death. Though they had honored the king as a leader and served him with nothing but excellence and integrity, they couldn't and wouldn't give him ultimate allegiance above God himself. This enraged the king to such a degree that he ordered the furnace turned up seven times hotter and commanded his strongest soldiers to bind them as captives. They trusted God so deeply that they felt no need to defend themselves. They boldly declared He'd deliver them—and even if He didn't, He was still the God of the universe. The soldiers who tossed them into the furnace died from the heat. But God joined them in the fire and walked among the flames with them. They prevailed unbound and unharmed. You might be young, but you can still hold fast to your convictions. Trust God to deliver you. You'll come through the fire without smelling like smoke.

ALIGN YOUR MIND Read Daniel 3.

ALIGN YOUR ACTIONS If you've compromised your convictions or kept your faith hidden, may you stand a little stronger today and trust God.

ALIGN YOUR HEART

> *Jesus, help me to be brave on Your behalf. No matter what I face, I will emerge unbound and unharmed because You are with me. Thank You. Amen.*

Becoming Accusation-Proof

At this, the administrators and the satraps tried to find grounds for charges against Daniel in his conduct of government affairs, but they were unable to do so. They could find no corruption in him, because he was trustworthy and neither corrupt nor negligent.

Daniel 6:4 NIV

When you honor God and trust Him to defend and deliver you, He'll lead you to high places and use you in profound ways. And this will ignite jealousy in others. Daniel was exceptional because, above all, he honored God. He determined not to do the wrong thing. And not to leave the right thing undone. When you walk with God this way, you become bulletproof. Though others will try to accuse you, they'll find no fault. Their accusations won't stick. Your character and God's favor are a shield around you. Yet as we see in Scripture and in history, when persecutors can't find fault, they'll change the rules to justify their attack against God's people. In the end, their plans will come to nothing. Jesus said, "Don't be bluffed into silence by the threats of bullies. There's nothing they can do to your soul, your core being. Save your fear for God, who holds your entire life—body and soul—in his hands."* Living above reproach protects you and honors Him.

ALIGN YOUR MIND　Read Daniel 6:1–5.

ALIGN YOUR ACTIONS　Ask God to show you how to live above reproach. What things do you need to stop doing? What things do you need to start doing?

ALIGN YOUR HEART

Father, You're my protection and shield. Help me to live in a manner worthy of Your name and of my high calling. My accusers and my destiny are in Your hands. Amen.

* The Message paraphrase of Matthew 10:28.

The Power of Prayer

"Give orders that for the next thirty days any person who prays to anyone, divine or human—except to you, Your Majesty—will be thrown into the den of lions."

Daniel 6:7

Daniel's accusers manipulated the king into issuing a decree that would trap—and kill—Daniel. Yet Daniel went to his usual prayer spot, opened the windows toward heaven, and with nothing to hide, prayed as earnestly and consistently as he always did. There were both natural and supernatural outcomes of Daniel's prayer life. Daniel was thrown into a pit with ravenous lions known for tearing their prey limb from limb: this was the natural outcome of disobeying a man-made law. Yet God shut the mouths of the lions, and Daniel not only lived, but he was promoted. This was the supernatural outcome of obeying and honoring God above anything man-made. There'll always be outcomes to saying no to the world in order to say yes to God. But if you cultivate a consistent, earnest, sincere prayer life, you will hear from God. He'll reward you publicly for the way you've pursued Him privately.* In the coming days, anyone who prays to God alone, refusing to bow down to idols, will suffer consequences. Yet anyone who truly seeks His face will see lions quieted.

 ALIGN YOUR MIND Read Daniel 6:6–28.

 ALIGN YOUR ACTIONS Start the habit of a consistent, humble, private prayer life now. What—and how—you pray today impacts tomorrow—and the rest of your life. Be known as a person whose prayers God answers.

 ALIGN YOUR HEART

> *Mighty King, I bow before You and honor You as my King. Give me courage to be Your representative on the earth today. Amen.*

* See Matthew 6:6.

O Lord, Hear, Forgive, and Act!

"O Lord, hear. O Lord, forgive. O Lord, listen and act! For your own sake, do not delay, O my God, for your people and your city bear your name."

Daniel 9:19

Daniel, like Joseph, could've been bitter and steeped in self-pity for bearing the consequences of sinful people. Neither deserved what happened to them. But even at young ages, they leveraged their hardship for the greater good of their people. They dug deep, rose up, and became great leaders. We live in a day when no one wants to take responsibility for their actions, let alone the actions of others. Yet that's exactly what Daniel did here. He knew Israel's history enough to know of God's faithfulness and Israel's sinfulness. He didn't mince words, make excuses, or complain about his captivity. Facedown, he fully named and owned the sins of his people. He appealed to God based on His goodness and mercy and nothing else. Daniel stood in the gap for his people and his nation. That's what leaders do. Gabriel, the archangel, came to Daniel to bring further insight and understanding. When we move past our personal discomforts and into a place of intercession for the greater purposes of God, heaven moves and God responds. Your school, city, and nation are desperate for redemption whether they know it or not.

ALIGN YOUR MIND Read Daniel 9:1–23.

ALIGN YOUR ACTIONS Even at your age, you can consider the sins of your nation. Like Daniel, humble yourself and pray. May God hear, forgive, and act.

ALIGN YOUR HEART

Father, we've abandoned You, neglected Your ways, and served idols of our own making. Forgive us, O Lord! Draw us back to You. Bring revival. Heal our land. Amen.

Shine like the Stars

"Those who are wise will shine as bright as the sky, and those who lead many to righteousness will shine like the stars forever."

Daniel 12:3

Everyone wants their five minutes of fame, even if it's for all the wrong reasons. It's attention they crave. Yet they're chasing after the wind. Even the true celebrities who've honed their craft and paid their dues will be in for a big surprise one day. The archangel Michael prophesied to Daniel about the anguish reserved for the last days. Nobody's stardom or platform will save them. But God will rescue His own. They *will shine bright for all the world to see*, and they'll shine like the stars *forever*. We as believers don't exhaust ourselves trying to be stars; we empty ourselves because we're servants. Our culture today values all the wrong things. Scripture says it this way: "Their destiny is destruction, their god is their stomach, and their glory is in their shame. Their mind is set on earthly things."* But we're of a different kingdom. May we, like Daniel, serve with wisdom, godliness, and integrity. He lived in *Babylon* yet kept his heart pure. You may feel surrounded by sinfulness, yet everything you do for the kingdom, every person you love and point to Jesus, adds to the future glory of your life. Keep living for Jesus. One day you'll shine for all to see.

ALIGN YOUR MIND ▶ Read Daniel 12.

ALIGN YOUR ACTIONS ▶ Ask God to show you how to shine for Him today.

ALIGN YOUR HEART

Mighty King, help me not to care about or be distracted by empty pursuits. I want to live for Your kingdom because it will last forever. Amen.

---

* Philippians 3:19 NIV.

Not a Back-Up Plan

"When she runs after her lovers
    she won't be able to catch them.
She will search for them
    but not find them. Then she will think,
'I might as well return to my husband,
    for I was better off with him than I am now.'"

Hosea 2:7

In a seemingly scandalous move, God instructed Hosea to marry a prostitute. Not just any prostitute, but one who'd leave him again and again, bearing children from other men. What? Why? To reflect Israel's wandering ways. And wander, Gomer did—it was both heartbreaking and tragic. Yet during one of her sinful pursuits, things fell apart. She returned to Hosea by default. How often do we do the same today? Both heartbreaking and tragic, we alternately run to Him when we're in trouble, then away from Him when we're bored or challenged, or both. God is patient with our growth process and loves us beyond measure. But He'll put up with selfish immaturity only for a season. When it's time for us to progress in our faith, but we refuse to grow up, God will discipline us. His majesty, power, and glory are matchless, and He's not to be trifled with. He's not a back-up plan. He's either Lord of your life, or He isn't.

ALIGN YOUR MIND   Read Hosea 2:1–13.

ALIGN YOUR ACTIONS   Ask God to show you which idols you run to. Cast them down in repentance and ask Him to do a maturing work in you.

ALIGN YOUR HEART

Mighty God, grow me up in You! Show me any attitudes, mindsets, or idols that hinder my maturity. Lead me to higher ground. I want to grow in Your grace and wisdom. Amen.

Led to the Desert

"But then I will win her back once again.
I will lead her into the desert
and speak tenderly to her there."

Hosea 2:14

God leads us into the desert—not to dismiss us, but to deliver us. After a time of discipline, God led Gomer to the desert to remind her who she was, to reset her course, and to reawaken her heart. Sometimes we arrive in the desert because we've lost our way. Sometimes it's through no fault of our own. One day we're thriving, and the next we feel cut off from God and community. Still other times we feel dead on arrival. Our souls are parched, we're exhausted, and we wonder if we'll ever feel whole again. God does some of His best work in our desert seasons. He reminds us that we're not what we do, we're someone He loves. The desert is the place where we break unhealthy attachments to the things of this world—even attachments to godly things that have been twisted into our identity and value. We need the desert seasons because we need continual reminders that first and foremost, we're made for Him. We're prone to wander, prone to strive, and prone to find our worth in things other than God. But if we embrace this season and listen for the Lord's tender voice, we'll come out of this wilderness leaning on the arm of our Beloved.

ALIGN YOUR MIND ▶ Read Hosea 2:14–16.

ALIGN YOUR ACTIONS ▶ When you're in the desert, look and listen for Jesus. This season will prove to be one of the most important in your life.

ALIGN YOUR HEART

Jesus, meet me here. Give me a fresh sense of Your love. Let me hear Your voice. Amen.

Prepare for His Blessings

"I said, 'Plant the good seeds of righteousness,
    and you will harvest a crop of love.
Plow up the hard ground of your hearts,
    for now is the time to seek the LORD,
that he may come
    and shower righteousness upon you.'"

Hosea 10:12

Throughout Scripture God appeals to His children to return to Him, follow Him, and trust Him so He can bless them. We're prone to wander. God sees it, knows it, and continually makes a way for us to return to Him. God longs to be gracious to us, to show us His kindness, mercy, and love. He's a good Father who withholds no good thing from those who walk uprightly before Him. But why does He call for such allegiance? Why are His blessings so conditional? Because He's the only true Source of life. He created us. He made us for His glory. His ways are higher than ours and His paths are our road to healing and redemption. We cannot sustain His blessings when we're outside of His will. We'd squander them or they'd crush us. So how do we prepare for the next season of God's blessings? We sow seeds of righteousness now. And we plow up the hardened places in our lives so that when His showers of blessings come, we're ready.

ALIGN YOUR MIND ▶ Read Hosea 10:1–12.

ALIGN YOUR ACTIONS ▶ If you have a dream that hasn't been realized yet, you might not be ready for it now. Ask God to help you plow up the soil in your heart, plant His good seeds, and prepare for His rain.

ALIGN YOUR HEART ▶

Gracious Father, show me where to plow and sow abundantly. I want to be ready for Your showers of blessings. Amen.

After Repentance Comes Refreshment

"Don't be afraid, O land.
Be glad now and rejoice,
for the LORD has done great things."
Joel 2:21

The prophet Joel's message took a sudden turn. He went from calling for repentance, with a warning about impending judgment, to charging the people not to fear. He even said, "Be glad *now*. For the Lord has done great things." Joel wanted the people to remember two things about God: He's holy and He's good. The Israelites would never know God's profound goodness until they came to grips with their capacity to defy Him. We'll never be free from sin that we refuse to acknowledge. And we'll never truly experience the depths of His goodness until we come to grips with the depths of our need for Him. However, when we are sincerely, truly sorry for our wandering ways and we repent (have a change of heart and a change of mind), times of refreshing do come.* But we can't have it both ways. We'll either enjoy a season of sin that ultimately destroys us, or we'll enjoy the refreshing, reviving, never-ending spring of God's goodness as we stay in the flow of His love. We don't keep repenting to ensure our salvation or to secure His love; we repent because we love God, we know His ways bring true Life, and we desire to enjoy the ultimate blessing: oneness with Him.

 ALIGN YOUR MIND Read Joel 2:12–27.

 ALIGN YOUR ACTIONS Ask God to search your heart for any unacknowledged sin. Repent and respond to what He shows you.

 ALIGN YOUR HEART

> *Precious Lord, search my heart. Show me what I need to see. Point out anything that offends You. Lead me onward, Lord. Amen.*

* See Acts 3:19.

When God Pours Out His Spirit

*"I will pour out my Spirit upon all people.
Your sons and daughters will prophesy.
Your old men will dream dreams,
and your young men will see visions."*

Joel 2:28

Many scholars believe that this prophesy was fulfilled in part at Pentecost.* Imagine the power of God's movement across ethnic, generational, and economic lines. He's no respecter of persons; He's a respecter of faith! Some scholars believe that another Great Awakening is coming, and that we will see an upsurge in the work of the Holy Spirit in our midst. But we don't have to wait until then to encourage someone with a prophetic word, dream dreams, and see visions. God is actively at work on the earth today in these very ways! Countless Muslims have come to Christ after seeing a vision that they knew was Jesus. Though I know there are differing views on this topic, I like to err on the side of faith and dare to believe God for more, not less. Several years ago my husband and I claimed this verse as our own: "Even at night my heart instructs me."† We asked God to give us dreams in the night hours, strategies on how to pray, and what to believe Him for. He's answered our prayers in too many ways to count. Don't wait for a great outpouring. Pray and believe God for more now.

ALIGN YOUR MIND ▶ Read Joel 2:28–32.

ALIGN YOUR ACTIONS ▶ Ask God to stretch you, to give you more, to pour out His Spirit on you. Be open to where He leads.

ALIGN YOUR HEART ▶

Precious Father, pour out Your Spirit on me and my family! May we discern Your ways with greater clarity! Amen.

---

* See Acts 2.
† Psalm 16:7.

Thousands Are Waiting in the Valley of Decision

Thousands upon thousands are waiting in the valley of decision.
There the day of the LORD will soon arrive.

Joel 3:14

A friend told me a story about a man who didn't know Jesus. A young believer befriended him and spent regular time with him. Thinking he was doing the appropriate thing by earning the man's trust before sharing the gospel, the young believer finally shared Jesus after an entire year had passed. The friend's reply? "No way this is true. And if it is true, why would you wait a whole year to tell me? What if I would have died suddenly? It's like I've been in a burning building, and you were waiting until we were close enough to death to warn me! What were you thinking?" Of course, the young man was jarred by the response, but it bears some consideration. Every single day, people die without knowing Jesus. They face a Christless eternity; once they've taken their last breath, there's no altering their eternal destiny. The ship is sinking. Lives will be lost. It's time to save them, time to tell them about the lifeboat God has provided. It's up to them to decide whether or not they'll trust Jesus for themselves. But right now, thousands privately wonder if there's a God in heaven who loves them. Be His brave ambassador today.

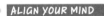 **ALIGN YOUR MIND** ▶ Read Joel 3:14–21.

 ALIGN YOUR ACTIONS ▶ Share your faith story with someone this week.

 ALIGN YOUR HEART ▶

Father, I'm sorry I prefer comfort over risk when it comes to sharing my faith. Give me a heart for the lost around me and the boldness and courage to reach out to them. Amen.

God's Surprising Prophet

Indeed, the Sovereign LORD never does anything
until he reveals his plans to his servants the prophets.

Amos 3:7

Amos was not the son of a prophet; he was not the son of a priest. As a humble shepherd, he could have stayed in Tekoa, doing his job, providing for his family, worshiping God. But God gave Amos a vision of the future. . . . Amos, a fiery, fearless, and honest shepherd from the south, confronted [the Israelites] with their sin and warned them of impending judgment."* Imagine this God-fearing man, working on the hillside, shepherding his sheep, when suddenly he's ambushed with a great vision from God of impending judgment on God's people. He'd heard about the wandering ways of his brothers and sisters in the north—how they worshiped idols, cheated the poor, and exploited the vulnerable. Suddenly, he felt God's fire in his bones. He had to do something about it. He spoke with precision and power. Some listened. Others didn't. Today, we are teetering on the edge of judgment as well. Yet, as Scripture says, God never does anything without first revealing His plans to His servants—at least to those who are awake, listening, and waiting for His word. And the ones God uses may surprise us. Maybe it won't be the person with the giant platform or spectacular ministry. Maybe it'll be a fast-food worker, a farmer, or a fellow student.

ALIGN YOUR MIND Read Amos 3.

ALIGN YOUR ACTIONS Ask God to speak to you about the times we're in. Write down your thoughts. Pray through them.

ALIGN YOUR HEART

> Jesus, help us to be humble enough to hear You speak. Amen.

* *Life Application Study Bible*, 1861.

Gloating Is Never Godly

"You should not have spoken arrogantly
in that terrible time of trouble."
Obadiah 1:12

A yelling match broke out at a Christian writers conference. The yellers were known Christian leaders who happened to stand on opposite sides of the political aisle. Their argument was so heated that it stirred up all kinds of angst and anxiety in the hearts of the other writers in attendance. Their conviction evolved into anger, which morphed into full-blown rage and prideful condescension—it became downright out of control. We live in a polarized culture politically, racially, economically, and denominationally. Because this is where we live, it matters deeply that we steward our perspective. It matters how we speak *to*, and *about*, those who look, live, believe, or think differently from us. There's no place in our hearts for arrogance, reactive rage, or selective love. Humble, bold conviction that compels us to stand up for the weak is one thing. But self-righteous, divisive condemnation is something altogether different. A good test of our hearts is to note how we react to political outcomes or the latest, hottest news report. Are we able to remember that God is on the throne and that He draws nearest to His humble servants? Or will we be ruled by fear and lash out? Will we gloat when the other guy loses? Our world desperately needs more saints who hold a godly perspective.

 ALIGN YOUR MIND Read Obadiah.

 ALIGN YOUR ACTIONS If you have to let go of love to hold on to your cause or argument, check your heart. Repent if you're anything but humble, hopeful, and expectant.

ALIGN YOUR HEART

> Lord, help me to guard my heart, temper my words, and reflect Your heart for others, no matter how different we are. Amen.

An Impossible Mission

"Get up and go to the great city of Nineveh. Announce my judgment against it because I have seen how wicked its people are."

But Jonah got up and went in the opposite direction to get away from the LORD.

Jonah 1:2–3

Picture the most anti-Christian city in the world today, where people are heartless, cruel, and wicked to their core. In Jonah's day, that city was Nineveh, the capital of Assyria. What if God called you to bring the good news to dangerous extremists who've tortured and killed countless Christians or those who openly worship satanic things? Jonah didn't want this assignment. He didn't want such wicked people to be saved. He wanted God's judgment—not His mercy—to fall. So Jonah got up and went the opposite direction. Jonah hated the people of Nineveh and all they stood for. He'd built up anger in his heart and spite in his soul. The mission *felt* impossible. Yet here's what's true: *Hiding from God is impossible*. Doing what He asks is always possible with His strength. If your heart's cold or you're postponing obedience, know this: You're heading into a storm. If you're willing to turn around and engage your faith once again, you'll find God more faithful than you ever dreamed possible.

ALIGN YOUR MIND Read Jonah 1:1–3.

ALIGN YOUR ACTIONS Are you hiding from God? Has your love grown cold toward a specific person or group? Ask God for His loving perspective and courage to fill you.

ALIGN YOUR HEART

Heavenly Father, give me faith, boldness, and courage to go where You call, love how You love, and run to You, not away from You. I know I can trust You. Amen.

What the Storms Reveal

The sailors were terrified when they heard this, for he had already told them he was running away from the LORD. "Oh, why did you do it?" they groaned.

Jonah 1:10

In my book *Fully Alive*, I wrote about a word God gave to me in one of the greatest storms in my life: *The storms reveal the lies we believe and the truths we need.* Jonah tried to escape God's call on his life by launching out onto the great sea. But he soon learned that God is the God of the land and the sea. The lie Jonah believed was that he could run from God. The truth he needed was this: Though nothing could ever separate him from God's love, we will experience consequences when we run from Him. I serve as a ministry coach for a group of women online. Just the other night, one of them pondered, "The men on the ship were paying a price for Jonah's disobedience, so who's paying a price for mine? Who am I putting in harm's way? Who am I not blessing, serving, helping because I'm hiding?"* What a powerful observation! Once the sailors threw Jonah overboard, the storm instantly stopped. The men were awestruck by the Lord's great power, and God arranged for a fish to swallow Jonah. Getting swallowed by a fish can help a man swallow his pride. Jonah's story was not over yet.

ALIGN YOUR MIND Read Jonah 1:4–17.

ALIGN YOUR ACTIONS What lies are you believing right now? What are they stopping you from doing? Who's paying the price?

ALIGN YOUR HEART

> Lord, reveal the lies I believe and the truths I need. Forgive my disobedience and use me to bless others. Amen.

* Paraphrase from Jeni Fobart.

The Lord Spoke a Second Time

Then the LORD spoke to Jonah a second time: "Get up and go to the great city of Nineveh, and deliver the message I have given you."

Jonah 3:1

When the Lord spoke to Jonah, Jonah ran in the opposite direction. When a storm came, Jonah was tossed overboard. When the Lord arranged for a great fish to swallow Jonah, he thanked God for not allowing him to drown. Once Jonah got his heart right before God, the Lord ordered the fish to spit Jonah out onto the beach. Then God spoke to Jonah a *second time*. We don't always get it right the first time. We delay obedience because of self-protection—to save face or stay comfortable or avoid risk. And when we mess up, the enemy is right there to condemn us for both our disobedience *and* the consequences of it, as if he cares about a lost soul or lost opportunity. But the opposite is true. He relishes the idea of such things. He loves to throw you into a self-defeating, self-condemning cycle. Determine to have none of it. God is the God of second chances. He cares far more about developing an intimate relationship with you, built on trust, than He does about you getting it right every single time. Accept God's grace and begin again. He's doing a great work in you.

ALIGN YOUR MIND Read Jonah 2–3.

ALIGN YOUR ACTIONS Refuse condemnation for missed opportunities. Look for God's invitation to new ones and embrace them.

ALIGN YOUR HEART

Lord, You're the God of second chances; Your patience with me is breathtaking. I know I've missed opportunities because I let self-preservation win. But I'm listening and watching. Show me my next assignment. Amen.

Is It Right for You to Be Angry?

The LORD replied, "Is it right for you to be angry about this?"
Jonah 4:4

Jonah warned the people of Nineveh judgment was coming. And, just as Jonah predicted, the people responded. The king stepped down from his throne, dressed in burlap, and issued a corporate fast. No one was allowed to eat or drink anything, not even the animals. Everyone needed to earnestly seek God. And they did. Their response moved God's heart, and in His kind and compassionate way, He showed mercy to a city previously doomed for judgment. And Jonah was furious. He was angry with God for having compassion on his enemies, for sparing such wicked people. His prejudice mattered more than Nineveh's predicament. "See?" he told God. "I *knew* you wouldn't let them die like they deserve. So just kill me instead; I'm too angry to even deal with this right now." And God, being gracious, asked, "Is it right for you to be angry about this?" It's not for you or me to decide who gets God's grace, mercy, and compassion; they're for everyone willing to bow their knee to Him. No one is out of his reach while they still have breath in their lungs. His intent is always that people might respond and repent. And if they do, we should rejoice. If we do not, we're the ones who need correction.

 ALIGN YOUR MIND Read Jonah 4.

 ALIGN YOUR ACTIONS Is there a person in your life you don't want to extend God's mercy and compassion to? Ask God's forgiveness, and pray for them daily.

 ALIGN YOUR HEART

> *Lord, forgive me for being so selective with my grace. Fill my heart with Your love and mercy for* all *people. Amen.*

A Beautiful Day Is Coming . . .

Everyone will live in peace and prosperity,
 enjoying their own grapevines and fig trees,
 for there will be nothing to fear.
The LORD of Heaven's Armies
 has made this promise!

Micah 4:4

Once, I shared about a particularly hard time in life, an interviewer asked me this surprising question: "Do you ever just get sick of the battle? Don't you ever feel like saying to God, 'Enough, already!'?" Honestly, yes; I do feel that way sometimes. But after losing a few loved ones to cancer, and after my own fierce battles, something has changed in me. The road of trials and tribulations led to a new perspective—one I couldn't grasp in the valley. I know now, this side of the storm, that life on earth is short and eternity is long. Pain and heartache and struggle are real, and the force of their blows can knock us off course, leaving us wondering *Why?* and *How long?* as we try to catch our breath. And yet, these days, these years—even your entire future stretching out ahead of you—are just a drop in the ocean of eternity. It's hard for us to understand, like an ant trying to comprehend the sky. But we don't need to understand to believe that the glory of eternity with Jesus will swallow every bit of the pain of our present.

ALIGN YOUR MIND   Read Micah 4:1–8.

ALIGN YOUR ACTIONS   Refuse to waste precious strength on whining, complaining, or worrying. When you're tempted to do those things, find a reason to praise God instead.

ALIGN YOUR HEART

> *Lord Jesus, thank You for the promise of eternity with You. Help me to see all my worries, pain, and troubles in light of eternity. Fill me with hope. Amen.*

Do Justly, Love Mercy, Walk Humbly

To do what is right, to love mercy,
and to walk humbly with your God.
Micah 6:8

Israel had a history of leaving God to worship idols. They'd still go through the motions, sacrificing what the law said they needed to sacrifice, but they also built shrines and sacrificed and prayed to other gods. It's like going to church on Sunday and saying your Bible verses, but living for yourself—or your music or your phone or your sports—the rest of the time. Oof. Hits close to home, doesn't it? And here's the thing: When God lovingly confronted Israel through His prophets, the people would throw up their hands. "What more do you want from us?" they'd ask. "We're doing what you said, sacrificing the bulls and the oil. Isn't that enough?" They went through the motions, but their hearts stayed cold. In the end, it's not our outward actions God cares about; He cares about changed hearts. "You do not delight in sacrifice," wrote King David, "but a broken and contrite heart You will not despise."* God doesn't want to be appeased. He wants to be loved, honored, followed, and even enjoyed. So what do a changed heart and life look like? Ones that, together, do justly. Love mercy. And walk humbly with the one true God.

 ALIGN YOUR MIND ▸ Read Micah 6:1–8.

 ALIGN YOUR ACTIONS ▸ Prayerfully take stock of your heart and life. Where are you just going through the motions? Where are your heart and actions aligned with God?

ALIGN YOUR HEART ▸

O Lord, how often I rely on outward performance when You're really after inward transformation. Heal me, change me, and grow Your likeness in me. Amen.

* See Psalm 51:16–18.

After Discipline Comes Deliverance!

Do not gloat over me, my enemies!
For though I fall, I will rise again.
Though I sit in darkness,
the LORD will be my light.

Micah 7:8

Discipline rarely feels loving. Yet God disciplines His children because He's a loving heavenly Father. He trains and course-corrects and refines now so we not only grow in strength and maturity, but we also don't get into worse trouble later. But when He does, our enemies gloat. Sadly, if you're walking through a season when God is addressing something in your life, your fellow Christians may look down their noses and make assumptions about you. God *hates* all of that. But He allows it so we can learn to discern and value His voice above the noise. The great challenge during times of discipline is to respond to God and refuse to react to your enemies and critics. It takes both humility and grit to submit to God's correction while also rejecting insecurity, inferiority, scarcity, and condemnation. None of those are in the heart of God. He disciplines those He truly loves and intends to use. And once the season of correction and refinement are through, God will deal with your enemies and critics in ways that will make them tremble. Gloating is never acceptable for a believer. God does His best work in and through His humblest saints.

 ALIGN YOUR MIND Read Micah 7.

 ALIGN YOUR ACTIONS If God is disciplining you or someone you know, stay humble and hopeful.

ALIGN YOUR HEART

Precious Lord, You're a good Father. Help me walk through any correction or refinement You give me with grit and humility. I bow before You. Amen.

God Promises Peace

> Look! A messenger is coming over the mountains with good news!
> He is bringing a message of peace.
>
> Nahum 1:15

Jonah warned the city of Nineveh that God's judgment was coming. The people sincerely repented and received God's mercy instead. Over time, though, Nineveh lost the spiritual ground it had gained. One hundred years later, God called Nineveh—the capital of Assyria—a city of murder and lies. And though Assyria was a military superpower and seemed impossible to defeat, God could reduce them to rubble in an instant. *Why would a loving God want to destroy a whole city?* When a city is so vile that it's known only for its wickedness, you can be sure that the weak and the vulnerable are the ones who pay the highest price. When lawlessness and corruption run rampant, the weak are exploited the most, suffer the greatest, and are most desperate for a defender. Here in the midst of this impossible situation, God proclaims good news and peace. Peace here translates this way: "Completeness, wholeness, peace, health, welfare, safety, soundness, tranquility, prosperity, perfectness, fullness, rest, harmony; the absence of agitation or discord."[*] Jesus brought the good news and brings the good news. He speaks peace to His people. And at the right time, He will deal with the wicked, defend the weak, and deliver His people.

ALIGN YOUR MIND Read Nahum 1–3.

ALIGN YOUR ACTIONS Use your prayers, your gifts, or your presence to bring the message of God's peace to a vulnerable person in your life.

ALIGN YOUR HEART

> *Father, cut off the strength of the wicked and increase the power of the godly.[†] Work wonders in our day. Amen.*

---

[*] *New Spirit-Filled Life Bible* (Nashville: Thomas Nelson, 2002), 1218.
[†] See Psalm 75:10.

Look Around and Be Amazed

The LORD replied,
"Look around at the nations;
   look and be amazed!
For I am doing something in your own day,
   something you wouldn't believe
   even if someone told you about it."

Habakkuk 1:5

Habakkuk looked around and felt utter dismay. His heart broke over the injustice and corruption around him. How long before God would intervene? He wasn't whining or complaining; he sincerely sought God for answers to heartfelt questions. Habakkuk's words could easily be declared today: "I am surrounded by people who love to argue and fight. The law has become paralyzed, and there is no justice in the courts. The wicked far outnumber the righteous . . ."* So how did God respond? Unbeknownst to Habakkuk, God was already working. "Look around and be amazed, for I am doing something . . ." In every generation, the godly lament over the wickedness in their midst. And in every generation, God's plan is already in motion before His people even know to ask for it. Your call today is to look around for the good and for God moving in your family, school, and community. In fact, grow expectant about what He's up to. May you see Him work in ways that utterly surprise and amaze you. You can be sure of this: He is working, moving, and arranging circumstances this very moment.

ALIGN YOUR MIND Read Habakkuk 1.

ALIGN YOUR ACTIONS Look for God's movement in your life. Be amazed. Let that realization sink deep into your bones. (It'll put faith in your heart.)

ALIGN YOUR HEART

Lord, let me see Your miracles! I want to see Your glory at work. Thank You for working in my day! Amen.

* Habakkuk 1:3–4.

Habakkuk's Priorities

> I will climb up to my watchtower
> and stand at my guardpost.
> There I will wait to see what the LORD says
> and how he will answer my complaint.
> Habakkuk 2:1

Many have lamented to God over the years because of the wickedness in their day. Sometimes God responded; other times He seemed silent. So why did God respond to Habakkuk with such clarity and assurance? Habakkuk had a humble, earnest heart. When it seems we're surrounded by sin and evil, many people either put their heads in the sand and entertain themselves to death, or they shake their fists at the dark, blaming God—and everybody else—for ruining their idea of what life should look like. But as this chapter says, the righteous shall live by *their faithfulness to God*. Habakkuk pursued God and positioned himself in such a way that he wouldn't miss Him. Habakkuk realized that he was appointed as one of the guardians of the kingdom and took his place at the guard post. There, he waited and listened for how the Lord would address the wickedness and decay around him. Habakkuk cared about righteousness and he longed for revival. He never *demanded* an answer from God; instead, he *appealed* to Him for one. What if we all did the same?

ALIGN YOUR MIND Read Habakkuk 2.

ALIGN YOUR ACTIONS See yourself as a guardian of the kingdom. Find your high ground so you can look and listen for God to address the sin around you. Share what He reveals with those who will listen.

ALIGN YOUR HEART

Mighty King, You've made me a guardian of the kingdom. Speak to me. Grant me opportunities to help others so that they may hear and be saved. Amen.

Yet I Will Rejoice

Even though the fig trees have no blossoms,
and there are no grapes on the vines . . .
yet I will rejoice in the LORD!
I will be joyful in the God of my salvation!
Habakkuk 3:17–18

In the verses above, the word *yet* carries so much meaning, so much depth, such great faith. We all walk through times of testing, discipline, or even reduction, all of which are critical for developing our faith. Testing proves and strengthens our faith. Discipline corrects and refines our character. Reduction prepares us for growth and abundance. God continually draws us deeper so we'll be more firmly rooted in Him. While we long for promotion, provision, and protection from hardship, we're also incredibly quick to shift our hope onto—and find our identity in—those very things. Suddenly the gifts become more important than the Giver of Gifts. But when God allows us to go for a time without such gifts, we see again that any gift from His hand pales to the treasure of knowing His heart. And we arrive at the profoundly liberating place where we look at our heartbreak and unfulfilled dreams, and then look up to Him and sincerely say, "*And yet. . . .*" It's where we find Him to be everything we need and more. It's where the things we thought we needed look like trifles. It's where our souls find joy.

ALIGN YOUR MIND ▸ Read Habakkuk 3.

ALIGN YOUR ACTIONS ▸ Write out your own "and yet" faith declaration.

ALIGN YOUR HEART

Father, You withhold no good thing from me. I will trust You while I wait on You. You are better than any gift I long for. And I already have You. Thank You. Amen.

The Danger of Complacency

"I will search with lanterns in Jerusalem's darkest corners
to punish those who sit complacent in their sins.
They think the Lord will do nothing to them,
either good or bad."

Zephaniah 1:12

The more Israel filled their days and nights with evil pursuits, the more they lost sight of God's majesty, power, and authority. And when God didn't send swift, disastrous judgment, they not only became indifferent to Him, but they also assumed He was indifferent to them. They shrugged their shoulders, believing He didn't actually care whether people did right or wrong, whether they walked in sin or righteousness. How short their memory was! The word *complacent* in this passage is akin to the process of curdling, thickening, or settling into. In other words, when we let go of our conviction, when we stop caring about sin (and worse yet, when we somehow think that God is on the same page), something destructive settles within us. Our faith curdles; our sin becomes normal, and we shrug our shoulders over the consequences of it all. God will have none of it. He is *not* indifferent about anything. *Never confuse God's patience with complacency.* Sin has very real consequences, and righteousness has very real rewards. Being complacent in your sin is no small thing to God. A day of reckoning is coming unless we wake up and repent.

 ALIGN YOUR MIND Read Zephaniah 1.

 ALIGN YOUR ACTIONS Prayerfully take stock of your life. Are you indifferent to God in any way? Has any sin become normal? Deal with it immediately. Ask for God's forgiveness.

 ALIGN YOUR HEART

> *Lord, I don't want to be complacent! Wake me up, humble my heart, and draw me near. Fill me with Your passion and convictions. Amen.*

God Delights in You with Gladness

"He will take delight in you with gladness.
With his love, he will calm all your fears.
He will rejoice over you with joyful songs."
Zephaniah 3:17

God is not indifferent about anything. He is passionate, kind, and true. He takes great delight in you and cares deeply about every nuance of your life story. He's well aware of the lies you picked up when life let you down, and He's wholeheartedly committed to helping you sort through your life in a way that heals you and restores your perspective. Every delay, every denial, every pause in your story has a purpose to it. Every hardship, steep hill, and harrowing experience has served to shape you into the person you are today. Though at times it may have felt as though He looked away or lost your address, He never did. And never will. Though the world continually distorts His character, He remains who He is. He is the everlasting Father, God of all comfort, and lover of our souls. You know what will heal your heart? The thought of His smile when you come into His presence. Imagine Him fixing His eyes on you with great delight as He listens to what you have to say. He's not in a hurry. He has time for you. His heart for you will forever change you.

ALIGN YOUR MIND Read Zephaniah 3.

ALIGN YOUR ACTIONS Picture God's delight in you. Imagine the kindness on His face as He listens to your prayers. Allow His song over you to reverberate in your heart.

ALIGN YOUR HEART

Father, I forget how much You love me. Help me to know and experience Your love in a way that changes me forever. Thank You, Lord. Amen.

When You Can't Seem to Get Ahead

> "This is what the LORD of Heaven's Armies says: Look at what's happening to you! You have planted much but harvest little."
>
> Haggai 1:5–6

The people had returned to their homeland to rebuild the temple after the armies of Babylon had destroyed it. They continually encountered opposition, delays, and frustrations, and so they lost their zeal, focus, and sense of purpose. When this happens to God's people, we tend to lose sight of our identity and our purpose. We begin to operate out of a scarcity mindset instead of out of the abundance of our heir status. We grab for ourselves and forget about the greater call on our lives. Haggai came onto the scene and asked the leaders why they were more focused on their own personal comfort and gain than they were on their God-given task. He then called people back to their original task of rebuilding the temple. There's a message in this story for us. Oftentimes when we encounter roadblocks, setbacks, and delays, we lose heart, and then we lose focus. We forget our purpose. We start grabbing for ourselves, trying to make things happen, but we never get ahead. What's the answer? Return first and foremost to keeping God at the center of your life. Seek His kingdom first. Follow His lead. Everything else will fall into place.*

 ALIGN YOUR MIND ▶ Read Haggai 1.

 ALIGN YOUR ACTIONS ▶ Have you abandoned a God-given task because you've lost heart? Re-engage today.

 ALIGN YOUR HEART ▶

Mighty God, give me laser focus and fierce faith. Help me to stay the course and be about Your work on the earth today. I know You'll provide everything I need. Amen.

---

* See Matthew 6:33.

Be Strong, Get to Work

"Be strong, all you people still left in the land. And now get to work, for I am with you, says the LORD of Heaven's Armies."

Haggai 2:4

The people of Judah had returned to God and reengaged in His purposes. They stepped back into the powerful river of His provision. It's the same with us. When we dabble on the shoreline of His purposes, we'll never experience the power of His provision. We miss so much when we're out of sync with His will. The river of God runs wild; it's strong and powerful. And when we jump in, we're strong and powerful, and He takes us on a wild ride. Why do we work so hard to avoid the work He puts before us? Maybe it's fear of failure, anxiety over the cost, or our flesh's aversion to challenge. And yet, we're made for the river! If you're postponing obedience for self-preserving reasons, or for any other reason, don't waste another day. Be strong and get to work. You will experience the Lord's provision, presence, and empowering grace in ways you never otherwise would. Don't fear what the rest of the world fears. You're safest in the center of His will. Jump into the river of God. Your life will never be the same.

ALIGN YOUR MIND Read Haggai 2.

ALIGN YOUR ACTIONS If your current assignment doesn't require faith of some kind, it's time to seek and trust God for more.

ALIGN YOUR HEART

Lord, I want to live in the flow of Your power and provision when I work and when I rest. Give me faith and courage to jump into the river and go where You lead. Amen.

Not by Might, but by His Spirit

"This is what the Lord says to Zerubbabel: It is not by force nor by strength, but by my Spirit, says the Lord of Heaven's Armies."

Zechariah 4:6

God's people had a monumental task before them: rebuild the temple. As they faced literal and spiritual opposition, the Lord reminded them that they'd never accomplish their call in their own strength. Military reinforcement wouldn't get the job done. Only by the Spirit's power would the mountains move, the enemies flee, and the way become clear for them to finish their task. It's the same with us. Our call is not an easy one. In fact, it's impossible apart from the grace of God and the empowering work of the Holy Spirit. Why does God invite us to partner with Him in a way that positions us to need Him every moment of every hour? Because we need Him that much whether we realize it or not. But when we're engaged in purposes that are beyond us, we learn something of God's character. We no longer fear our limits. We grow confident in His abilities, assured of His strength. We stop looking to our accomplishments to validate our worth. We instead look at every task, large or small, as an opportunity to trust God and see what He will do with a heart of faith. And then we offer it back to Him. It's the only way to live.

 ALIGN YOUR MIND Read Zechariah 4.

 ALIGN YOUR ACTIONS Are you relying on your own strength or abilities in any way? Invite His Spirit's intervention, and see what He'll do.

 ALIGN YOUR HEART

Precious Father, forgive me for doing things in my own strength. Holy Spirit, please do a mighty work in and through me. Amen.

Seeds of Peace and Prosperity

"For I am planting seeds of peace and prosperity among you. The grapevines will be heavy with fruit. The earth will produce its crops, and the heavens will release the dew."

Zechariah 8:12

God's people wandered far away from His best for them. They sinned, practiced idolatry, cheated the poor, and exploited the weak. They looked more like the world than their Maker. Then their temple was destroyed, and they were carried off into captivity. After seventy years they returned to their homeland and began the work of rebuilding the temple. And yet they lost heart once they encountered opposition and delay. Their apathy led them to care more about their personal comfort than God's kingdom. This grieved the heart of God. But then they heeded the prophet's charge to get back to work. As a result, God pronounced blessing over their lives and land for their obedience. Though we have to be careful not to always attribute blessing to obedience or hardship to disobedience, it's important to note that something changes in the land and in our lives when we sincerely seek the heart of God. He plants seeds of peace and prosperity in our midst. He offers us an otherworldly peace and He prospers our soul. Worldly treasures may come and go, but these treasures belong to anyone who sincerely seeks Him.

ALIGN YOUR MIND Read Zechariah 8:1–13.

ALIGN YOUR ACTIONS Nurture the seeds God has planted in your life. Water them with His Word. Seek peace and pursue it. Trust God to prosper your mind, body, and spirit.

ALIGN YOUR HEART

Father, I want life to spring up all around me. Show me how to nurture the seeds You plant in my soil. Amen.

We Have Heard God Is with You

"Please let us walk with you, for we have heard that God is with you."
Zechariah 8:23

Zechariah pronounced an end to the old and a declaration of the new. He prophesied about a day when Israel would no longer be the object of scorn; instead, she'd be a symbol of God's grace and power. Over the centuries, God's chosen people have loved Him, wandered from Him, rebelled against Him, and then repented before Him, only to wander again. But a day is coming when the Jewish people will recognize Christ as their Messiah and will seek Him wholeheartedly. "Jerusalem will be a holy place—highly respected throughout the world because its people will have a change of heart toward God. People from other nations will see how God has rewarded His people for their faithfulness and want to be included in their great blessings."* Though this is a prophecy for the nation of Israel, there's a potential promise here for us as well. Imagine walking so closely with the risen Lord, listening so intimately for His voice, and obeying Him so wholeheartedly that those around you run to catch up with you, long to walk with you, and seek to learn what you know about the great God of heaven. May your life reflect God's active and real presence on the earth today.

ALIGN YOUR MIND ▶ Read Zechariah 8:14–23.

ALIGN YOUR ACTIONS ▶ What needs to change in you so others see God in your life? Make the change.

ALIGN YOUR HEART

> *Lord, I want my life to so reflect Your heart of grace and power that when others encounter me, they encounter You. Raise me up to reflect Your glory. Amen.*

* *Life Application Study Bible*, 1959.

Righteous and Victorious, yet Humble

> Look, your king is coming to you.
> He is righteous and victorious,
> yet he is humble, riding on a donkey—
> riding on a donkey's colt.
>
> Zechariah 9:9

Zechariah prophesied the coming Messiah five hundred years before His birth. The people of Jerusalem needed a victorious king, a warrior to defend them and protect them. But nobody expected Him to be the kind of King that He is. He's righteous, victorious, and humble. Though the prophecies described Him, much of the world missed Him. And so it goes today. Even the disciples who knew Jesus personally expected Him to use His miracle-working power to rise up and defeat Rome. But He wasn't that kind of king. He lived a righteous, humble life, and defeated sin and death victoriously. He turned the world upside down and started a kingdom movement that's still going strong today. One day He will gather His people together, He will overthrow wicked governments, unseat wicked leaders, confront evil forces, and disarm them all. He'll restore everything the enemy stole from us. The Israelites tried to get it right, but they couldn't. We try to get it right, but we can't. So our King came to us. He lived and died for us. Rose again for us. And now, finally, we can live righteous, victorious, humble lives, just like our King.

ALIGN YOUR MIND Read Zechariah 9.

ALIGN YOUR ACTIONS Do you live like your King—righteous and victorious, yet humble? Ask the Spirit to shape your life to look like Jesus'.

ALIGN YOUR HEART

Father, thank You for sending Your Son. Jesus, thank You for coming to earth. Holy Spirit, thank You for empowering me to live like my King. I am forever blessed. Amen.

Testing God

"Bring all the tithes into the storehouse so there will be enough food in my Temple. If you do . . . I will open the windows of heaven for you. I will pour out a blessing so great you won't have enough room to take it in! Try it! Put me to the test!"

Malachi 3:10

Every time I read Malachi chapter 3, I cringe when I read how God asks His children to return to Him and they respond with, "How can we return if we've never wandered away?" They go on to question if it even pays to obey Him. Pays? There's no fear of God. No sense that He's right about anything. They want their will, their way. Still, God asks them to bring in the tithe, to sow seeds into the kingdom. He even invites them to test Him and see if He doesn't unlock provision and blessing beyond their imagination. This passage has been misused as a license to use God for personal gain. But that's not the invitation here. Instead, He's saying, "If you will dare to see me as your provider, you will find me faithful to the point where you trust me with every other area of your life." It's still true today.

ALIGN YOUR MIND Read Malachi 3:1–14.

ALIGN YOUR ACTIONS What are you not giving back to God? Time? Money? Your talents and abilities? Today, trust that whatever you offer up to Him with a humble heart He will bless beyond what you imagine for His glory and His kingdom.

ALIGN YOUR HEART

Lord, forgive us for trusting ourselves more than You! Forgive us for hoarding resources that ultimately come from and belong to You. Give me faith to sow generously. Amen.

The Lord Listened and Remembered

Then those who feared the Lord spoke with each other, and the Lord listened to what they said. In his presence, a scroll of remembrance was written to record the names of those who feared him and always thought about the honor of his name.

Malachi 3:16

That time you leaned across the table, grabbed your friend's hand, and encouraged her to hang in there and trust God—the Lord listened and wrote it down. That time when you were on the phone crying your eyes out and your friend prayed for you? He was there. That moment when you anxiously shared your story of faith, He leaned in, listened, and opened His book. He's so taken by your faith that He remembers every faith conversation, every heartfelt moment of worship, every act prompted by your faith. When you bow and sincerely give thanks for food that blesses and sustains, God's right there. He is well aware of those who disregard Him. And He's intimately aware of those who honor Him. On earth the lines seem blurry between believers and unbelievers. Hard to tell them apart sometimes. But in heaven? There's perfect clarity. Absolute distinction. Make no mistake about it.

ALIGN YOUR MIND ▸ Read Malachi 3:16–18.

ALIGN YOUR ACTIONS ▸ Find someone to encourage today. Look for God's presence when you do. Praise Him for His attentiveness.

ALIGN YOUR HEART

> *Lord, I forget sometimes how much my faith matters to You. How much I matter to You. When I'm encouraging another in the faith, help me to be as attentive to You as You are to me. I love You, Lord. Amen.*

The Sun of Righteousness Will Rise

"But for you who fear my name, the Sun of Righteousness will rise with healing in his wings. And you will go free, leaping with joy like calves let out to pasture."

Malachi 4:2

One night I had a vivid dream. I walked through a large field with a fence surrounding its perimeter. Outside the fenced area were mountains and streams and wildflowers. It was beautiful enough inside the fence, but I longed for the freedom beyond. When I approached the edge of the field, I saw a gate that was bolted and chained shut—like there was no way out. Suddenly, out of nowhere, the enemy unleashed a fury of creatures that swarmed and attacked and pushed me back, away from a gate that was impenetrable anyway. I woke up and realized afresh how desperately the enemy wants us to stay captive. Yet if we contend for our freedom and trust God's promises, we will experience a measure of freedom we never dreamed possible. And there's a day up ahead when the gates of hell will no longer prevail against us in any way. We will go free and leap with joy, like calves let out to pasture. Keep walking. Keep believing. The Sun of Righteousness will one day rise with healing, redemption, and restoration in His wings.

ALIGN YOUR MIND Read Malachi 4.

ALIGN YOUR ACTIONS Can you imagine a new level of freedom in your life? Ask God for a picture of what that would look like. Pray until it becomes a reality.

ALIGN YOUR HEART

> Lord Jesus, it's for freedom that You've set me free. And one day, my soul will know a joy I never imagined. Show me what freedom looks like today. Amen.

He Will Save His People from Their Sins

"And she will have a son, and you are to name him Jesus, for he will save his people from their sins."

Matthew 1:21

I blew it the other day. I woke up full of condemnation and berating thoughts—none of which come from the Father's heart. I then remembered mercy, forgiveness, and grace. I relished afresh the precious gift of God's Son. Our flesh pulls us toward the very things that drain the life and purpose right out of us. Sin of any kind destroys the prospect of the new things God wants to do in and through us. Jesus stepped in to interrupt sin's curse and hold on us. He came to save us from the downward cycle that would ultimately destroy us. Consider what Jesus has done. He stepped down from His throne in heaven, came to earth, endured crucifixion, took *our* punishment, died *our* death, defeated *our* enemy, forgave us of *our* sins, gave us His Holy Spirit, grafted us into the royal family, offered us heir status along with Him, and made us active participants of His promises, and He ultimately secured *our* eternity. We won't fully grasp all we've inherited until we see Jesus face to face. But know this today: He will save you from your sin if you allow Him to. He wants life for you, wholeness for you, freedom for you.

ALIGN YOUR MIND Read Matthew 1.

ALIGN YOUR ACTIONS Ask the Lord if you have any sinful habits He wants to deal with in your life. No condemnation. Just a holy invitation.

ALIGN YOUR HEART

Precious Lord, thank You for all You've done for me! Set me free to worship You with everything in me! You are Lord. Amen.

Provision, Protection, and Promotion

> Then Jesus was led by the Spirit into the wilderness to be tempted there by the devil.
>
> Matthew 4:1

The Spirit led Jesus into the wilderness to be tempted by the devil. The wilderness is where we are tested and proven time and again. We're vulnerable in the wilderness, but it's where we must learn to resist temptation and remember what's true. People in recovery often use the HALT acronym to help them stay out of trouble. If you're *hungry, angry, lonely,* or *tired,* then you're at risk, so be careful. In His wilderness, Jesus was no doubt hungry, possibly tired and lonely too. And when He was most vulnerable, the enemy went after God's faithfulness in three areas that he'll go after in us as well: provision, protection, and promotion. The enemy wanted Jesus to take matters into His own hands, to force an early outcome in hopes that He'd thwart His ultimate purposes for you and me. But Jesus saw right through the enemy's scheme and prevailed even in His weakest moments. Notice too how the devil attacked and questioned Jesus' identity with every temptation. It's the same for you. *Is God faithful? Will He really come through for you? Does He really love you? Are you really the heir He says you are?* These are truths we must settle in our souls before those wilderness seasons come.

 ALIGN YOUR MIND Read Matthew 4.

 ALIGN YOUR ACTIONS Consider the questions above. Ask God to make those truths unshakable in your soul.

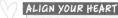 **ALIGN YOUR HEART**

Lord, You kept the big picture in mind in Your weakest moments. Help me to do that too. I want to believe You and prevail, even when my heart is faint. Thank You, Lord. Amen.

Congratulations, the Kingdom Is Yours!

"God blesses those who are poor and realize their need for him,
for the Kingdom of Heaven is theirs."

Matthew 5:3

Oftentimes when we come to the edges of ourselves, we tend to despair. And our enemy wants it that way. But when we notice our limits in our capacity to love another, have patience, or hold on to faith, we have a place to go with those limits. Jesus says that blessed—most happy and to be envied—are those who finally grasp that they'll never be enough in themselves. Because now, finally, they can step forward and inherit more of the kingdom. We come to Christ for the first time through the low door of humility. We admit our need for a Savior. We grow in much the same way. If the enemy can't get you to strive in your own strength, he'll try to get you to despair over your lack of it. Either way, he wants you to keep your focus on yourself. But once you come to the edges of yourself, manage a smile, look up, and wiggle your toes in the fresh grass of kingdom territory, you'll never have to despair over your limits again. You'll see yourself as blessed beyond measure. For every limit, God offers lavish grace and an endless landscape of kingdom territory just waiting to be apprehended.

ALIGN YOUR MIND Read Matthew 5:1–16.

ALIGN YOUR ACTIONS Identify a limit that most troubles you. Now smile, look up, and apprehend God's limitless grace and provision just waiting for you!

ALIGN YOUR HEART

Father, I open my arms, put a smile on my face, and ask for more of You! Increase my capacity for all that You are. I am blessed beyond measure. Amen.

Hold Heaven Close

"Store your treasures in heaven, where moths and rust cannot destroy, and thieves do not break in and steal. Wherever your treasure is, there the desires of your heart will also be."

Matthew 6:20–21

God wants us to live with the end in mind. He's set eternity in our hearts. How we live *here* deeply impacts how we'll live *there*, when we're forever with Him. How we steward our time, treasure, and talents impacts what kind of stewardship awaits us on the other side. And when it comes to our desires, Jesus reminds us that they start with what we treasure. Whatever we hold closest to our hearts fuels our daily desires. Hold heaven close. Treasure Jesus most. Storing up treasures in heaven means living like His promises are true, valuing what He values, and tending to His concerns on the earth today. We lose our reward when we live out of our insecurities or misuse our time, treasure, and talents. But when we—out of loving response for all God has done—give a cup of water, offer a kind word, give a gift, forgive an enemy, move forward in faith, or pray a bold prayer, heaven takes note and Jesus rewards. This earth will pass away. Sin, self-ambition, and pride in our accomplishments will all pass away too. Whatever you do for Jesus will last.

 ALIGN YOUR MIND ▶ Read Matthew 6.

 ALIGN YOUR ACTIONS ▶ Impact eternity today: offer a kind word, give a gift, forgive an enemy, move forward in faith, pray a bold prayer. Focus your heart on heaven-bound things and not earthbound.

 ALIGN YOUR HEART ▶

Father, help me to align my desires with You and store up my treasures in heaven. Awaken the reality of eternity within me. Amen.

The Power of Persistence

"Keep on asking, and you will receive what you ask for. Keep on seeking, and you will find. Keep on knocking, and the door will be opened to you. For everyone who asks, receives. Everyone who seeks, finds. And to everyone who knocks, the door will be opened."

Matthew 7:7–8

Some take these verses to mean that, if we bother God long enough, He'll give us whatever we want. But we don't dictate to God. He's not a means to an end, especially selfish ends. He's The End as well as The Beginning. However, Jesus himself charged us in this passage to persist and keep persisting. Why? Because we give up too soon. Our dreams are too small. And we often don't want to pay the price. Our hope isn't in an outcome—it's in Jesus, who invites us to persist in faith and to believe for the impossible for the sake of His name and His kingdom. Life's twists and turns have left me breathless at times, but my persistence has changed me. I've either seen miraculous breakthroughs around me, or I've experienced personal breakthroughs within me. God knows what He's doing when He invites us to run hard after Him. It's interesting that Jesus inserted this invitation amid His caution about judging others. What if we sought God for wisdom and perspective on those we're tempted to judge with the same passion we seek Him for His blessings in our lives?

ALIGN YOUR MIND Read Matthew 7.

ALIGN YOUR ACTIONS Consider how God might be asking you to persist in prayer. Engage with Him today.

ALIGN YOUR HEART

Lord, stir up a passion in my soul. Help me to persist in prayer in a way that honors You and changes me! Amen.

Rest for the Weary, a Burden That's Light

> Then Jesus said, "Come to me, all of you who are weary and carry heavy burdens, and I will give you rest. . . . For my yoke is easy to bear, and the burden I give you is light."
>
> Matthew 11:28–30

Jesus has incredible compassion for the weary soul. He'll never ask us to grind our gears to the point of exhaustion. That's not to say we won't experience seasons of hard work, long hours, and exhausting opposition. But always, amid such times, God offers provisions of grace, exit ramps for rest, and His shoulders to help carry the weight of our burden. No matter if you're exhausted because you've committed to more than God asked of you, deadlines are looming, or you're in a battle through no fault of your own, bring your weary self to Jesus. Find rest for your soul. If the weight of your burden is more than you can bear, ask Him to hold it for you. He'll do the heavy lifting. It's not only possible to experience replenishment right in the midst of these trying seasons, it's essential. Take Jesus up on His offer to fill you back up again. Your need for rest is natural. God's provision for you is *super*natural.

 ALIGN YOUR MIND ▸ Read Matthew 11.

 ALIGN YOUR ACTIONS ▸ Unplug and take some time to rest in God's presence. Give your burdens to Him. Ask for more of His empowering grace.

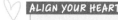 **ALIGN YOUR HEART**

Dear Jesus, help me find rest in You. Here's the burden of my heart. Will You carry it for me? Flood my heart with peace and rest today. Amen.

A Great Separation Awaits Us

"But when the Son of Man comes in his glory, and all the angels with him, then he will sit upon his glorious throne. All the nations will be gathered in his presence, and he will separate the people as a shepherd separates the sheep from the goats. He will place the sheep at his right hand and the goats at his left."

Matthew 25:31–33

It might be hard to comprehend the magnitude of what these verses are saying—the end of time seems so far away, and not nearly as pressing as school assignments or even the peer pressure around you. But think of it this way: For those who trust Christ for salvation, life on earth is as bad as it gets—your bad days now are the worst you will ever deal with. Forever. For those who've rejected Jesus' precious gift of grace, life on earth is as good as it gets. Sorrow and terror will be their only friends. Forever. God knows which souls belong to Him, and a day is coming—sooner than we know—when His true children will be revealed. May the reality of that important day fuel you to care about those who are lost. May God give you courage to share the Good News with those who are headed for an eternity without Him.

ALIGN YOUR MIND Read Matthew 25.

ALIGN YOUR ACTIONS Who needs to hear the Good News in your life? Pray for them. Share the gospel.

ALIGN YOUR HEART

> *Lord, forgive me for being so wrapped up in my earthly concerns that I forget about the day to come. Help me to live ready and to help others live ready too. Amen.*

True Story

The Roman officer and the other soldiers at the crucifixion were terrified by the earthquake and all that had happened. They said, "This man truly was the Son of God!"

Matthew 27:54

*J*esus was content to be misunderstood. He was on a mission to save all who would believe in Him. The King of Kings humbled himself so low as to die a criminal's death on the cross. He endured abhorrent dishonor and disrespect. He was mocked by fools and killed by religious hypocrites. He was abandoned by His friends and felt forsaken by His Father. At any moment He could have called the whole thing off and thousands of angels would have come to His aid. But He endured it all—all for love. Once He gave up His Spirit, the thick temple veil tore from the top to the bottom. The earth quaked. The sky turned black. The dead rose. It took all of these earthly phenomena for the guards and soldiers to finally declare, "Truly, this was the Son of God." Eventually the truth will be revealed—always. We waste so much precious energy and lose valuable perspective when we try to manage others' opinions of us. What if we just stayed on-mission? What if we were content to be misunderstood? What if we entrusted our story to the One who knows the whole truth? Like Jesus, we'd become a force to reckon with.

 ALIGN YOUR MIND Read Matthew 27–28.

 ALIGN YOUR ACTIONS Put a stop to any thoughts about what others might think about you. Renew your mind with thoughts of God's fierce love for you.

ALIGN YOUR HEART

> *Lord, help me to stay on-mission. Give me fierce faith and courageous conviction. Just like You. Amen.*

The Wonder of Good Soil

"Listen! A farmer went out to plant some seed."

Mark 4:3

Jesus talked about four kinds of soil (heart conditions): not guarded; not grounded; not given to the things of God; and nurtured soil that produces thirty, sixty, and even one hundred times what was planted. These are metaphors for the condition of our hearts. The first soil speaks of the person who lives in proximity to the Word but doesn't see its value. They may attend church or watch online, but it's really a side note in their lives. The second speaks of the person who values the Word, but only when it suits them. When life gets hard, they look for other solutions and forget what they already know. The third speaks of the person whose heart is divided and conquered. They're pulled between competing earthly desires and worries, but they love their faith too. It's just not their highest priority. The fourth soil speaks of the person who understands and embraces the wonder of the seed that's planted in good soil. They've experienced enough hardship and heartache to see the value of tending their soil and guarding their heart. They treasure the Word, love new growth, pull the weeds of sin, and are continually receptive to the living, active Word of God. Theirs is a full life that nourishes many. Jesus wants this for all of us.

ALIGN YOUR MIND Read Mark 4:1–25.

ALIGN YOUR ACTIONS Tend to the soil of your heart by dealing with anything that disrupts your peace, flourishing, and hope.

ALIGN YOUR HEART

Lord, I want my heart to be healthy soil that nurtures and nourishes the Word You've planted in me. May what You've planted in me multiply one hundredfold. Amen.

Peace and Authority

When Jesus woke up, he rebuked the wind and said to the waves, "Silence! Be still!" Suddenly the wind stopped, and there was a great calm.

Mark 4:39

I once followed Jesus right into a storm. I stepped out in faith thinking Jesus was about to take me to a place of peace and rest, when in fact, He led me right into a storm because He had a few things to teach me. Jesus did the same for the disciples. He knew that once they got into the boat and sailed for a while, these seasoned fishermen would encounter such fierce winds and overpowering waves that they'd fear for their lives. Did Jesus brace for impact? No. He fell asleep! The disciples actually had to wake Him up (this was no light nap). Jesus got up and rebuked the wind and the waves. He called for peace and stillness. The disciples watched in awe. While the storm raged, they questioned Him, "Lord, don't You care?" Once He spoke peace over the storm, He questioned them, "Where's your faith?" Given what awaited the disciples on the other side of the lake, they needed to learn how to access peace and rest when chaos swirled. We do too. But you don't have to wait for the storm to start. Cultivate a heart of peace and rest today. Stand in your authority. When the storm does hit, you'll be able to stand strong.

 ALIGN YOUR MIND Read Mark 4:35–41.

 ALIGN YOUR ACTIONS Today, remind your heart to receive God's peace. Ask Him to infuse it with His bold authority.

ALIGN YOUR HEART

> Lord, grant me a peaceful heart that rests in You and help me to stand in the authority You've entrusted to me! Amen.

Optimistic Resilience

She replied, "That's true, Lord, but even the dogs under the table are allowed to eat the scraps from the children's plates."

Mark 7:28

The Jewish people once considered Gentiles scavengers. Dogs. And not the cuddly, house-pet kind. One day a Syrian-Phoenician woman approached Jesus, fell at His feet, and begged Him to deliver her little girl who was possessed by a demon. At first it seemed as though Jesus refused to help her and insulted her in the process. I used to struggle with Jesus' response to this situation until I looked a little deeper into it. John Eldredge said this, "Picture a glint in Jesus' eye as He spoke to her. He knew she was up for this banter. He was trying to teach the disciples a lesson." The study note in my Bible goes deeper: "On the surface, Jesus' words may seem harsh and unsympathetic, but the woman recognized them as a wide-open door to God's throne. Jesus did not use the negative term for 'dogs' that referred to scavengers; instead, He used the term for a household pet. The woman took the cue and added to his analogy of pets under a family dining table. Her attitude was expectant and hopeful, not prickly and hypersensitive. . . . We could learn from this woman's singular purpose and optimistic resilience. Jesus really does want to meet our needs. When we pray, we're talking to a friend."*

 ALIGN YOUR MIND Read Mark 7.

ALIGN YOUR ACTIONS Determine not to take things personally even if they're intended that way. And pray earnestly with joy and optimistic resilience.

ALIGN YOUR HEART

> *Lord, I desire more faith, confidence, and resilience! Do a miraculous work in me! Amen.*

* *Life Application Study Bible*, 2124–25.

Practicing the Art of Remembering

"'You have eyes—can't you see? You have ears—can't you hear?' Don't you remember anything at all?"

Mark 8:18

Our brains hold on to negative experiences more readily than they do the positive ones. We remember fear, trauma, pain, and betrayal because we feel them all the way down to our bones. But positive memories can actually play a part in healing our hearts, and redemptive memories remind us of God's faithfulness—and that we actually have a very real history with Him. Imagine the toll on our souls when we carry painful memories with us wherever we go. We end up living in *reaction* to our circumstance instead of in *response* to God's leading. Jesus wants us to travel light. He wants to redeem our perspective. He was trying to warn the disciples about the influence of ungodly leaders. But the disciples were still stuck on the small issue of who forgot the bread, and they were arguing about it. They'd completely forgotten about His ability to multiply the loaves! We'll never see ourselves in the bigger story until we allow God to change our most repetitive, negative thoughts. Determine to practice the art of remembering a few minutes every day. It'll open your ears and eyes to the presence of God in your midst. You have a history with God. You have a future with Him too. And He's very much at work in your present moment.

ALIGN YOUR MIND Read Mark 8.

ALIGN YOUR ACTIONS Practice remembering your favorite moments in life—times when you laughed, felt loved, and sensed God's nearness. It'll do wonders for you.

ALIGN YOUR HEART

> *Lord, change my thoughts and perspective. Help me to remember things that glorify You and heal me. Amen.*

People Just like Us

> John said to Jesus, "Teacher, we saw someone using your name to cast out demons, but we told him to stop because he wasn't in our group."
>
> Mark 9:38

One day my friend's toddler son wrapped his arms around her leg and said, "I love my mommy." My friend smiled until her son gripped her leg tighter, looked at his sister, and declared, "*My* mommy!" To which her daughter replied, "She's *my* mommy!" They went back and forth until they were in an all-out brawl. This frequently happens within the church. Different denominations claim to have cornered the market on truth, or a special relationship with God and His Word. But Scripture tells us that there are many tribes and tongues that will gather together for the Marriage Supper of the Lamb. We must not confuse a narrow mind with the narrow way. Yet we must season everything with discernment. There's a difference between accepting fellow *believers* and accepting every *belief*. Even Jesus warned that false teachers would appear inside the church. How do you know the difference? Test the fruit of their words and actions. Do you see love, joy, peace, patience, kindness, goodness, faithfulness, gentleness, or self-control?* If so, welcome them as family, even if they look or worship differently than you. Jesus promised we'd all be tested to prove our faith. And He asked us to live at peace with one another.

ALIGN YOUR MIND ▶ Read Mark 9.

ALIGN YOUR ACTIONS ▶ Ask a trusted adult to help you find a blog or podcast from a Christian outside your denomination. Talk about the differences with them.

ALIGN YOUR HEART

> *Lord, give me a grander picture of what Your kingdom looks like! Grant me discernment in all things. Amen.*

* Galatians 5:22–23

Let God Direct the Conversation

They were now on the way up to Jerusalem, and Jesus was walking ahead of them. The disciples were filled with awe, and the people following behind were overwhelmed with fear. Taking the twelve disciples aside, Jesus once more began to describe everything that was about to happen to him.

Mark 10:32

The disciples were filled with awe. The people were filled with fear. Jesus wanted His followers prepared. He opened His mouth and led with this important word: *Listen*. But, apparently, they weren't listening. Jesus went on to describe the horrific events that awaited Him in Jerusalem, down to the details that He'd be mocked, spit upon, flogged, whipped, and then killed. Why didn't this jarring news suddenly stop them in their tracks? Somehow, James's and John's minds had wandered elsewhere. They were thinking about status and position. Jesus spoke about suffering. They wanted to talk about promotion. We must discern the conversation God wants to have with us. He always loves us—always wants what's best for us. So we must listen when He cautions, corrects, or redirects. He wanted the disciples prepared so that when the unthinkable happened, they'd remember the rest of the story—that He would rise again. Amazingly, God promoted the disciples to places of honor that they could never imagine during their time on earth. He answered their prayers, and then some. But the prize never comes without the process of preparation. Don't get ahead of God. He's always watching out for you.

 ALIGN YOUR MIND Read Mark 10.

 ALIGN YOUR ACTIONS Spend some quiet time listening for God's voice. Open His Word. Let Him speak.

 ALIGN YOUR HEART

> *Father, help me to discern the conversation You want to have with me today. Amen.*

People Used to Say . . .

"What's more, your relative Elizabeth has become pregnant in her old age!
People used to say she was barren, but she has conceived a son and is now
in her sixth month. For the word of God will never fail."

Luke 1:36–37

There was intense shame and disdain attached to barrenness, the inability to have children, in Elizabeth's day—it was one of the worst things to happen to a woman. But as He often does, God called Elizabeth to wait longer than most to see her dream fulfilled, because the answer to her prayers served a greater purpose than she could imagine. God is always redeeming stories. People used to say that I was weak and fragile. That's no longer true. I used to berate myself because my short-term memory was messed up. That's not an issue anymore. What about you? Do you believe God can change the narrative of your story? Are you remaining hopeful and expectant? People will say what they say and think what they think. But may their limited perspectives have zero impact on your faith. For nothing is impossible with God.

ALIGN YOUR MIND Read Luke 1.

ALIGN YOUR ACTIONS What disparaging things have people said about you? What berating things have you said about yourself? What if God moved in such a way that those things were no longer true? And what if the lies no longer felt true? Can you picture it? Pray with hopeful expectancy today; God's not done with you yet.

ALIGN YOUR HEART

> Lord, I refuse to be bound by my past limitations or by others' perspectives of me. You are the God who saves, redeems, and restores. Change my story for Your glory. Amen.

The Power of Good News

"The Spirit of the LORD is upon me,
   for he has anointed me to bring Good News to the poor.
He has sent me to proclaim that captives will be released,
   that the blind will see,
that the oppressed will be set free. . . ."

Luke 4:18

Jesus first stepped into ministry when He was baptized in the Jordan River. When He came up out of the water, the Holy Spirit descended upon Him like a dove. The heavens opened and His Father declared His affection for Him. Then Jesus, full of the Holy Spirit, went into the wilderness to be tempted and tested by the devil. He emerged from that spiritual battle victorious and, in the power of the Holy Spirit, went to the synagogue, stood up, and read a prophecy from Isaiah that was being fulfilled before their very eyes. He proclaimed Good News to the poor, freedom for captives, and sight to the blind. He *is* the Good News. Love came down to rescue us! The gospel of Jesus Christ is more than a four-step prayer to secure our eternity. It's the very power and the presence of God to radically change a life—from captive to totally, completely free. As the Father sent Jesus, and with the same power, He also sends you.

 ALIGN YOUR MIND ▶ Read Luke 4.

ALIGN YOUR ACTIONS ▶ The Good News isn't just a ticket to eternity. It's about changed lives, about God's power and presence moving through you to build His kingdom—now. Think about and praise God for this truth today.

ALIGN YOUR HEART ▶

Father, lead me to those who would love You if they knew You. Prepare their hearts and speak mightily through me. Set them free, Lord. Amen.

When Increase Comes

And this time their nets were so full of fish they began to tear!

Luke 5:6

When Jesus had finished speaking from their fishing boat, He instructed the disciples to go out to the deep and let down their nets to catch some fish. Simon replied, "We worked hard all last night and didn't catch a thing, but if you say so, I'll try again." This time their nets were so full they began to tear. They needed help to bring in all of the fish. The abundant catch almost sunk their boat! When Simon Peter witnessed the Lord's great power, he also realized his own sinful state and begged Jesus to leave his presence. When the Lord takes you deeper, several things happen almost at once. The increase that you prayed for will likely stretch you beyond your capacity. Things may pull apart at the seams. You may feel like you're sinking. And in the midst of increase, growth, and the stress that goes along with it all, you'll be acutely aware of your own humanity and sinfulness. The enemy will spew in your ear that you're in over your head. Do not fear these growing pains. Instead, grow in grace. Grow your team. And grow in your dependence on Jesus. You're made for this.

ALIGN YOUR MIND ▸ Read Luke 5.

ALIGN YOUR ACTIONS ▸ If you long for kingdom increase, ask for it. If you're managing much now, don't lose perspective. He's only answering your prayers.

ALIGN YOUR HEART

Lord, lead me to the deep places with You! Increase Your work in and through me. Multiply my offering and give me grace to manage all You've entrusted to me. Amen.

Judging Others

> "Do not judge others, and you will not be judged. Do not condemn others, or it will all come back against you. Forgive others, and you will be forgiven. Give, and you will receive. Your gift will return to you in full—pressed down, shaken together to make room for more. . . ."
>
> Luke 6:37–38

We live in a culture where people are quick to believe the worst, not the best. Quick to dismiss with hurtful comments, not understand. People are pronounced guilty even if they're proven innocent. We must not get caught up in the groupthink so prevalent in our day. Jesus wants His followers to live and love a different way. Though Scripture calls us to rightly discern good from evil, right from wrong, the word *judge* in this passage refers to our tendency to separate, pick apart, and put ourselves above another. And the word *condemn* is to determine a verdict against someone else. Honestly, our opinions don't matter as much as we think they do. Unless we're directly involved and impacted by someone, we're best to hold our tongues *and* our thoughts and pray about what we think we see. In this passage, I love how Jesus turned on a dime from judgment to generosity. When we're gracious, generous, and forgiving like our Savior, we will walk in a fullness that the world desperately needs.

ALIGN YOUR MIND Read Luke 6.

 ALIGN YOUR ACTIONS Pray earnestly for the person you're most tempted to judge. It'll bless God's heart and change your perspective.

 ALIGN YOUR HEART

> *Lord, give me eyes to see others the way You do. Help me love them and pray for them even when I don't know the whole story. You do. And that's enough. Amen.*

Today Might Be the Day

"Daughter," he said to her, "your faith has made you well. Go in peace."

Luke 8:48

I wish I knew her name. We know her as the woman with the issue of blood. Her story moves me to tears and inspires me to courage. She bled continually, profusely for twelve years. She not only endured chronic illness, body odor, fatigue, and financial brokenness, but she was also painfully shunned by society. She had to yell, "Unclean!" when others were nearby so that no one would defile themselves by touching her. Imagine. How does a person keep their hope alive under such circumstances? I'm sure she had many days of discouragement and defeat. But one day, she heard Jesus was in town. And that day, she tossed aside her labels and social stigmas. She pressed through the crowd with persistence and faith. The throng of people pressed up against her and jostled her. But then she grabbed a fistful of Jesus' robe and everything changed. Sheer power surged down her arm, throughout her body, and no doubt made her cheeks flush. She was instantly healed. Jesus stopped in His tracks to find out who had touched Him with that kind of faith. He wanted her to know that she hadn't taken healing from Him. He'd freely given it to her. Don't give up hope. Keep pressing in. Today might be the day.

ALIGN YOUR MIND Read Luke 8.

ALIGN YOUR ACTIONS Are you waiting for breakthrough in any area? Tell your soul, "God sees me. He knows. Today might be the day."

ALIGN YOUR HEART

Lord, give me faith and persistence to lay hold of Your promise. Break through for me. My soul waits for You. Amen.

Authority and Awe

"Look, I have given you authority over all the power of the enemy, and you can walk among snakes and scorpions and crush them. Nothing will injure you."

Luke 10:19

Years ago I stood in my living room, overwhelmed by fear and anxiety. Lyme disease raged in my body. Painful neurological symptoms surged in my face, on my head, and down my arms. Bill collectors called every day about our medical debt; we were in over our heads. I thought the whole battle might swallow me whole. There, in that moment, the Lord's voice thundered in my soul, "Susie, are you a believer simply because you've secured your eternity? Or do you actually believe this stuff? When are you going to shift your weight off your fears and on to my promises? Fear and faith are opposing forces. You have to turn your back on one to behold the other. I've given you authority. Now's your time to take authority." That was a game-changing moment for me. The disciples marveled that the demons obeyed them. Jesus wanted them to walk in their authority but with humility. The devil's pride and lust for power were his downfall. Jesus said, "Don't marvel that the demons obey you. Marvel that your name is written in the Book of Life."* Take authority. Marvel that He saved you. What a mighty God we serve!

 ALIGN YOUR MIND ▶ Read Luke 10.

 ALIGN YOUR ACTIONS ▶ Put any enemy harassment and overwhelming circumstances in their place today. Marvel at the miracle of your salvation.

 ALIGN YOUR HEART ▶

> *Lord, help me to stand in authority and to stay in a place of awe. What You've entrusted to me, what You've accomplished for me, is miraculous. Help me to walk accordingly. Amen.*

* See Luke 10:20.

He Rewards Those Who Are Ready

"He may come in the middle of the night or just before dawn. But whenever he comes, he will reward the servants who are ready."

Luke 12:38

When Jesus talked about the parable of the soils, He addressed distraction, immaturity, and divided affections. Here He similarly addresses how the worries of this life pull us away from the kingdom life and power to which our souls are heir. Jesus wants us to remove every distraction, shut every door that offers the enemy access, and fan the flame within us so we will not only discern the times, we'll be ready for His return. That posture of holy readiness means so much to God that He promises to greatly reward anyone who lives this way. Jesus' heart will be so overwhelmed by your faith that He'll serve you at a banqueting table, and then pull up a chair and share a meal with you! Imagine it. If holy readiness blesses Jesus' heart that much, don't you think it should occupy our hearts as much? Though Jesus said it's unwise to try to guess the date of His return, it is wise to pay attention to the times. Moments before Christ's return, some—including Christians—will be partying, indulging, and even rejecting everything that matters to God. But may you live ready.

 ALIGN YOUR MIND Read Luke 12.

 ALIGN YOUR ACTIONS What distractions and worries keep you from living ready? Deal with them today. Imagine sharing a celebratory meal with your friend Jesus.

ALIGN YOUR HEART

Jesus, You deserve my highest praise and my holiest life! I can't wait to see You face to face. Stir up a passion in my soul. Help me to cultivate a life of holy readiness. Amen.

Communion

He took some bread and gave thanks to God for it. Then he broke it in pieces and gave it to the disciples, saying, "This is my body, which is given for you. Do this in remembrance of me."

Luke 22:19

Though His betrayal was in motion, Jesus served communion. Jesus knew that in a few short hours He would face rejection, torture, and execution. Before His followers had a chance to be traumatized by the devil's evil schemes, Jesus, in so many words, said to them, "*Remember* this. *Remember us. The enemy hasn't taken my life. I have freely given it. Though your badness once disqualified you, the Father's goodness has saved you. This is the new covenant. Though I am well aware of what lies ahead of me on that cross, my deepest desire beforehand is to be with you, break bread with you, and remind you that my promises are true. Though schemes are being devised behind my back, I want you, my beloved ones, to see my face.*" How many times do you think the disciples replayed that night in their minds, impacting them in the years to come?* When we come to the table, we honor the memory of Christ's sacrifice. We embrace the power of His transforming love. And we believe in His ability to heal, restore, and redeem every aspect of our lives.

 ALIGN YOUR MIND Read Luke 22.

 ALIGN YOUR ACTIONS The next time you have communion, slow down, be still, and ponder Jesus' heart for all who call Him Lord.

 ALIGN YOUR HEART

> *Lord, You were broken that I might be whole. Bring healing and redemption to me and through me. Amen.*

* Adapted from my book *The Uncommon Woman* (Chicago: Moody Publishers, 2008), 134–35.

The Prayer of Salvation

And Jesus replied, "I assure you, today you will be with me in paradise."
Luke 23:43

One day on my radio show, a man called in to ask about eternity. His voice quaked as he searched for answers. There were only a few minutes left before the show ended. I didn't want to miss an opportunity to pray with the man, but I didn't want to put him on the spot either. I whispered a prayer for wisdom. My clock counted down with two minutes to spare. I asked, "Sir, would you like to follow Jesus and trust Him with your eternity?" He immediately said yes. I led him in a prayer of confession, repentance, trust, and declaration that Jesus is Lord. It was beautiful. Listeners emailed afterward and said they had to pull to the side of the road because they had too many tears in their eyes to drive. We stood in awe of God's faithfulness. Then I received a jarring email from an angry listener telling me they were pulling their funding because I hadn't prayed the "Romans Road" prayer. She added a few exclamation points to make sure I felt her fury. Plenty have prayed the "right" prayer with the wrong heart. Jesus saved the thief on the cross because of a simple, heartfelt confession. Trusting in Jesus is so much more about a surrendered heart than it is about the perfect words. Thank You, Jesus.

ALIGN YOUR MIND Read Luke 23.

ALIGN YOUR ACTIONS God always cares more about your heart than He does the fanciness of your prayers. Consider your heart condition today. Confess. Realign. Pray simply.

ALIGN YOUR HEART

Lord, I surrender my heart to You. May my words and life honor You. Amen.

Light Always Wins over Darkness

The light shines in the darkness,
and the darkness can never extinguish it.
John 1:5

Dr. Jim Wilder is a Christian counselor and a neuropsychological expert. One day during an interview I asked him, "If someone battles fear, do you tell them to face it head on?" He gently said, "No. Not at all. Imagine a child afraid of the dark. A loving father would pick up his little one, embrace him, and assure him of his father's love. Once the child is at home in his father's love, together, they walk into the dark room and turn on the light. Everything starts and ends with the Father's love. From there, you start to heal."* A thick darkness covers the earth, and it's only getting darker. But the glory of the Lord shines upon us.† We don't have to fear the darkness, and we won't, as long as we're at home in the Father's love. God's love heals the heart and will heal the world. The more you allow His love to impact you, the brighter your light will shine. Jesus gives life to everything and everyone. May His life—mightily at work within you—heal your soul, make you whole, and shine brightly through you so the world will know Him too.

 ALIGN YOUR MIND Read John 1.

 ALIGN YOUR ACTIONS Consider the things that frighten you. Take some time in God's presence and reflect on God's fatherly love. Stay there until your heart is at rest once again.

 ALIGN YOUR HEART

Lord, the more I understand Your love, the less I fear the darkness. I am with You and You are with me. I have everything I need. Amen.

* My paraphrase of Dr. Wilder's answer.
† See Isaiah 60:2.

You Will See the Kingdom

> Jesus replied, "I tell you the truth, unless you are born again, you cannot see the Kingdom of God."
>
> John 3:3

Nicodemus met Jesus in the dark of night, likely to avoid the attention of his colleagues, who were continually antagonistic toward Jesus. And he sincerely wanted answers. He'd heard about Jesus' many miracles. Jesus told Nicodemus that unless he was willing to be born again, he wouldn't see the kingdom of God. We walk by faith, not by sight. We come to Jesus by faith, but then He opens our eyes to a spiritual dimension, and we begin to really see. The word *see* in the passage above translates this way: to perceive, experience, or discern. In other words, those of us who have been born again get to *see, perceive,* and *experience* the kingdom of God! When you're born again, God's Spirit takes up residence in your soul. Suddenly your tastes change. Your values are rearranged and your spiritual eyes open up. You begin to see things differently. You see status as little more than a house of cards. You see humility as a sign of high-ranking honor. Those who the world overlooks, you see and embrace as treasured souls, bearing the image of God. Surrounded by overindulgence and selfishness, you experience the outrageous joy of radical generosity. You discern the importance of faithfulness over achievement and lasting joy over fleeting sinful pleasure. Once you've been born again, you're a part of a living, active, powerful kingdom.

 ALIGN YOUR MIND Read John 3.

ALIGN YOUR ACTIONS Ask God to open your eyes to the kingdom all around you. What do you see?

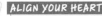 **ALIGN YOUR HEART**

Father, help me perceive, experience, and discern Your kingdom! I want more of You. Amen.

Saving Face or Saving Grace

"Come and see a man who told me everything I ever did! Could he possibly be the Messiah?"

John 4:29

She went to the well at midday to draw water, avoiding the gossip and the glares from other women. Jesus, tired from a long walk, sat down by the well. He asked for a drink of water. This woman had three strikes against her. She was a Samaritan (considered an inferior race), a woman (considered an inferior gender), and known to be living in sin. No "respectable" Jew would ever talk to someone in public under even *one* of those conditions. But Jesus will cross every social barrier to get to us. He is full of grace and truth. He treated her with honor and respect, but He also addressed the sin that He knew would destroy her. She soon realized her path to freedom. She left her water jar and ran back to face the people she'd worked so hard to avoid. The townspeople got one look at this woman and realized that their opinions held no more sway over her. Saving face had been swallowed up by saving grace. Because one woman was willing to be known as someone who needed saving, nearly a whole town decided to follow Jesus. Can you imagine the impact today if God's people cared more about saving grace than saving face?

ALIGN YOUR MIND ▸ Read John 4.

ALIGN YOUR ACTIONS ▸ Do you manage your image more than your heart? Are you more concerned about what others think than what God does? Ask God for a fresh infusion of grace and courage.

ALIGN YOUR HEART

Jesus, swallow up my tendency for saving face with Your saving grace. May others know You because of it. Amen.

Do You Want to Get Well?

When Jesus saw him and knew he had been ill for a long time, he asked him, "Would you like to get well?"

John 5:6

This story in John chapter 5 takes an interesting turn. Jesus approached a man who'd been stuck on a mat for thirty-eight years, an outcast and beggar, and asked him, "Do you want to get well?" If you've never endured long periods of pain or hardship, this might seem like a strange question. But when you suffer a long time, you get used to it, losing any sense of hope or expectancy. You build your identity around the pain—even make excuses to *not* get well. The first three words out of this man's mouth were "I can't, sir." Sometimes Jesus heals instantly. But some of us need a healing journey more than an instant miracle. We need to confront the lies we believe and the excuses we make. Like the lame man, we need a deeper healing. When Jesus told the man to stand up, pick up his mat, and walk, it took incredible courage and faith for him to obey. Because Jesus wasn't just healing him; He was confronting his fear, changing his identity, calling him into a whole new way of living. Have you identified more with your pain than God's promise? If so, it's time to rise up and walk.

ALIGN YOUR MIND ▶ Read John 5.

ALIGN YOUR ACTIONS ▶ Have you settled for pain instead of God's promises? Do you want to get well? Ask Jesus to help you rise up in hope and walk forward in faith.

ALIGN YOUR HEART

Lord, heal me from the inside out. Replace fear and lies with Your love and truth. I want to be well! Amen.

Making God in Our Image

Jesus told them, "If God were your Father, you would love me, because I have come to you from God. I am not here on my own, but he sent me."

John 8:42

*I*n every generation there's always a remnant—a small group—that fears God and honors His name. Unfortunately, the Pharisees were not this group. They fell in love with their own power, believed in their own grandeur, and used their position to manipulate systems and exploit the vulnerable. They'd fallen so far from the heart of God that they didn't recognize Him when He came to earth. Everything they accused Jesus of, they themselves were guilty of. Jesus finally replied to them, "If God were your Father, you would love Me." The same is true today. When we refuse to allow the Word of God to truly challenge and change us, we'll twist our faith to match our complacent lives, we'll pick and choose what we want to be true about God, and we'll ultimately find the Jesus of the Bible hard to understand—even offensive at times. But when we discern God's heart for righteousness, holiness, redemption, and deliverance, we will see Jesus as the much-needed Savior of the world. Jesus is the Way, the Truth, and the Life. Once we've seen Him for who He is, we've seen God for who He is.

 ALIGN YOUR MIND Read John 8.

 ALIGN YOUR ACTIONS Have you made God in your own image? This week, read the Gospels back-to-back. Ask God for a fresh revelation of himself as you read.

 ALIGN YOUR HEART

Jesus, help me to see and know You as You are—not as I think You should be. I will follow Your terms, not mine. Amen.

A More-Than-Enough Life

"The thief does not come except to steal, and to kill, and to destroy. I have come that they may have life, and that they may have it more abundantly."

John 10:10 NKJV

Our enemy searches for every opportunity to disrupt our lives, destroy our influence, and kill any hint of new life that springs up within us. Yet every time the devil makes a move, God already has a plan. Jesus came not only to destroy the devil's influence in your life, but also to give you *abundant* life, which translates this way: "Superabundance, excessive, overflowing, surplus, over and above, more than enough, profuse, extraordinary, above the ordinary, more than sufficient."* How many of us live in the overflow and surplus of God's blessings for us? This is not a prosperity gospel message. It's not about material blessings, which come and go. The truly abundant life is a life healed and whole; restored and redeemed; free and secure; full of faith, hope, and love. Those are the things the devil wants to destroy. But if we put on our spiritual armor and contend against enemy influence, we'll find the fullness Jesus offers here. The most joyful people on the planet are not the rich or famous; it's those who wholeheartedly follow Jesus and live like His promises are true.

ALIGN YOUR MIND Read John 10.

ALIGN YOUR ACTIONS Do you live the spilling-over, abundant life Jesus came to give? Why or why not? Ask God for a vision of what this kind of life looks like for you.

ALIGN YOUR HEART

Jesus, I don't want to settle for less than Your best for me! Show me what Your abundance looks like in my life. Amen.

---

* *New Spirit-Filled Life Bible*, 1461.

Remain in His Love

"I have loved you even as the Father has loved me. Remain in my love."

John 15:9

I've noticed that whenever my spiritual disciplines—like having a dedicated quiet time, making time pray, listening to worship music—start to feel like should-do's (instead of get-to's), I've lost sight of God's love. When I take beautiful practices and turn them into a checklist, I fall down every time. I lose heart. It's the Father's love that changes us, keeps us, and renews us each day. Because we're sinners, we have an uncanny aversion to grace. This takes a toll on the soul. But Jesus' victory settled all that for us. He wants us to live wholly in response to His great love for us. And though Scripture says that nothing can ever separate us from God's love,* Jesus still instructs us to remain in His love. *Why? Remain* translates this way: to be held, kept continually, to continue to be present with.† When Jesus tells you to remain in His love, He's inviting you to be continually present with Him; continually reminded of His affection for you and consistently aware of His righteousness through you. We lose our way when we lose sight of His love. This is Jesus' great gift to us—this invitation to be continually present with the One who loved us first and loves us most.

ALIGN YOUR MIND Read John 15.

ALIGN YOUR ACTIONS Spend fifteen minutes a day pondering Jesus' deep affection for you. It will change your life.

ALIGN YOUR HEART

Jesus, help me to remain continually aware of Your nearness, patience, and love. I'm held, loved, and blessed. Thank You, Lord. Amen.

---

* See Romans 8:31–39.
† Strong's Interlinear Bible Search, StudyLight.org, John 15:9.

Make Us One, Lord

"I pray that they will all be one, just as you and I are one—as you are in me, Father, and I am in you. And may they be in us so that the world will believe you sent me."

John 17:21

Some of the most powerful events I've been involved with included multiple Bible-believing denominations working together for the good of their community. They refused to divide along denominational, racial, or economic lines. For the sake of the gospel (and not at the cost of gospel truth), they joined together in biblical Christianity to bless and serve their community. Together they prayed for businesses, families, children, and the hurting and broken. Together they planned an exciting and effective event that communicated the love of a Savior who is accessible to all who would call on His name. God promises that when He sees that kind of unity, He cannot help but command a blessing.* When we identify more with our divisions than we do with our Savior's deepest desire for unity, we've lost our way. One of the last things Jesus prayed before His death was that His followers would be one—and by our unity, the world would believe God sent Him. If unity matters so much to Him, shouldn't it matter as much to us?

ALIGN YOUR MIND ▶ Read John 17.

ALIGN YOUR ACTIONS ▶ Talk with your parents or a trusted adult about denominational differences. What are ways you can support biblical unity in your home, school, church, or community?

ALIGN YOUR HEART

> *Jesus, forgive us for so easily dismissing Your heart's desire. Start with me, Lord. Show me what to do. My eyes are on You. Amen.*

* See Psalm 133:3.

Harnessed Power

As Jesus said, "I am he," they all drew back and fell to the ground!
John 18:6

Jesus gathered with His disciples in an olive grove, a place where He'd be pressed, and His will surrendered, for our sakes. The guards arrived with blazing torches and weapons at the ready. Jesus knew precisely why they'd come, so He stepped forward to meet them. Nobody took His life. He freely gave it. Imagine the scene in the heavenly realm: The angels held their breath with their swords drawn, watched every move, waited for the slightest signal from the King they loved so much. Yet He never exerted His will. He surrendered it. He asked the guards who they were looking for. They replied, "Jesus the Nazarene." As soon as He uttered the words "I am He," the power of the Godhead burst forth from Him and knocked the soldiers off their feet! It's estimated that as many as six hundred soldiers were on the scene that night to arrest Jesus. Imagine Him stepping forth in surrender and then opening His mouth in power. We in our finite minds cannot fathom what we've gained because we have Jesus, but this we know: He is our King. And there is none like Him.

 ALIGN YOUR MIND Read John 18.

 ALIGN YOUR ACTIONS Imagine the scene in the garden. Picture Jesus, confident yet humble. Think about the kind of force needed to knock six hundred soldiers to the ground without hurting them. Write out a prayer of thanksgiving.

ALIGN YOUR HEART

Jesus, there is no one like You. I want to know You more. I want to reflect Your humility, pray from a place of intimacy, and walk in Your power. Lead me onward, Lord. Amen.

Power, Not Preference

He replied, "The Father alone has the authority to set those dates and times, and they are not for you to know. But you will receive power when the Holy Spirit comes upon you. And you will be my witnesses, telling people about me everywhere—in Jerusalem, throughout Judea, in Samaria, and to the ends of the earth."

Acts 1:7–8

During the forty days after His resurrection, Jesus periodically appeared to His disciples to prove that He was alive and talk with them about the kingdom of God. The disciples asked, "Has the time come for You to free Israel and restore our kingdom?" A fair question considering they'd walked through both the trauma of their Savior's execution and the elation of seeing Him resurrected. Wouldn't the obvious next step be to overthrow Rome and liberate the Israelites? But Jesus didn't give the answer they wanted. They were still thinking about salvation through a finite earthly kingdom, not quite yet grasping the eternal implications of His mission: salvation through an everlasting heavenly kingdom for *anyone* who would trust Him—in every generation to come. He didn't placate their preferences, as understandable as they were. Instead, He promised power—a power that would give sight to the blind, strength to the weary, healing to the broken, and salvation to the lost. A power that is still changing the world today.

ALIGN YOUR MIND Read Acts 1.

ALIGN YOUR ACTIONS If God's not giving you what you want at the moment, perhaps His plan is bigger than you can imagine. Ask Him to help you see your life from an eternal perspective.

ALIGN YOUR HEART

Lord, help me to think, pray, speak, and live in proportion to Your unfailing power and love. Amen.

Death Could Not Hold Him

"But God released him from the horrors of death and raised him back to life, for death could not keep him in its grip."

Acts 2:24

When Jesus surrendered himself to die for our sins, death grabbed Him in its clutches. The devil thought he'd won. But death could not hold Him in its grip. And since Jesus destroyed the devil's claim on us, death and destruction will not have the final say in our lives. Consider Peter. Before Jesus' resurrection, he was impetuous and inconsistent. He even denied knowing Jesus! After the resurrection, Peter became bold as a lion, consistent in faith, and powerful in speech. He spoke with such authority that when people heard him, they were cut right to the heart. Whatever weaknesses, insecurities, or inconsistencies have pulled you down or defeated you, know this: The reality of Christ's resurrection is great news for you! Since death could not hold Jesus down, nothing can hold you down. You now have a High Priest, sitting at the right hand of the Father, constantly interceding for you.* Can you picture it? Jesus sits next to the Father and continually prays for you, intervenes on your behalf, and makes a way where there is no way. What's holding you back today? It's no match for the resurrection power Christ has made available to you.

ALIGN YOUR MIND Read Acts 2.

ALIGN YOUR ACTIONS What's holding you back today? Ask God to show you how He's interceding for you. Pray along with Him.

ALIGN YOUR HEART

> Lord, I sometimes forget that You are always for me. Show me what You see and how You're praying for me. I want to live in step with You. Amen.

* See Romans 8:34.

Embrace Expectancy

But Peter said, "I don't have any silver or gold for you. But I'll give you what I have. In the name of Jesus Christ the Nazarene, get up and walk!"

Acts 3:6

A man who was lame from birth was brought to the temple gate each day so he could beg. When Peter and John entered the temple, the man did what he had done every other time: He asked for money. I imagine he kept his head down when he spoke, hoping for a few coins. Peter refused to help this man remain a beggar. In his fierce, powerful way, Peter charged him, "Look at us!" Repetition makes us look down. Expectancy compels us to look up. Author and pastor Jeff Manion once said, "It's one thing to stick with something for a long time. It's another thing altogether to keep your heart in it." So true. We so often settle for a powerless life without even realizing it. And, like the men who brought the lame man to the temple to beg, the people around us accommodate our settled-for life. Peter raised the standard that day. He offered what God had entrusted to him: resurrection power. Before everyone's eyes, the man's feet and ankles were instantly healed and strengthened. Refuse to settle. Don't just go through the motions. Embrace expectancy that God will move—and will do a work greater than you imagine. Resurrection power is available to you today.

ALIGN YOUR MIND Read Acts 3.

ALIGN YOUR ACTIONS Ask God to show you where He wants your sense of expectancy to make a comeback.

ALIGN YOUR HEART

Jesus, I don't want to settle for less than Your best for me! Raise up a new standard of faith and expectancy within me. Amen.

Unschooled and Ordinary

> When they saw the courage of Peter and John and realized that they were unschooled, ordinary men, they were astonished and they took note that these men had been with Jesus.
>
> Acts 4:13 NIV

I've always admired those with multiple degrees. Several times over the years, I've applied and been accepted to a university to further my education. Each time I prepared to return to the fray of textbooks, tests, and hours of study, I was offered a new book contract. The timing was just never right. Truth is, I wanted to go back to school for validation, but validation is never a good reason for a believer to do anything. Education is wonderful and important. But after seeking the Lord for my path, I realized He wanted me to move forward in faith, trusting that He's more than enough validation for me. Scripture says that He's given us everything we need for life and godliness. The very power that raised Jesus from the grave is alive in us. The people who watched Peter and John were astonished because they were unschooled, ordinary men whose lives were marked by an otherworldly power, boldness, and wisdom. Clearly, they'd been with Jesus. Whether you head to college, trade school, or straight into the workforce after high school, there's no substitute for the power of God that comes through intimate oneness with Jesus.

 ALIGN YOUR MIND Read Acts 4.

 ALIGN YOUR ACTIONS Ask God if you've allowed anything to disqualify you from serving Him powerfully.

 ALIGN YOUR HEART

Jesus, You have a different plan for each of us. Help me to follow where You lead. When I look to anything but You, I miss the resurrection power that comes from You. You're more than enough for me. Amen.

The Danger of Facade

He brought part of the money to the apostles, claiming it was the full amount. With his wife's consent, he kept the rest.

Acts 5:2

The Church had begun. People, filled with the Holy Spirit, worshiped and shared meals together. The wealthy sold their possessions so the poor had enough to eat. There were no needy people among them. In come Ananias and Sapphira. They sold some property—and then lied about the amount of their offering. Nobody forced them to sell their property, and nobody demanded they give a certain amount. So why lie? Greed. Pride. Appearance. Maybe, in their minds, saying they gave *all* their money might make them seem more spiritual, get them praise and attention, even position them for a prominent role in the budding Church. We are guilty of the same when we create a false image of who we are—and it's so easy to do in the age of social media. We want the attention, praise, and promotion, so we edit the pictures, conceal part of the truth, control the narrative and image we present to the world. But when we put on a facade, we open the door to the enemy's destruction in our lives. The enemy is the father of lies. Jesus is the Truth that sets us free. God doesn't have unrealistic expectations of us, but He does expect us to be honest and real so we can grow. Jesus intends to redeem the real person. Not the pretend one.

ALIGN YOUR MIND Read Acts 5.

ALIGN YOUR ACTIONS In what ways are you controlling your image? Be honest and real—and shut down any facades.

ALIGN YOUR HEART

> *Lord, here I am. All of me. Change me from the inside out. Amen.*

If God Has Made It Clean

Peter told them, "You know it is against our laws for a Jewish man to enter a Gentile home like this or to associate with you. But God has shown me that I should no longer think of anyone as impure or unclean."

Acts 10:28

I once walked away from a conversation I so wished I'd handled differently. A woman shared someone's redemption story, but instead of celebrating the new things God had done, she wrinkled her nose and spoke disdainfully of the sordid details from this redeemed woman's past. I tried to move the conversation to the positive, but to no avail. I wish I would have stopped the flow completely and reminded the speaker that if Jesus has chosen to forget this woman's sins *and ours*, we should too. After Jesus' resurrection, the Holy Spirit empowered the disciples to turn the world upside down. He also blew to smithereens their preconceived ideas. One day during a time of prayer, the Lord showed Peter that the Gentiles were not unclean or inferior people. Jesus loved and came to save them too. Your journey and mine—with all of its twists and turns, highs and lows—is sacred, holy ground to our Father. We'd be wise to treat one another's stories with the kind of love, honor, and consideration our Father has shown us. Don't call something unclean that Jesus has declared clean, precious, forgiven, and free.

ALIGN YOUR MIND Read Acts 10.

ALIGN YOUR ACTIONS Are you hanging on to salacious parts of your story or another's? Give those to God and thank Him for washing us clean.

ALIGN YOUR HEART

Lord, I remember all of the wrong things. Purify my heart so I see every story through Your eyes. Amen.

When Prison Walls Shake

Suddenly, there was a massive earthquake, and the prison was shaken to its foundations. All the doors immediately flew open, and the chains of every prisoner fell off!

Acts 16:26

Paul and Silas were severely beaten and thrown into a deep dungeon, but something happened in that dark dungeon that thwarted the enemy's plans. Paul and Silas prayed and worshiped, and the other prisoners heard them. The earth quaked, the prison walls shook, and the chains of every prisoner fell off! Paul even had the opportunity to lead the jailer *and his household* to faith in Jesus. When life circumstances throw us into a pit and we're at the end of ourselves, the most powerful, strategic thing we can do is to pray and worship. After all, we have access to the inner throne room of the Most High God. And He makes His home among the praises of His people. People are always watching how we respond to hardship; our response to our trials has the potential to set captives free. During one of my dark seasons, God seemed silent and I felt abandoned. In the blackness of my bedroom, I dropped to my knees, lifted my hands, and worshiped—and I could feel the oppression lift. We worship because He's worth it, regardless of our circumstances. And He promises to strengthen those whose hearts are turned toward Him.*

ALIGN YOUR MIND ▶ Read Acts 16.

ALIGN YOUR ACTIONS ▶ How do you respond to trials? Next time you face hardship, turn your heart toward God, pray with persistence, and worship with passion.

ALIGN YOUR HEART ▶

> *Father, may I always shine for You, even in my darkest moments. Give me strength to worship in all seasons of life. Amen.*

* See 2 Chronicles 16:9.

Face the Facts, yet Still Believe

> And Abraham's faith did not weaken, even though, at about 100 years of age, he figured his body was as good as dead. . . . Abraham never wavered in believing God's promise. In fact, his faith grew stronger, and in this he brought glory to God.
>
> Romans 4:19–20

I once heard a story about a woman who, when given heartbreaking news, laughed at it as a twisted act of faith. My heart broke for this dear woman. Faith isn't about denial. It's about deliverance. Faith faces the facts head on and declares, "While you may be true, truer still is God's Word and His promise to me. I will err on the side of faith (not fear) until my own eyes see how the Lord will come through for me." I once wrote a paraphrased prayer after studying Abraham's faith in Romans chapter 4. May it encourage you: *Without weakening in my faith, I will face the fact that there are many reasons I should not be able to fulfill the call of God in my life. But I will not waver in unbelief regarding the promises of God. No, I will be strengthened in my faith, giving glory to God because I am fully persuaded that God has the power and is able to do what He's promised. Therefore, I put no confidence in my weaknesses or obstacles. I put all of my confidence in the faithfulness of almighty God, who daily establishes His purposes for me!*

 ALIGN YOUR MIND ▶ Read Romans 4.

 ALIGN YOUR ACTIONS ▶ Personalize the prayer above and make it your own.

 ALIGN YOUR HEART ▶

> *Lord, give me strength to face the facts and faith to see mountains move, hearts restored, and lives forever changed. Amen.*

A Place of Undeserved Privilege

Because of our faith, Christ has brought us into this place of undeserved privilege where we now stand, and we confidently and joyfully look forward to sharing God's glory.

Romans 5:2

Several times in my life, I've been invited to a place at the table among notable leaders. Each time, I looked around and couldn't help but feel I didn't belong. I felt utterly in over my head and completely dependent on the Lord. I even prayed I wouldn't make a fool of myself. That sense of undeserved privilege will never be lost on me. In Christ Jesus, we have a place at the table of grace. In fact, we have the same right standing before the Father as Jesus does. Righteous. Holy. Redeemed. Without fault. We've not earned our way there. We don't deserve such status and advantage. Yet we now have the rights of an heir. We have the privileges of royalty. We have access to God himself and heavenly help. We are no longer earthbound travelers. We are citizens of heaven. We've placed all of our trust in Christ and in His death and victory over our sin. God will never look at us the same way again. He'll never see you through the filter of your sins or wandering ways. He's not hung up on your weaknesses. When He looks at you, He sees pure, spotless righteousness. What a blessing to stand in this place!

ALIGN YOUR MIND ▶ Reads Romans 5.

ALIGN YOUR ACTIONS ▶ Do you see yourself as royalty? What's stopping you from living as an heir?

ALIGN YOUR HEART ▶

Father, I stand before You in a place of divine privilege. Help me to grasp it and live in a manner worthy of Your name. Amen.

Shut the Door

When he died, he died once to break the power of sin. But now that he lives, he lives for the glory of God. So you also should consider yourselves to be dead to the power of sin and alive to God through Christ Jesus.

Romans 6:10–11

Oftentimes after major output, we're tired, weary, and especially susceptible to enemy attack. The recovery community uses the acronym HALT to remind them when to guard their hearts and their steps. Hungry. Angry. Lonely. Tired. These apply to us too. One day after a big event, I sensed the enemy waiting for me to stumble and fall. I felt weak and vulnerable, so I alerted my intercessors and asked them to pray. One friend shared a dream she'd had the night before. In the middle of the night, a man tried to break in the front door. She ran to the door to find his arm reaching through, trying to pull down the chain lock. She slammed the door shut and called the police. She said, "We have the spiritual reinforcements we need, but sometimes we need to build a stronger door." We all leave certain doors open—or unlocked—which grants the enemy easy access to our lives at just the wrong time. Maybe you need to shut the door on fear, unforgiveness, worry, rebellion, overindulgence, performance, or self-pity. Remember, the enemy's intent is to destroy you, so shut the door on him. Live the full, rich life Christ died to give you.

ALIGN YOUR MIND ▸ Read Romans 6.

ALIGN YOUR ACTIONS ▸ Ask God to show you any open doors in your life. Shut them.

ALIGN YOUR HEART

Jesus, show me where I'm vulnerable. Help me to build a stronger door. Amen.

Life to Your Body

The Spirit of God, who raised Jesus from the dead, lives in you. And just as God raised Christ Jesus from the dead, he will give life to your mortal bodies by this same Spirit living within you.

Romans 8:11

When we trust Jesus for salvation, His Spirit takes up residence in our souls. Jesus was buried under the heap of the world's sin. And the very power that raised Him from the grave is now alive in us. The phrase *lives in you* translates "dwells." His Spirit actually abides—finds its home—within us. And the phrase *give life to your mortal bodies* means, "spiritual power that invigorates, restores life, endues with new and greater power in life."* Is God's Word true? Yes! Is His power alive within you? Yes! Is it possible that the same Spirit that raised Christ from the grave is able to give strength to your bones and add fresh energy to your steps? Yes, yes, it is. Yet as we contend for His power and health in our physical bodies, it's incredibly important to engage our faith by doing what we can, and then trusting God to do what only He can. Every step we take toward healing and wholeness matters. May Jesus show you your next steps.

ALIGN YOUR MIND ▶ Read Romans 8:1–17.

ALIGN YOUR ACTIONS ▶ You're never too young to make healthy adjustments. Prayerfully ask God to show you one thing you can change today that will put you on a healthier path.

ALIGN YOUR HEART

Lord Jesus, Your Spirit is alive and at work in me! Show me what needs to change in my life. Infuse my body with the power of Your Spirit. Amen.

* Strong's Interlinear Bible Search, StudyLight.org, Romans 8:11.

A Foretaste of Glory

And we believers also groan, even though we have the Holy Spirit within us as a foretaste of future glory. . . .

Romans 8:23

The time I was devastated by a friendship betrayal, I felt the Lord's comfort and peace. The Holy Spirit whispered to me to rise up and pray for my enemies. There have been countless moments when God's love has flooded my soul and swallowed up my insufficiency: the time I felt prompted to call a friend with a precise and powerful word of encouragement, or the time I stepped up to speak, feeling fragile and weak, only to have His power rise up within me with great clarity and boldness. There's nothing like the movement of God's Holy Spirit within us; this is how we know we belong to Him.* Those profound otherworldly moments are just a taste of things to come. Jesus gave us His Holy Spirit as a promise to us that He's coming for us. And when He does, He'll redeem every aspect of our stories. We'll see with new eyes. And what we see will take our breath away. Never minimize or underestimate the power and the presence of the Holy Spirit in your life. He offers peace, comfort, correction, and direction. He empowers and awakens. The more deeply you know God's Word, the more clearly you'll discern His voice.

ALIGN YOUR MIND Read Romans 8:18–39.

 ALIGN YOUR ACTIONS Memorize Romans 8:38–39 this week. Recall the Holy Spirit's recent activity in your life, and thank the Lord.

 ALIGN YOUR HEART

> *Father, thank You for Your presence in my life. Fine-tune my ears to hear Your voice above all others. Amen.*

* See Romans 8:16.

Everything

For everything comes from him and exists by his power and is intended for his glory. All glory to him forever! Amen.

Romans 11:36

Have you ever walked through a long battle, fought valiantly, taken ground inch by inch, only to wonder if and when God might step in? I've had to fight hard for my health. One day my attitude ventured into dangerous territory. I went from crying out to God to questioning when He would do His part. I shudder to remember or even admit this now. In His fatherly, authoritative way, He questioned me, *"Susie, who provided you with the funds to go to the doctor and purchase what you need?"* Immediately, I buckled. "You, Lord." He wasn't finished with me. *"Who keeps your heart beating and puts breath in your lungs without fail? Who has offered you a support system to weather this battle? And who has promised that you'd emerge stronger and wiser than you were when you started?"* Again, I could barely speak. "It's You, Lord. Only You." The next morning, this passage from Romans absolutely undid me. Everything comes from Him, is sustained by His power, and exists for His glory. Even our faith is a gift from Him, to be offered back to Him. We own nothing that didn't first come from His hand. Our very life-breath is His intentional gift to us. May we never forget it.

ALIGN YOUR MIND ▸ Read Romans 11.

ALIGN YOUR ACTIONS ▸ Thank God for the gifts that you've either taken credit for or taken for granted.

ALIGN YOUR HEART ▸

Lord, You've given me Your life and breath and purpose and promises. Help me not to forget that everything comes from You and is sustained by You, for Your glory. Amen.

Surrender and Be Revived

And so, dear brothers and sisters, I plead with you to give your bodies to God because of all he has done for you.

Romans 12:1

One day on my show, Chip Ingram shared some interesting insight. "People often ask me how to get unstuck," he said. "My answer always surprises them. I say, 'Surrender. Let go of whatever you're white-knuckling right now. Let it go and offer your whole self to God with a heart of surrender. I believe personal revival will come.'"* We lose power when we cling to our own way. We lose heart when we strive to force an outcome. And we lose perspective when our thoughts get stuck on our own will. Rest, rejuvenation, and revival come when we simultaneously release our cares and cling more firmly to Jesus. We then reset our gaze and renew our mind with thoughts of God's goodness, His faithfulness, and His sovereignty in our lives. When we walk in step with Him, He leads us even when we're unaware. A mind conformed to the world is obsessed and occupied with the small story, with things that will burn up and pass away. When your mind is transformed by God, you see redemption possibilities all around you. You're occupied with God's presence and His profound affection for you. You trust Him because you know Him.

ALIGN YOUR MIND Read Romans 12.

ALIGN YOUR ACTIONS What are you clinging to too tightly? Close your eyes, open your hands, and prayerfully release whatever comes to mind.

ALIGN YOUR HEART

> *Lord Jesus, I surrender my whole life to You! Forgive me for clinging to things I cannot control. I trust You, Lord. Revive my heart once again. Amen.*

* My paraphrase of Chip's insight.

An Accumulative Spiritual Wealth

Through him, God has enriched your church in every way—with all of your eloquent words and all of your knowledge.

1 Corinthians 1:5

We so often measure God's ability and our capacity in small increments. I remember a time when I was heading into a big weekend of ministry, yet I felt so drained from sickness, sleepless nights, and a glaring sense of my own weak humanity. I went to my knees and asked the Lord for strength. He reminded me that He'd forged a deep well within me over the years. That we have a history together. He's not limited by a bad week, so I don't have to be either. In his devotional *Sparkling Gems from the Greek*, Rick Renner writes about the word *enriched* in the passage above; it's *ploutizo*, where we get the word "plutocrat"—someone who is so wealthy that his handlers cannot give him a definitive number on his wealth because it's accruing at such a fast rate. When we walk with the Lord day in and day out, we accrue a spiritual wealth that multiplies faster than we can imagine. We gather a lifetime of wisdom, experiences, and insights from walking with our Savior. Don't let a bad day or a bad week throw you off. You're richer than you know.

ALIGN YOUR MIND ▶ Read 1 Corinthians 1:1–9.

ALIGN YOUR ACTIONS ▶ When you have an off day, step back and remind yourself how rich you are in Christ Jesus. Tell your soul what's true.

ALIGN YOUR HEART ▶

Father, I can be so shortsighted at times. I'm supremely wealthy in You! When my well feels dry, help me to draw from Your endless supply. Thank You, Lord. Amen.

God Chooses the Weak

God chose things despised by the world, things counted as nothing at all, and used them to bring to nothing what the world considers important.

1 Corinthians 1:28

Mine was an impossible situation. How could God possibly take a terminally insecure girl, full of self-contempt and fear, and deliver her from all of those things? I feared trauma. I feared rejection. I feared others' opinions. I was my own worst enemy; I didn't know how to cut myself some slack. Yet somehow, by the miracle of God's grace, He first saved my soul, and then over the years has made me whole. People who see me now think of me as strong, feisty, and bold. Maybe parts of me really are, but I have more healing to go. And I remember so well who I was when He found me. I've met many Christians along the way who'd say the same thing. They operate at high levels even by the world's standards, but there's no hint of pride or self-importance in them—only humility and gratitude. They remember where they came from and how God saved them. God specializes in taking nobodies and making them somebodies. The world can't figure it out because it makes no sense. God gets the most glory when He's the one who writes our story.

 ALIGN YOUR MIND Read 1 Corinthians 1:10–31.

 ALIGN YOUR ACTIONS When you feel unimportant, weak, or less than, remind yourself that God chose you—and He's not done writing your story. When you feel on top of things, stay humble, remembering where your strength comes from.

 ALIGN YOUR HEART

Lord, I was nobody, and You're making me a somebody. I'm forever grateful. Use my weakness for Your glory. Amen.

What God Has Freely Given You

We have received God's Spirit (not the world's spirit), so we can know the wonderful things God has freely given us.

1 Corinthians 2:12

A listener who called in to my show struggled to get her words out. She'd had an abortion and couldn't get out from underneath the weight of shame and guilt. My heart broke for her. I felt nudged to ask, "Dear one, have you ever prayed and asked Jesus to forgive your sins, heal your soul, and save you for all eternity?" "No," she said through tears. "That's why I called in." My heart beat quickly as I led her through the prayer of salvation. Together we declared Jesus as Lord and asked God to forgive her, cleanse her, and fill her to overflowing. I pictured the Holy Spirit taking up residence in her soul and guiding her all her days. She cried tears of joy as we said good-bye. Life is so painful, yet we're not meant to sort it out on our own. We need Jesus. We need our heavenly Father. We're desperate for the Holy Spirit's influence. One of the reasons God gave us the Holy Spirit is so we can know the things He has freely given us: Access. Grace. Forgiveness. Mercy. Grace. Power. Insight. Direction. Grace. Wisdom. Freedom. Redemption. Oceans and oceans of grace. A life redeemed. Promises fulfilled. Praise His Name.

ALIGN YOUR MIND Read 1 Corinthians 2.

ALIGN YOUR ACTIONS Ask the Spirit to direct you to a Scripture passage you need today. Write a prayer of praise for all God has given you.

ALIGN YOUR HEART

> Father, You've given me everything. Help me to discern all You've offered and let it change me forever. Amen.

What You Think of Me

As for me, it matters very little how I might be evaluated by you or by any human authority. I don't even trust my own judgment on this point. My conscience is clear, but that doesn't prove I'm right. It is the Lord himself who will examine me and decide.

1 Corinthians 4:3–4

Even Paul, an apostle highly regarded, was not immune to others' judgment. And while most of us rush to defend ourselves, if only in our own minds, he does the opposite—not even trusting his own judgment. He knew the truth that we only see as through a glass dimly,* and the opinions and wrath of others will come to nothing.† Only God is eternal, just, and all-knowing. Only His opinion counts—and He gave His only son for *you*. So today, refuse to waste any more brain space worrying about people's ever-changing opinions. Instead, fill your mind with this truth from Isaiah: "Because the Lord, the Eternal, helps me I will not be disgraced; so, I set my face like rock, confident that I will not be ashamed."‡

ALIGN YOUR MIND > Read 1 Corinthians 4.

ALIGN YOUR ACTIONS > Practice a zero-tolerance policy when it comes to thoughts about others' opinions. If you catch yourself worrying over what others think of you, stop in your tracks and say out loud (in private might be best ☺), "It matters little what you think of me. It doesn't even matter what I think of me! With God as my helper, I will not be ashamed."

ALIGN YOUR HEART

> *Father, I'm done allowing others' opinions to dominate my mind, time, and self-esteem. Fill my heart and mind with thoughts of You. Amen.*

---

* See 1 Corinthians 13:12.
† See Isaiah 51:13.
‡ Isaiah 50:7 VOICE.

Purpose in Every Step

So I run with purpose in every step. I am not just shadowboxing.
1 Corinthians 9:26

Have you ever seen a boxer warming up before a match? They're crouched in their fighting stance, bouncing on their toes, throwing punches at the empty air. That's shadowboxing. It serves a purpose, but if all you ever do is punch the air, you'll never win a match. Disciplined athletes know this, and we should too. There's a distinct purpose for every season in our lives. Training will look different from one season to the next. People who do the same thing in every season rarely gain momentum and often lack vision. There's a time to gain ground, to hold your ground, and to recover lost ground. There's a time to learn new skills, to reaffirm timeless truths, and to receive fresh input. There's a time to pull back and recover and a time to step out and take risks. Paul reminds us in this passage that to run your race with purpose in every step, you need discipline. You need to discern the season God has you in right now. And remember, wisdom's path is always peace.

ALIGN YOUR MIND ➤ Read 1 Corinthians 9.

ALIGN YOUR ACTIONS ➤ Spend time with a parent or trusted friend and talk through the season you're in right now. Prayerfully discern where your focus should be.

ALIGN YOUR HEART

Father, help me to discern where You have me right now. Help me run this race to win the prize. Show me the wisdom in discipline and the weight of my choices. Amen.

The Four I-Sins

These things happened as a warning to us, so that we would not crave evil things as they did. . . .

1 Corinthians 10:6

The Israelites had experienced God in miraculous ways, yet their history with Him was never compelling enough to keep them from repeatedly wandering toward self-destruction. Their painful journey serves as a cautionary tale for us. Consider their four I-sins: Idolatry, Immorality, Irreverence, and Irritation. The first two say to God, "I want more!" while the second two shout, "I am more!" *Idolatry* is born out of discontentment. When we loosen our grip on God's goodness, our eyes start to wander. Once our spiritual amnesia kicks in, we try lesser gods to see if they might satisfy. *Immorality* is often born out of unhealed brokenness, and sometimes out of just plain decadent sinfulness. Yet we destroy our bodies and our souls when we walk through this door. *Irreverence* comes from pride and ignorance: we value our opinion above God's and before we realize it, honor and awe fall by the wayside. *Irritation* springs from entitlement: we think we deserve more than God, or others, are giving us at the moment. If we rehearse those four thought patterns long enough, they'll spew out of us. What's the remedy? Identify and then rid yourself of those thoughts and patterns. Strengthen your walk with the Lord. Remember His love. Rely on His goodness.

 ALIGN YOUR MIND Read 1 Corinthians 10.

 ALIGN YOUR ACTIONS Identify which I-sin you're most drawn to and why. In prayer, shut those doors and ask God to fill your soul with true satisfaction. Make a note to do this every few months.

 ALIGN YOUR HEART

> *Lord, I'm prone to wander. Bind my heart to Yours. You are good. I love You. Amen.*

Love Heals and Redeems

Three things will last forever—faith, hope, and love—and the greatest of these is love.

1 Corinthians 13:13

Curled up in a ball in my bed, I held fistfuls of my bedsheets and blinked back my tears. We had just returned from the ER, where doctors had told Kev they thought I had multiple sclerosis (MS), a disabling neurological disease.* I could barely look at my husband. We were so young, with three little boys, and he'd already endured so much with me. Fear put such a choke-hold on my perspective that I asked my husband to divorce me. Sobbing, I begged, "Please. Marry someone who loves Jesus, who will love and play with our boys." Clearly, I wasn't thinking. My pain was speaking. Kneeling at my bedside, Kev put his finger over my lips and said, "You stop that right now. You are my bride and always will be. If I have to kneel down and kiss you because you're in a wheelchair, then that's what I'll do." I was honestly shocked. I'll never forget that tangible display of the Father's love. Unconditional love heals the heart like nothing ever could. We self-sabotage and push others away because of fear and insecurity. Yet every heart is desperate to be loved amid their brokenness. May you know and experience the kind of love that heals and redeems.

ALIGN YOUR MIND Read 1 Corinthians 13.

ALIGN YOUR ACTIONS You don't need to be married to love in a way that heals and redeems. Ask God to love through you in a way that's beyond you.

ALIGN YOUR HEART

Father, thank You for the countless ways You love me. Heal me completely so I can love that way too. Amen.

* My diagnosis turned out to be Lyme disease.

Strong and Steadfast

So, my dear brothers and sisters, be strong and immovable. Always work enthusiastically for the Lord, for you know that nothing you do for the Lord is ever useless.

1 Corinthians 15:58

I've spoken to many ministry leaders who've gone through painful seasons when they've been easily dismissed or replaced. They poured their hearts into serving the Lord, only to be tossed aside as if none of it meant anything to anybody. They're not the only ones. Friends pour into a friendship only to have the other betray their trust. Athletes pour hours and hours into honing God-given talents only to be benched the entire season. You do a selfless act of service for someone only to have them make fun of you for it. Only God knows why things shake out the way they do. But one thing He promises: your work for Him, your faith steps, your heartfelt prayers, your selfless love and service are never wasted. Every time a believer serves God in any capacity, heaven takes note. Records are kept for a future reward. And the current atmosphere is changed because you—as a faith-filled person—are part of it. You won't know this side of heaven how profoundly your service impacted the greater kingdom story, but someday you will. Let it be enough for now to know that nothing you do for Jesus is ever wasted.

 ALIGN YOUR MIND Read 1 Corinthians 15.

 ALIGN YOUR ACTIONS This week, add faith and joy to every one of your deeds. Picture the eternal impact. Leave the results to God.

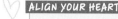 **ALIGN YOUR HEART**

Father, You are so good to me. You've collected my tears of sorrow and frustration and remembered my service for future reward. My delight is in You. Amen.

Comforted Comforters

He comforts us in all our troubles so that we can comfort others. When they are troubled, we will be able to give them the same comfort God has given us.

2 Corinthians 1:4

I once ran into an author friend whose son is in prison. This woman has taken a parent's worst nightmare and turned it into a mighty ministry for those whose lives have been turned upside down by crime. She's someone who is very present and looks deep into your eyes when you speak. When I saw her and she saw me, her compassion undid me. I couldn't hide it anymore. I broke down and told her about my son who'd lost his way. She wrapped me up in a hug and cried with me. My trial was akin to a mud puddle if hers was a tsunami. Yet she'd received such comfort from the Lord, she had more than enough comfort for me when I needed it. God comforts us in our pain and sends messengers when we need them most. And as we arise out of the ashes of our pain, we're wiser and braver so we can truly help those God puts in our path. My son returned to the faith and is now a godly husband and father. I'm a grateful momma who has endless compassion for parents of prodigals. Christlike comfort changes us.

ALIGN YOUR MIND Read 2 Corinthians 1.

ALIGN YOUR ACTIONS How has God comforted you? Ask Him to bring someone into your path whom you can comfort with what you've received. Watch God grow your compassion before your very eyes.

ALIGN YOUR HEART

God of all comfort, hold me close and heal my heart. Use me for those who need what You've imparted to me. Amen.

Where the Spirit of the Lord Is

For the Lord is the Spirit, and wherever the Spirit of the Lord is, there is freedom.

2 Corinthians 3:17

When the Holy Spirit is given free rein in our lives, He gives us the desire to do the very things that bring Him glory, allow us to flourish, and move His purposes forward.* It's the precious Spirit of God that winces within us when we say something we shouldn't, do something we ought not do, or consider something that would ultimately destroy us. It's that same Spirit who fills us with peace when we're on the right track, about to make the right decision or take a faith risk that makes no sense. The word *freedom* in this passage isn't a freedom to live as we want; it's the freedom to be everything God intended us to be. When the Spirit moves in our midst, He moves obstacles out of our way, and sometimes those obstacles are within us. When we set our minds on the things above, on the things of the Spirit, we experience life and peace.† When we come to Christ for the first time, He fills us with His Holy Spirit and does so continually as we walk with Him and stay sensitive to His guidance in our lives. God gets the glory and we are set free when we're continually in step with the Spirit of God.

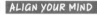 **ALIGN YOUR MIND** Read 2 Corinthians 3.

 ALIGN YOUR ACTIONS Where have you not given the Holy Spirit free rein in your life? Why? Repent today, listen to His whisper, and pay attention to His nudge inside you.

 ALIGN YOUR HEART

Holy Spirit, fall afresh on me. Lead me onward. Amen.

---

* See Philippians 2:13.
† See Romans 8:6–8.

We Carry This Treasure

> But this beautiful treasure is contained in us—cracked pots made of earth and clay—so that the transcendent character of this power will be clearly seen as coming from God and not from us.
>
> 2 Corinthians 4:7 VOICE

I have a nephew who, when he was little, was the clumsiest little fellow I knew. Yet his momma still allowed him to carry the breakables from the car to the house at family gatherings. One time I watched him carry a glass casserole dish, cheering him on, but in a matter of moments, I heard him holler from outside, "Whoooaaa!" and I knew he'd landed in the shrubs. Which he did. The squirrels were thrilled. I think of that moment every time I ponder the idea that Jesus lives in me—someone who all too often falls in the shrubs and drops the dinner. It's like He's entrusted the family heirloom to a toddler. More so, He has made us a kingdom of priests, a holy nation, His prized possession. We carry this treasure—the presence and the power of the living God—in these earthen vessels so that we'll constantly remember that this power comes from Him. We lose heart when we're more surprised by our badness than we are His goodness. God knew who He was getting when He saved us. He's thrilled to count us as His own. With our mistakes and missteps, we're still His treasure, where He dwells.

ALIGN YOUR MIND Read 2 Corinthians 4.

ALIGN YOUR ACTIONS You carry the greatest treasure in the world—what will you do with it? How will your life change?

ALIGN YOUR HEART

Father, I'm so honored that You dwell with me. All glory and honor belong to You. Amen.

Live by Believing, Not by Seeing

For we live by believing and not by seeing.
2 Corinthians 5:7

Why do we need to live by faith and not by sight? Because oftentimes, what our eyes see contradicts what God's Word says. We'd like to place God's promises over every moment of our lives and see them perfectly aligned at all times, but that will never be our experience this side of heaven. God's promises come to pass over time, much like His prophecies. We will experience times and seasons when it looks, feels, and seems like God's promises aren't true at all. But they are. *That's what faith is for.* If we tether ourselves to a specific outcome, we'll be disappointed. If we expect God to operate on our timeline, we will be disappointed. "Paul reminds us that though we may think we are at the end of our rope, we are never at the end of our hope."* Remember, faith is for the long journey, and promises take time to come to fruition. But ask any serious praying believer and they'll tell you this: The answers do come. Once you've learned the secret of abiding in Christ, relying on His Word, praying His promises, and staying in it for the long haul, you'll never rely on anything else like you rely on God. Live by faith today.

 ALIGN YOUR MIND Read 2 Corinthians 5.

 ALIGN YOUR ACTIONS What circumstances are holding your gaze and stealing your joy? Switch your gaze to God's promises and engage your faith by believing them.

 ALIGN YOUR HEART

> *Father, I look to You. I believe You. I will wait for You. Your promises are true, and You are faithful to Your Word. Amen.*

* *Life Application Study Bible*, 2569.

We Serve God No Matter What

We serve God whether people honor us or despise us, whether they slander us or praise us. We are honest, but they call us impostors. We are ignored, even though we are well known.

2 Corinthians 6:8–9

This faith journey isn't for sissies. We endure hardship, betrayal, accusation, and slander. But we also see miracles and lives changed, and we get to partner with God in a way that transforms us. The tricky thing is that we live in a time when Christian ministry and service can quickly turn to status points, morphing well-intentioned Christians into celebrities, even if just in their own churches or communities. That's when motives may falter, and we may develop an attachment to our position, the power or status that comes with it, and the idea that our worth is tied up in it all. That's why God allows our house of cards to come crashing down. It's not good for us, and it doesn't glorify God when we "serve" Him in a way that mostly serves us. Paul modeled this better than anyone. If you've been dissed, dismissed, or overlooked, don't squander your influence by taking offense or taking it out on God. Determine that you'll serve your King no matter who's looking. He's the ultimate authority and the One who rewards your faith. When it's all about His kingdom and not yours, you'll not only survive your battles, you'll thrive in spite of them.

ALIGN YOUR MIND Read 2 Corinthians 6.

ALIGN YOUR ACTIONS Take some time to consider your motives today. Are you seeking first His kingdom or yours?

ALIGN YOUR HEART

> *Heavenly Father, I bow before You. I'm at Your service. Show me what obedience looks like in this season. Amen.*

Waves of Increase

You will be made rich in everything so that your generosity will spill over in every direction. Through us your generosity is at work inspiring praise and thanksgiving to God.

2 Corinthians 9:11 VOICE

Our finances were a mess, yet we longed to live freely and generously. When God brought us to this passage, it jumped off the page and into our hearts. He whispered to us His truth: *I will provide seed for you as you begin to sow. I will supply and increase your store of seed and enlarge the harvest of your righteousness. You'll be made rich in every way so that you can be generous on every occasion, causing many to thank me because you dared to trust me as your provider.* Suddenly I had a vision of being generous not just with our finances, but also with our time, our prayers, our kindness, and our compassion. We were fearful financial sowers at the time, giving sparsely, not generously. But we began applying biblical principles to our finances, added generous sowing, and literally saw the enemy's plan for our resources fall apart. Looking back, I am awestruck by God's faithfulness to His word. The more we sowed, the more waves rippled back to us so that we could become even more generous than before. I have a dream to see every believer walk in the flourishing generosity God offers them.

 ALIGN YOUR MIND Read 2 Corinthians 9.

 ALIGN YOUR ACTIONS How do you steward your resources—things like your time, abilities, possessions, money, prayer, kindness? Do you give generously or joyfully? Why or why not? Today, give generously and joyfully to someone.

ALIGN YOUR HEART

Lord, help me be a cheerful and generous giver for Your glory. Amen.

God's Mighty Weapons

For though we walk in the world, we do not fight according to this world's rules of warfare. The weapons of the war we're fighting are not of this world but are powered by God. . . .

2 Corinthians 10:3–4 VOICE

Given the spiteful contempt we see on social media today, even among Christians, you'd think that our hope lies in the government, getting the "right" leaders in office, and protecting the "right" rights at all costs. Of course, we long for righteous leaders and a healthy government. And our freedoms are precious. But these aren't necessary for Christianity to thrive. The opposite is actually true. Across the world, the kingdom is bursting at the seams where Christianity is most vehemently opposed. We hope because Jesus died and rose again. Now, you who are filled with His Spirit have the power and the authority to take out the spiritual forces that not only oppose you, but that oppose the truth about God and His kingdom. You don't and won't win the war with clever arguments or savvy talking points. Overexposure to snide and vindictive media will only fuel your fear and empower your anger. Refuse to fight your battles as the world does. Determine to get on your knees and, in Christ's authority, pull down every stronghold and arrogant thought that exalts itself above the knowledge of God. Unless you fight your battles in the spiritual realm, you'll lose your battles in the earthly realm.

ALIGN YOUR MIND Read 2 Corinthians 10.

ALIGN YOUR ACTIONS Take your fears to God and pray against the spiritual forces that oppose His truth.

ALIGN YOUR HEART

Father, You've positioned me to fight my battles from a place of victory. Give me faith to believe. Amen.

Where Power Is Perfected

"My grace is sufficient for you, for my power is made perfect in weakness."

2 Corinthians 12:9 NIV

Paul said something very interesting in this chapter. He opted not to share too much about his experiences so that others wouldn't think more highly of him than they ought. He wanted his life to speak for itself. Most of us are the opposite: We prefer that others think more highly of us than we deserve. But Paul was so confident in his identity in Christ that he determined not to manipulate the opinions of others. God kept Paul humble so He could use Paul greatly. Paul begged for relief from his thorn in the flesh, some limitation that no doubt slowed him down and made him more dependent on God. God said no and then promised that through Paul's continual, humble dependence, he'd come to know a power he'd know no other way. We strive to manage others' opinions of us, and we beg for relief from our weaknesses. And yet when we cease striving and let our lives speak for themselves, we'll settle into a holy sense of identity. And when, in our weakness, we look for God's power to be perfected in us, we'll settle into a holy sense of contentment amid our limitations. God's grace is all about His presence, His power, and His enough-ness. And we have His grace.

ALIGN YOUR MIND Read 2 Corinthians 12.

ALIGN YOUR ACTIONS Do you strive for appearance's sake or berate yourself for your weaknesses? Ask God to help you settle into His grace and use your weakness for His glory.

ALIGN YOUR HEART

Lord, thank You for empowering me by Your grace. Keep me humble and dependent on You for Your great glory. Amen.

Setting Aside
God's Unmerited Favor

I do not set aside the grace of God, for if righteousness could be gained through the law, Christ died for nothing!

Galatians 2:21 NIV

At the end of every year, our family gathers around the table to reflect on these three questions: (1) What did God teach you this past year? (2) What life lesson will you take with you into the coming year? (3) What do you want from the Lord in the year to come (e.g., wisdom, faith, understanding, etc.)? One of our sons shared this with raw eloquence: "Launching into adulthood challenged me. Though you raised me to believe that my identity is rooted in Christ, I realized there were places of unbelief in my own soul. I looked inward at myself to try to reason with my sense of not-enough-ness, but that only left me in greater despair. Then one day the Lord impressed upon my heart that He actually *likes* my presence, likes to be with me. And that I bring value to the places where He leads me. He reminded me that as much as my earthly father loves me, He loves me that much more. I really do believe I have value because Jesus said so." We're surrounded by His favor, yet too often we set it aside to strive our way out of a hole that we're not actually in. May God give you a fresh revelation of your intrinsic value in Him.

ALIGN YOUR MIND > Read Galatians 2.

ALIGN YOUR ACTIONS > Sit with God. Ask for a deeper understanding of how much you're worth.

ALIGN YOUR HEART >

Lord, help this to sink in! I want to revel in Your unmerited favor, swim in oceans of grace, and live like I'm free! Amen.

Do We Earn Our Miracles?

I ask you again, does God give you the Holy Spirit and work miracles among you because you obey the law? Of course not! It is because you believe the message you heard about Christ.

Galatians 3:5

Isn't it something that God reached down from on high to save the lowest, most needy of humanity? None of us can proudly line up and receive a trophy because we've fulfilled the requirements of the law. With wide-eyed wonder, we stand amazed that we have a prize we did not earn. God gave us the Holy Spirit as a sign of our future inheritance and a gift of His grace. There's not one single righteous act on our part that prompted God to do such a thing for us. Even our faith is a gift from His heart to ours. It's the same with miracles. My son was miraculously healed from a serious back injury. He didn't earn it, but he did believe for it. I once interviewed Lee Strobel about his book *A Case for Miracles*, in which he researched indisputable, documented cases of miracles that cannot be explained away. I said to Lee, "It's a mystery as to why God heals some and not others. Have you noticed any common denominators?" He replied, "Only that everyone He healed believed that He could and embraced a humble, expectant posture before Him." May we all embrace such humble belief and expectancy!

 ALIGN YOUR MIND Read Galatians 3.

 ALIGN YOUR ACTIONS Do you have an impossible situation in your life? Ask for a gift of faith. Believe that miracles still happen in our day.

 ALIGN YOUR HEART

Lord, thank You for the undeserved gift of the Spirit in me—move in power through me! Amen.

How You Fall from Grace

For if you are trying to make yourselves right with God by keeping the law,
you have been cut off from Christ! You have fallen away from God's grace.

Galatians 5:4

How do you fall from grace? By trying to earn your own way. The Jewish Christians tried to impose their Jewish laws and traditions onto the Gentiles who had recently come to Christ, as if to say, "You're a substandard Christian unless you add these elements to your faith walk." Paul stepped in and said that the opposite is actually true. He went on to say, "I am a sinner if I rebuild the old system of the law I already tore down."* Dallas Willard once asked John Ortberg, "Who uses up more grace? Believers or unbelievers?" John guessed the unbelievers. Dallas replied, "No, John. Believers burn up more grace than a 747 burns up jet fuel!"† Of course our choices matter, and they'll always have consequences. We will fall into sin; it's part of being human—but that doesn't mean we automatically fall from grace. Because grace is another matter altogether. When we try to earn our way, we've lost our way. When we rely wholeheartedly on the saving, empowering grace of Jesus Christ, we find ourselves freer and happier than we had ever imagined. Amazing grace.

ALIGN YOUR MIND Read Galatians 5.

ALIGN YOUR ACTIONS In what areas do you try to earn your own way? Repent and ask for God's empowering grace to fill you.

ALIGN YOUR HEART

Lord, I marvel at Your grace. May Your Spirit constantly and continually awaken me! Amen.

* See Galatians 2:18.
† John Ortberg shared this story on my show one day.

Don't Grow Weary, the Harvest Will Come

So let's not get tired of doing what is good. At just the right time we will reap a harvest of blessing if we don't give up.

Galatians 6:9

Seattle Seahawks staffer Ben Malcolmson told a story on my show one day. When he was in college, he tried reaching his teammates for Jesus. He held prayer meetings, but no one showed. He offered to teach a Bible study; no one showed. He fasted and prayed. One day he had an idea. He put a Bible in every player's locker. He arrived at practice expectantly the next day, hoping for a breakthrough. The guys had torn their Bibles to shreds and thrown the pieces on the locker room floor. He was devastated and felt like a fool. Years later he ran into a teammate who told him a story that blew Ben away. This guy was raised in a Christian home but had wandered from the faith. He partied a lot in college. That day in the locker room, another player asked this guy about the Bible. The fallen-away Christian sat down and explained the gospel. The player came to Christ, and then died suddenly not too long after. Ben found out way after the fact that God had used his efforts to save one soul for eternity and bring another back to the faith. Never doubt God's faithfulness. Keep on keeping on. One day you'll hear stories that will take your breath away.

ALIGN YOUR MIND Read Galatians 6.

ALIGN YOUR ACTIONS When it seems like all your actions are fruitless, keep sowing. Look up. Live expectantly. The harvest will come.

ALIGN YOUR HEART

Lord, You are up to something good! Give me faith to keep sowing and believing. Amen.

Every Spiritual Blessing

All praise to God, the Father of our Lord Jesus Christ, who has blessed us with every spiritual blessing in the heavenly realms because we are united with Christ.

Ephesians 1:3

When the pandemic hit full force in 2020, an atmosphere of fear and scarcity smothered the globe. As friends and families were torn apart by lockdowns and politics, entire industries shut down, and goods and resources dwindled. People brawled in grocery stores over *toilet paper*. It was hard not to fear. But then I read this passage from Ephesians, and I felt like I could breathe again. *Help me grasp what You're saying here, Lord*, I prayed. And in the middle of a global crisis, I suddenly sensed that there were countless untapped storehouses in heaven, provisions that had never been claimed, virtues that had never been pursued. I sensed the invitation to reach up by faith and lay hold of the things I needed and longed for. When we, as Christians, give in to the earthly, not-enough mindset, it's as if we choose to live in a drought when God actually has flourishing, unending fields overflowing with all we need. We just have to ask. We're invited into the throne room, assured that we can approach the throne of grace with confidence, and make our request with humble boldness.* Seek first His kingdom, and all these things will be given to you†—not for your glory, but for His.

ALIGN YOUR MIND Read Ephesians 1.

ALIGN YOUR ACTIONS Prayerfully read Ephesians chapter 1. Dwell on His promises. Boldly ask for what you need to bring His kingdom to earth.

ALIGN YOUR HEART

> *Father, grant me the audacity to ask You for everything You long to impart to me. Amen.*

* See Hebrews 4:16.
† See Matthew 6:33.

God's Work of Art

For we are the product of His hand, heaven's poetry etched on lives, created in the Anointed, Jesus, to accomplish the good works God arranged long ago.

Ephesians 2:10 VOICE

Every Saturday our son drops our grandson off at 6:30 a.m. and picks him up at 1:30 p.m. Before they leave, we all have lunch together and spend an hour or two on the floor thoroughly enjoying our little treasure. I know others thoroughly enjoy their grandkids too, but I'm completely smitten by our little guy. I see parts of his mom and his dad in him. He is a true masterpiece. I whisper in his ear that he is mighty in God, and I tell him regularly how much his family loves him. I'm always happy to see him. I'm human and yet I love him with an otherworldly love. God is divine and yet loves you with the same passion I've described times a million. He's completely taken with you. He loves what makes you smile. He aches over what breaks your heart. He hears the silent whispers in the night. And He's right now arranging good work for you to do. God created you. You are His masterpiece, His work of art. And He didn't create you so you can sit on a shelf as wall art. He created you to change the world.

 ALIGN YOUR MIND ▶ Read Ephesians 2.

 ALIGN YOUR ACTIONS ▶ Imagine God's joy in creating you. Linger with that thought. Ask Him what good work He has assigned you in this season of your life.

 ALIGN YOUR HEART

> *Lord, I want to grasp this truth. Show me how You feel about me. Give me faith and clarity to fulfill my God-given call in this season. Amen.*

Above and Beyond

Now all glory to God, who is able, through his mighty power at work within us, to accomplish infinitely more than we might ask or think.

Ephesians 3:20

My health relapse lasted about three years. I'm on the other side now—about 95 percent recovered. Quite honestly, that journey felt like a walk through hell. When surges of symptoms overtook me, so did fear and anxiety. As I mentioned in an earlier devotion, God whispered to my heart one day, and it began a battle to uproot the lies I believed and replace them with the truths I needed. I fasted, prayed, cried out to God. I meticulously followed doctors' orders. I curled up in a ball in my dark bedroom and watched sermon after sermon. I hung on for dear life because I know God, and I knew He'd come for me. And He did. I stand here now redeemed, set free, and utterly amazed at the inner work God accomplished in me. Above and beyond what I could have imagined. God can only do through us what He's first done in us. This is a promise packed with meaning. We like to dream about the big things God might do through us. And we should. But dare to believe that God will use every enemy attack on your life to transform you into a warrior you never dreamed you could be.

ALIGN YOUR MIND Read Ephesians 3.

ALIGN YOUR ACTIONS Identify what God is working on in you. Imagine your freedom and transformation. Keep marching.

ALIGN YOUR HEART

Father, I don't like to suffer! I'm not fond of battles. But I know they'll come. So have Your way in me! Do the impossible in and through me. Amen.

Live a Life Worthy of Your Calling

Therefore I, a prisoner for serving the Lord, beg you to lead a life worthy of your calling, for you have been called by God.

Ephesians 4:1

Until Jesus returns, our two natures will constantly war within us. Our carnal nature bids us come, take the bait, eat the fruit, justify sin, hide from God. And our soul shrivels. Our spiritual nature calls us upward, into His presence, to walk in His way, taste His goodness, tremble in His presence, and experience redemption. And our soul flourishes. William MacDonald writes, "From heaven the angels are compelled to admire His unsearchable ways past finding out. They see how God triumphed over sin to His own glory. They see how He has sent heaven's Best for earth's worst. They see how He has redeemed His enemies at enormous cost, conquered them by His love. . . They see that through the work of the Lord Jesus on the cross, more glory has come to God and more blessing has come to [believers] than if sin had never been allowed to enter. God has been vindicated; Christ has been exalted; Satan has been defeated; and the church has been enthroned in Christ to share His glory."* Oh, the victory He won! Be done with lesser things. Rise up and live in a manner worthy of your calling.

 ALIGN YOUR MIND Read Ephesians 4.

 ALIGN YOUR ACTIONS Refuse to allow pettiness, drama, or distractions to keep you from the best of what God has for you.

 ALIGN YOUR HEART

> *Father, You are high and lifted up. Glorify Your Name in me. Call me higher, Lord. Amen.*

* William MacDonald, *Believer's Bible Commentary* (Nashville: Thomas Nelson, 1989), 1928.

Make the Most of Every Opportunity

Make the most of every opportunity in these evil days.
Ephesians 5:16

Once a month, my husband and I go on Facebook Live to share a few devotional thoughts and to pray for those in need. The prayer requests come in so fast, we can barely keep up with them all. We love standing in the gap with those who suffer. Recently I sensed God wanted some extra time with me prior to our session. I love spending time with Him, but this particular night, I kept saying, "Just one more minute" as I worked to gather some Bible verses for an upcoming event at our radio station. A good use of time, right? But not the *best* use of time. Though we had a great time praying for others, I felt a spiritual oppression throughout the session. Then, wouldn't you know, a troll hopped on and repeatedly called us false teachers, urging folks to stop listening to us. It was unnerving. I felt deeply convicted by God after the fact. He was only calling me to himself to prepare me ahead of time. To make the most of every opportunity is to discern God's highest and best will for you at every given moment. It translates this way: *to make wise and sacred use of every opportunity.*[*] These are evil days. Trolls are everywhere. Listen to the Lord.

ALIGN YOUR MIND Read Ephesians 5.

ALIGN YOUR ACTIONS Slow your pace and turn your face to the One who loves you most.

ALIGN YOUR HEART

> Lord, You're always watching out for me. Help me to take my every cue from You—to redeem my moments and to live a listening kind of life. Amen.

---

* Strong's Interlinear Bible Search, StudyLight.org, Ephesians 5:16.

Spiritual Warfare, Explosive Power

Above all, taking the shield of faith with which you will be able to quench all the fiery darts of the wicked one.

Ephesians 6:16 NKJV

Years ago I read the book *This Present Darkness*, and it forever changed my prayer life. Author Frank Peretti paints a graphic picture of the spiritual world, of the battle between demonic influences and spiritual forces. I remember one scene where a beaten-down pastor of a small congregation cried out to the Lord for help. From outside the church, you watch as a spirit of despair zeroes in on the church window, going in for the kill. Your heart skips a beat as you watch this vulnerable, discouraged pastor, unknowingly about to take another hit. At precisely the right moment, a white-winged angelic warrior swoops down and hurls the leathery winged creature into space. I literally dropped the book and cheered when I read that line. In the book of Ephesians, we read about the shield of faith, with which we are equipped to extinguish every fiery dart the enemy sends our way. "The Greek word used here is the word *dunamis* which denotes explosive power or dynamic power and is where we get the word 'dynamite.'"* We need to get better at using our NO. No, you can't have my family, my friends, my calling, my community! When you raise your shield of faith, explosive things happen in the spiritual realm.

 ALIGN YOUR MIND ▸ Read Ephesians 6.

 ALIGN YOUR ACTIONS ▸ When the enemy's lies start flying, say NO. Raise your shield.

 ALIGN YOUR HEART ▸

> *Father, You've equipped me to win in battle. Teach me to stand in faith. Amen.*

---

* Rick Renner, *Sparkling Gems from the Greek* (Tulsa, OK: Teach All Nations, 2003), 659.

He'll Finish What He Started

And I am certain that God, who began the good work within you, will continue his work until it is finally finished on the day when Christ Jesus returns.

Philippians 1:6

Whenever we try to rush maturity, or sprint through grief, or blow past our weaknesses, we actually slow down our spiritual development. We'll bend toward sin management, self-editing, and fear responses, all of which turn us inward instead of upward. God started this work, and He's the one who will finish it. I have a unique vantage point now that my sons are grown. We were purposeful in teaching them to know God's love, treasure His voice, and understand His ways are best. Yet each of them walked through their share of hurts, missteps, and trials that left me unnerved and wondering what would happen to their precious faith. Two of our three sons actually wandered for a season. But as I've learned to entrust their stories to God, I've watched His guiding hand gently move them back to the center of His will. He's not in a hurry. He's okay with the process. He's not worried about their missteps. He loves and leads, guards and guides, protects and provides. He'll do the same for you and for those you love. He will finish what He started.

ALIGN YOUR MIND Read Philippians 1.

ALIGN YOUR ACTIONS Have you wandered from God's path? Felt frustrated by the limits of your age? Envied older teens? Humble your heart, refocus your gaze, and trust that the path God has you on is for your best.

ALIGN YOUR HEART

> *Father, You've begun a good work in me. Help me humble myself to Your process and timing. Thank You for Your patience. Amen.*

Leveraging Your Power

Though he was God,
he did not think of equality with God
as something to cling to.

Philippians 2:6

One day I stood a mother's-distance away while Jordan, age four at the time, stood in line for an order of fries. After the fourth person butted in front of him, I stepped up and asked him about it. He shrugged his shoulders, unsure of himself. I realized that though our son was kind, he was also insecure. We began to pump him full of truth. "Jordan, when God looks at you, His heart beats out of His chest because He loves you so much. You're no better than others, but you're not less than, either. Your opinion matters and God made you for a purpose." Over time we saw him rise up with a newfound confidence. One day Jordan was back in line. And just like before, people stepped in front of him, and he did nothing to hold his spot. When I approached him, he said, "Oh, don't worry, Mom. I know I could keep my place in line if I wanted; it's just that all these people look hungrier than me!" Suddenly, Philippians 2:6 passed through my mind. Jesus didn't consider equality with God something to leverage for His benefit. In fact, He leveraged it for ours, and in a way that cost Him everything. You have power for a purpose. May everyone around you benefit because of you.

 ALIGN YOUR MIND Read Philippians 2.

 ALIGN YOUR ACTIONS God has entrusted you with a sphere of influence. How can you wield your influence for the sake of others today?

 ALIGN YOUR HEART

Lord, forgive me for trying to grab power for myself. Help me to use Your power to help others. Amen.

Eyes Upward, Press On

I focus on this one thing: Forgetting the past and looking forward to what lies ahead, I press on to reach the end of the race and receive the heavenly prize for which God, through Christ Jesus, is calling us.

Philippians 3:13–14

If anybody had bragging rights, it was Paul. Yet he considered all of his achievements, all of his accomplishments, pure rubbish compared to the surpassing greatness of knowing Jesus. It's premature to forget about your past if God hasn't healed you of your past. Paul spoke here of past laurels, missteps, and sins as things to leave with Christ Jesus. If we rush past our pain, it will catch up with us. If we rest on past laurels, they'll trip us up. "Paul's desire to know Christ sprang from no other motive but to enjoy Him. He wanted Christ for Christ's sake, not his own. He was a lover of God, not a user of God. And whether he moved in Christ's resurrection power or was stretched to his last ounce of endurance, it mattered little. For Paul, it was all a part of the most fulfilling journey of all: truly knowing God."* While it seems far off right now, there is a heavenly prize waiting for you on the other side. Your current status, your past sins, carry no weight when you're under grace. Jesus cleanses, calls, and qualifies you. Treasure the prize and run to win.

ALIGN YOUR MIND ▸ Read Philippians 3.

ALIGN YOUR ACTIONS ▸ Ask God what it looks like to give your sins to Him and embrace His all-empowering grace instead.

ALIGN YOUR HEART

Jesus, help me to run my race until I see You face to face. Amen.

* *New Spirit-Filled Life Bible*, 1664.

Fix Your Thoughts

Fix your thoughts on what is true, and honorable, and right, and pure, and lovely, and admirable. Think about things that are excellent and worthy of praise.

Philippians 4:8

My friend Dr. Troy once shared with me these amazing insights on the power of our thoughts: "I don't think we fully comprehend how important our thought process is. Insecurity has its consequences. It fosters unhealthy thought patterns, which lead to unbelief, which then lead to poor choices—anything from eating terrible food to making destructive life-altering choices. But it doesn't stop there. When you harbor thoughts of insecurity, you are creating a divided kingdom within you, which cannot stand, let alone thrive. Your brain is wired to help you survive. God made it that way. When you embrace thoughts that are contrary to life, it's like putting one foot on the gas pedal and one foot on the brake. Imagine what that would do to your motor. Your brain wants you to survive and heal and to move forward. And yet the insecure person consistently feeds the brain a contrary message. Insecurity is bad for our system. We're made for more." Indeed, we are.* God has wired us to thrive. Any thoughts contrary to that which is pure, right, lovely, and excellent are destructive for your system and your soul. It takes both grit and grace to contend for a renewed mind, but it will change your life.

 ALIGN YOUR MIND Read Philippians 4.

 ALIGN YOUR ACTIONS Refuse thoughts that diminish. Fix your thoughts on what is good.

 ALIGN YOUR HEART

> *Lord, call me higher. Give me a vision for what a renewed mind looks like. Amen.*

---

* Excerpt taken from *Fully Alive* (Minneapolis: Bethany House Publishers, 2018), 174.

Rescued from a Kingdom

For he has rescued us from the kingdom of darkness and transferred us into the Kingdom of his dear Son.

Colossians 1:13

We were born into a kingdom of darkness. Stuck there. Unable to rescue ourselves. Destined for ever-increasing levels of captivity. Without hope. The word *darkness* translates this way: "ignorance of respecting divine things; accompanying ungodliness; consequent misery in hell; persons in whom darkness becomes visible and holds sway."* You've no doubt seen people so steeped in evil that the darkness is actually visible on them. We were once darkness's captives—until Jesus came. He died our death and paid our ransom. He broke our chains. He embraced us with great passion and transferred us into His family, the kingdom of Light. There, He bestowed upon us royalty, dignity, power, and authority. We now walk in love, boldness, kindness, and truth. The old kingdom can no longer claim us. We now work with God to help set other captives free. Paul opened this chapter with prayers for grace and peace. These are ours as well. *Grace* translates this way: "joy, pleasure, delight, sweetness; favor, merciful kindness; exerting holy influence upon the soul that keeps, increases, and strengthens." *Peace* translates "fearing nothing from God and content with its earthly lot."† Do you see what we've inherited here? An unshakable kingdom. We have every reason for joy, thanksgiving, and holy confidence.

ALIGN YOUR MIND Read Colossians 1.

ALIGN YOUR ACTIONS Write out the distinctions between the two kingdoms. Then praise the One who rescued you from darkness!

ALIGN YOUR HEART

Father, I cannot fully grasp what You've done for me. I bow low, raise my hands high, and worship You. Amen.

* Strong's Interlinear Bible Search, StudyLight.org, Colossians 1:13.
† Strong's Interlinear Bible Search, StudyLight.org, Colossians 1:2.

Continue the Way You Started

And now, just as you accepted Christ Jesus as your Lord, you must continue to follow him.

Colossians 2:6

I was in eighth grade when I first turned my heart toward God. I sat on a picnic table, looked up into the night sky, and prayed, "God, I know You're real. If there's more to You than what I know, please make Yourself real to me. I'll start to read the Bible, though I think it's kind of boring. But if You can help me out with that, we have a deal." I had no idea what I was saying. But God did. I found a Bible, began to read, and absolutely fell in love with Jesus. We all have different salvation stories, but we have this in common: We came through the low door of humility. We admitted our need and confessed our sin. We decided to believe that what Jesus did, He did for us. We asked Him to forgive us, cleanse us, and fill us. Then we reoriented our whole lives to follow Him. Salvation isn't about checking a box and praying the right prayer. It's about radical transformation from the inside out because Jesus becomes Lord of your life. Just as you embraced Him wholeheartedly when you came to Him, follow Him in that same way. Stay on His heels. Listen for His voice. Do what He says. He is a Good Shepherd. You can trust Him.

 ALIGN YOUR MIND Read Colossians 2.

 ALIGN YOUR ACTIONS List out ways you can draw closer to, and stay deeply rooted in, Him. Do one each day.

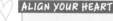 **ALIGN YOUR HEART**

Jesus, bind my heart to Yours. Keep me close to You. Draw me nearer still. Amen.

Let Peace Decide

And let the peace that comes from Christ rule in your hearts. For as members of one body you are called to live in peace. And always be thankful.

Colossians 3:15

After I got my license, I was looking to buy a car. A friend suggested I buy his because he wanted an upgrade—and he promised a good price. He showed me the car, took me for a ride, and immediately asked what I thought. I smiled and said, "I'll have to pray about it." He looked a bit perturbed but nodded okay. After praying, I felt very unsettled in my spirit. I let him know I wouldn't be buying his car. He got angry because he didn't understand my reason—faith. He ignored me after that. And the car died within a month. I felt grateful I listened to the Holy Spirit's leading. The word *peace* in this verse translates "umpire; to decide, direct, control, to rule."* When you are in Christ, Christ is in you. The Prince of Peace has taken up residence in your soul. His peace should always be your guide. Not people's opinions. Not your own reasoning. Not the pressure of the moment. If His peace is present, move forward. If there's no peace, stay put. And find your way back to peace again. Let God's peace be your constant companion throughout your day. Wisdom's path is always peace.

ALIGN YOUR MIND ▶ Read Colossians 3.

ALIGN YOUR ACTIONS ▶ Ask God to show you how to cultivate and prioritize His peace in your life.

ALIGN YOUR HEART

> *Prince of Peace, fill me afresh with a sense of Your presence. I treasure Your direction in my life. Lead me on. Amen.*

* Strong's Interlinear Bible Search, StudyLight.org, Colossians 3:15.

Mature and Fully Assured

Epaphras, who is one of you and a servant of Christ Jesus, sends greetings. He is always wrestling in prayer for you, that you may stand firm in all the will of God, mature and fully assured.

Colossians 4:12 NIV

I'm mentoring a young woman who is a gifted writer, full of insight, rich in character. She's walking through the fires of betrayal, abandonment, and rejection. I encouraged her to start a blog and podcast. She smiled thinly. "I'd love to," she replied. "But every time I start, the enemy rails in my ear, *'Who do you think you are?'*" I smiled. "Well, there's your assignment. Figure out the answer to that question. Who *do* you think you are?" I asked. "I see who you are. God loves who you are. But *you* need to know who you are. First discern God's heart for you, then discern His will; and then move forward with a face like flint. Next time the enemy spews that question, I want you ready with a feisty, faith-filled answer: 'I'll tell you who I am!'" Epaphras told Paul about the ungodly influences infiltrating the Colossian church. He wrestled in prayer so they might stand firm in the will of God, mature in the faith, and live fully assured of their place because of grace. You face the same battles. Live assured. Persevere. Stand firm in His will. Know His ways.

ALIGN YOUR MIND Read Colossians 4.

ALIGN YOUR ACTIONS Craft an answer for this question: Who do you think you are?

ALIGN YOUR HEART

Lord, You love me. You've called me. And You invite me to persevere and stand firm in spite of enemy opposition and ungodly influence. Strengthen me to that end today. Amen.

A Holy Momentum

As we pray to our God and Father about you, we think of your faithful work, your loving deeds, and the enduring hope you have because of our Lord Jesus Christ.

1 Thessalonians 1:3

Experts say that you find momentum in your life's calling when you combine your passions, your gifting, and your people. You'll become a force to reckon with. Paul commended the Thessalonians for their faithful work, their loving deeds, and their enduring hope. Passion, gifting, and people are extremely important. But without faith, hope, and love, you will lean away from God's best, not toward it. What's the faithful work God has assigned to you? Have you signed up for more than God has asked of you? Research shows that work is actually good for us. It's taking on more than God asked that slows us down and wears us out. Have you found a healthy rhythm in your pursuits? An ebb to your flow? And how about loving deeds? Are you going through the motions? Easy to do. Much harder to keep your heart in it. But oh, the power and the momentum when our hearts are engaged! And then there's enduring hope. Did you know that hope actually propels you forward? "Hope is never inferior to faith but is an extension of faith. Faith is present possession of grace; hope is confidence in grace's future accomplishment."* Want to be a triple threat? Master these: faithful work, loving deeds, enduring hope.

ALIGN YOUR MIND ▶ Read 1 Thessalonians 1.

ALIGN YOUR ACTIONS ▶ Identify what you need to adjust to have a healthy, powerful momentum.

ALIGN YOUR HEART ▶

> *Lord, empower my faith, inspire my deeds, and awaken new hope within me. Amen.*

---

* *New Spirit-Filled Life Bible*, 1684.

Your Proud Reward

After all, what gives us hope and joy, and what will be our proud reward and crown as we stand before our Lord Jesus when he returns? It is you!

1 Thessalonians 2:19

We hear so much bad news that we sometimes forget that good news is thriving all over the world. Countless Christians are living out their faith in their everyday lives. Communities are changed, people are restored. Paul was overjoyed for the way the Thessalonians loved and followed Jesus in spite of intense persecution. He looked ahead to heaven, and he imagined these redeemed lives as his crowning achievement. Two things may surprise us on Judgment Day. First, we'll be undone by the things God remembers and rewards. Our hearts will skip a beat when Jesus rewards us for the ways we loved when it didn't suit us, prayed when we didn't feel like it, and pointed someone to Jesus though we felt ill-equipped or self-conscious. But the second equally surprising reality is that some will arrive empty-handed. They may have had flashy ministries on earth, but they built them on earthly fame, not kingdom passion. And there are those who lived like atheists. They sincerely trusted Christ for salvation but lived much of their lives for themselves. Sobering questions to ask ourselves before Jesus returns are these: *Do I have people and fruit to show for my labors? Or are my efforts just for show?*

ALIGN YOUR MIND Read 1 Thessalonians 2.

ALIGN YOUR ACTIONS Ask yourself the questions above. Which efforts are fruitless, a distraction, or a drain? What needs to change for you to live fully engaged for the kingdom of God?

ALIGN YOUR HEART

God, help me to live a faithful, fruitful life. You are my great reward. Amen.

Filling in the Gaps of Your Faith

Night and day we pray earnestly for you, asking God to let us see you again to fill the gaps in your faith.

1 Thessalonians 3:10

As I've mentioned before, I'm almost fully recovered from my health battle. My most recent lab report revealed strong progress with just a few weak spots. My doctor likens it to plugging up holes so health can prevail. In the same way, we all have gaps in our faith, places where God wants to shore us up, strengthen us with truth, and establish us in freedom. For instance, because of my history with God, I have confidence that He is the one who will establish me. I don't need to posture or position for opportunities. But there are other places in my life where my gaps become evident. When pressure comes at me from all sides, I feel fear rising up within me. I fear the toll it will take on my health. I fear that it will disrupt my sleep. I fear that I'll make a mistake. Jesus modeled faith. He slept through the storm. He wants to shore up our faith and teach us how to embrace peace amid great pressure. When we experience wholeness and freedom, we're able to fill in the gaps for others. God is working even now. Don't fear your weaknesses. Embrace the process. Respond in faith. You're on your way to freedom. And many will benefit as a result.

ALIGN YOUR MIND ▶ Read 1 Thessalonians 3.

ALIGN YOUR ACTIONS ▶ Identify your gaps and ask Jesus to fill them.

ALIGN YOUR HEART

Lord, I want to be mature, whole, and free. Strengthen and establish me, I pray. Amen.

A Quiet Life

> Make it your goal to live a quiet life, minding your own business and working with your hands, just as we instructed you before. Then people who are not believers will respect the way you live, and you will not need to depend on others.
>
> 1 Thessalonians 4:11–12

We live in a day when everyone wants their five minutes of fame, no matter the cost or reason. Paul's words carry even more weight today than they did when he first delivered them. To lead a quiet life means to be secure in your lot. To fill *your* space and run *your* race, not whipping here and there, overcommitted, over-striving, over-proving to be something you're not. People are watching our lives more than we realize. I once received a scathing email from a listener letting me know that my guest was her neighbor. She said, "He has this big platform and looks so spiritual on social media, but he's a terrible neighbor. His dog poops in everybody's yard, and we watch him watching the pup from his window. He's unapproachable and acts better than everyone else. Like his goal is to be famous." Ouch. Now, maybe there's more to the story, but the point is, our lives send a message. Paul charges us to live so honorably that even those who don't share our faith will respect us. It's what gives our message credit when we share God's love with them. Your life is a living, breathing gospel message.

 ALIGN YOUR MIND ▶ Read 1 Thessalonians 4:1–14.

 ALIGN YOUR ACTIONS ▶ Does your life showcase the gospel? How might you more honorably run your race?

 ALIGN YOUR HEART ▶

Lord, sometimes I forget that people are watching how I live. Call me higher, call me deeper. Amen.

We'll Meet Him in the Air

Then, together with them, we who are still alive and remain on the earth will be caught up in the clouds to meet the Lord in the air. Then we will be with the Lord forever.

1 Thessalonians 4:17

Scripture teaches us that Satan is the prince of the power of the air.* The enemy has authority where Christ's authority is not enforced. He has the power (and has used it strategically) to influence media, entertainment, education, and science. The prince of the air has clearly occupied his space in a way that has shaped our culture. One might despair if thoughts stayed there. But did you know that it's in *this* space where Jesus will gather us to meet Him in the air? We will be glorified where the enemy has been magnified. "The air is Satan's sphere, so this is a triumphal gathering in open defiance of the devil right in his own stronghold."† Think about it. We will meet Jesus *in the air*! We will behold Him, be like Him, and be restored because of Him. That day is coming! "God will turn tragedy into triumph, poverty to riches, pain to glory, and defeat to victory. All believers throughout history will stand reunited in God's very presence, safe and secure."‡ Turn your eyes upward today. Live as one who is spoken for. Be joyful and expectant.

ALIGN YOUR MIND Read 1 Thessalonians 4:17–18; 5.

ALIGN YOUR ACTIONS Today, be encouraged. The enemy's doom is sure. And so is your victory.

ALIGN YOUR HEART

> *Father, thank You for what You have done for me. What You have won for me. Amen.*

* See Ephesians 2:2.
† *Believer's Bible Commentary*, 2038.
‡ *Life Application Study Bible*, 2673.

What Faith Prompts You to Do

> So we keep on praying for you, asking our God to enable you to live a life worthy of his call. May he give you the power to accomplish all the good things your faith prompts you to do.
>
> 2 Thessalonians 1:11

Some of the Thessalonians misinterpreted Paul's first letter and needed to be redirected. He charged them to live ready for Christ's imminent return. So they quit their jobs, lived idly, and waited around to be snatched up into the air. Paul followed up with a second letter, urging them to live ready while living *responsibly*. There were tasks to complete, needs to meet, people to love, and a God to serve. We have work to do. Paul prayed they'd not only fully engage their faith and live robust lives, but that God would give them the power to accomplish everything their faith prompted them to do. *Power to accomplish* translates this way: "miracle power, moral power, excellence of soul, power resting upon forces; to abound, furnish supply, render complete, filled to the brim."* My faith prompted me to attend a writers conference, to go on several mission trips in spite of my fears, and to sow generous amounts of resources back into the kingdom. With each faith step, I've experienced God's power and provision. I've developed an appetite for faith. How about you? What is your faith prompting you to do?

 ALIGN YOUR MIND ▶ Read 2 Thessalonians 1:11.

 ALIGN YOUR ACTIONS ▶ What is your faith prompting you to do? Engage your faith and take some risks.

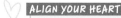 **ALIGN YOUR HEART**

Father, lead me out of the boat onto the water. Prompt me over and over again to live by faith. Amen.

---

* Strong's Interlinear Bible Search, StudyLight.org, 2 Thessalonians 1:11.

Your Life Prevents Evil

For this lawlessness is already at work secretly, and it will remain secret until the one who is holding it back steps out of the way.

2 Thessalonians 2:7

A Bible scholar suggested on my show one day that the enemy has an antichrist waiting in the wings in every generation because he doesn't know the day or the time of the Lord's return. This verse definitely speaks of the evil lurking in the shadows, of how lawlessness is already at work. So what's holding back this force bent on annihilating mankind? One thought is that the Holy Spirit, at work in the lives of believers, is the resistance that stops the enemy from unleashing pure evil on the earth. Once we're gone, taken up, the firewall is removed and lawlessness will abound. Think of how God uses believers to stand in between the wicked and the weak. How much evil is held at bay because a grandma prays for her grandchildren, or a pastor stands in the gap for his community, or godly students reach out in love to those on the margins of their school? The godliest saints endure the greatest opposition because they pose a threat to the dominion of darkness. You're never too young to be a part of God's resistance army. How might your life shut down an enemy scheme?

ALIGN YOUR MIND Read 2 Thessalonians 2.

ALIGN YOUR ACTIONS Ask the Holy Spirit to show you who to pray for or reach out to. Then move in love and your God-given authority.

ALIGN YOUR HEART

Father, I have nothing to fear, for You are with me. Help me to stand in the gap against the evil around me. Victory belongs to me because I belong to You. Amen.

What's a False Teacher?

> They set themselves up as experts on religious issues, but haven't the remotest idea of what they're holding forth with such imposing eloquence.
>
> 1 Timothy 1:7 MSG

It breaks my heart how freely some wield the "false teacher" label against sincere Bible-believing Christians simply because they hold different opinions on secondary doctrine. I love people in many Bible-believing denominations. We'll be in heaven together. Is it possible to love and respect our fellow Christians while holding to our convictions? Yes. Not one of us sees with perfect clarity.* We're all works in progress. Yet God is patient with us, so why are we not with one another? What is a false teacher? "They teach what is contrary to the truth found in Scripture (1 Timothy1:3, 1:6–7; 4:1–3). They promote trivial and divisive controversies instead of helping people come to Jesus (1:4). They aren't concerned about personal evidence of God's presence in their lives, spending their time on 'meaningless discussions' instead (1:6). Their motivation is to make a name for themselves (1:7)."† "Some will accomplish great things for God and preach gospel truth effectively but will depart from the faith and gradually turn to seducing spirits and false doctrines. Because of their former anointing and zeal for God, they will mislead many."‡ Pray for grace and discernment.

 ALIGN YOUR MIND Read 1 Timothy 1.

 ALIGN YOUR ACTIONS Ask God to help you discern the difference between a difference of opinion and a departure from His Word, and talk with a parent or trusted adult about it.

 ALIGN YOUR HEART

> *O Lord, fill me with discernment and grace. I need both in increasing measures. Amen.*

---

* See 1 Corinthians 13:12.
† *Life Application Study Bible*, 2687.
‡ *Life in the Spirit Study Bible*, 1915.

Pray for Everyone, Leaders Too

I urge you, first of all, to pray for all people. Ask God to help them; intercede on their behalf, and give thanks for them. Pray this way for kings and all who are in authority so that we can live peaceful and quiet lives marked by godliness and dignity.

1 Timothy 2:1–2

One day on my radio show I said, with great care and gentleness, "We live in a highly polarized culture; even Christians stand on opposite sides of the political aisle. However, if you call yourself a Christian, you're called to pray for your leaders whether you like them or not." Many appreciated it. One listener did not—and she wrote a letter, with many capital letters and exclamation points, telling me how thoroughly uninformed I am. Yes, we all could be more informed, but I know what Scripture says. And when it comes to the leaders you despise, don't you think they'll be better off if they get more of Jesus? We're to pray for everyone, ask God to help them, intercede on their behalf. What if every Christian prayed for *everyone* with that kind of passion and sincerity? The answer? We'd live peaceful, quiet lives, marked by godliness and dignity. God wants this for us. May we do what He says and see what He will do.

ALIGN YOUR MIND Read 1 Timothy 2.

ALIGN YOUR ACTIONS Check your heart today. Do you only pray for those you like? Repent and make it a practice to pray for whomever God brings to mind each day—even those you don't like.

ALIGN YOUR HEART

Lord, I forget the power of my prayers. Give me a passion for praying for everyone, including those I don't agree with. Amen.

Do Not Neglect Your Spiritual Gift

Do not neglect the spiritual gift you received through the prophecy spoken over you when the elders of the church laid their hands on you.

1 Timothy 4:14

Once there was an accountant who was gifted with spreadsheets, numbers, and financial projections. But he didn't appreciate the value of his gifts, so he became a pastor. He led a few people to Christ over the years, but not many. He saw some growth in his people, but not what he'd hoped for. He wrestled to find joy. Then he died and went to heaven. Jesus rewarded his faith and thanked him for his heartfelt service. Then He lovingly said, "I never asked you to become a pastor. I appointed you to become an accountant so you could help manage a large organization. I gifted you with numbers for a reason." God has gifted *you* in special ways for a special purpose. Don't fall for the trap of spiritualizing some gifts over others. God has an important role for *you* to fill. Don't neglect your spiritual gifts. If you're called to speak, speak with precision and power. If you're called to serve, do so with all of the enthusiasm and gusto you have in you. If you're called to create, create with excellence and joy. Your gifts are meant to be some of God's great gifts to the world.

ALIGN YOUR MIND Read 1 Timothy 4.

ALIGN YOUR ACTIONS Do you know what your spiritual gifts are? Even now, God is training you in them. Spend time reflecting on your passions and talents, and ask God to reveal and strengthen your gifts.

ALIGN YOUR HEART

Lord Jesus, stir up a new passion within me! Grow my gifts for Your glory! Amen.

Godliness with Contentment

But godliness with contentment is great gain.
1 Timothy 6:6 NIV

I once knew a young woman who battled perpetual discontentment. She completely missed out on her beautiful life because she was always anxiously looking ahead to all of the things she wanted but didn't yet have. One day she asked me why she was always so miserable. "Discontentment," I gently answered. "It blinds us to our current blessings and hinders us from forward-moving faith." Godliness is a reverent, holy pursuit of God. It's what compels us to lean in and listen for that still, small voice. It's what allows us fresh revelation around our next place of promise. It's what positions us for wisdom about what our next steps should be. And contentment? We're all in the not-yet in some ways. It takes great maturity to have forward-moving faith and vision while embracing your current lot and assignment. Most people leave before they actually leave. They abandon their current assignment before God releases them. If you want forward-moving faith that propels you to great maturity, don't run after the next shiny thing. Run after God. With all your might. And thank Him for your lot, right here, right now. Look around and thank Him for the blessings you'd miss if they went away tomorrow. Godliness with contentment is great gain.

ALIGN YOUR MIND ▸ Read 1 Timothy 6.

ALIGN YOUR ACTIONS ▸ Take time each day to thank God passionately for your current blessings and assignment. Ask Him to make you ready for what's next while you serve him right where you are.

ALIGN YOUR HEART

Lord, thank You for the life You've given me. Show me how to live here and dream with You about my future. Amen.

Enough with the Fear!

For God has not given us a spirit of fear, but of power and of love and of a sound mind.

2 Timothy 1:7 NKJV

I've battled fear my whole life. But it wasn't until recently that I learned of fear's toxic effect on our health. When your fears go rogue, they actually cause a cascade of inflammation inside your body. And inflammation is the soil where sickness and disease grow. Crushed under the weight of fear because of a health relapse, I finally declared war on my fears. The spirit God has given us compels us to walk in power, to love sacrificially, and to keep our wits about us in a world gone mad. God has wired us to live and thrive in love. Fear has to do with punishment. Love has everything to do with redemption, wholeness, and restoration. Fear makes us cower, pull inward, and forget who we are. Love makes us open up, look up, and remember again that we're someone God loves. When fear drives us, nothing good comes of it. Fear affects our brain's ability to process information and to make sound decisions. Fear diminishes our body's ability to rightly absorb and use the nutrients we ingest. Fear compels us to make self-sabotaging decisions. Can you see why fear is such a tool of the enemy? Fear is a spirit, and it's not from God.*

ALIGN YOUR MIND ▸ Read 2 Timothy 1.

ALIGN YOUR ACTIONS ▸ Memorize 2 Timothy 1:7; repeat it when your fears loom large. With God's help, deal with your fears.

ALIGN YOUR HEART ▸

> Father, You've given me a spirit of power, love, and sound mind. Help me to walk accordingly. Amen.

---

* Adapted from *Fully Alive*, 61.

A Soldier, a Farmer, and an Athlete

Endure suffering along with me, as a good soldier of Christ Jesus.
2 Timothy 2:3

As God's people, we need to learn how to suffer well. We hear much about prosperity and promises and not enough about endurance and perseverance. Those who've suffered and emerged from the ashes have much to teach the world. I owe some of my greatest lessons to the school of suffering. Paul not only calls us to suffer well, but he also charges us to think like soldiers, farmers, and athletes. What do they have in common? They know discipline, patience, and focus. They're not idle; they're engaged with an end-goal in mind. They know how to endure hardship when opposition comes. Soldiers don't get tangled up in affairs that distract and derail them from their mission. Farmers know how to sow seeds and wait patiently for the harvest. Athletes discipline their bodies, practice their drills, and master their skills. You and I are called to see ourselves as citizens of heaven, part of the Lord's army. We're called to sow the gospel, with ample seeds of faith, kindness, generosity, hope, and love. We're called to live expectantly as we wait for the promised harvest. Finally, we're to get into the habit of saying no to ourselves, of denying fleshly indulgences that only weaken us and make us vulnerable. This is how we live lives of influence and impact for the kingdom.

 ALIGN YOUR MIND Read 2 Timothy 2.

 ALIGN YOUR ACTIONS What do you need to change to live more like a soldier, farmer, and athlete? Start today.

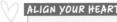 **ALIGN YOUR HEART**

> *Father, I want to be a good soldier for You! Train me, teach me, lead me onward. Amen.*

A Form of Religion
yet without Power

They will act religious, but they will reject the power that could make them godly. Stay away from people like that!

2 Timothy 3:5

*I*n this sobering chapter, Paul warns Timothy of the perilous times ahead: "For people will love only themselves and their money. They will be boastful and proud, scoffing at God, disobedient to their parents, and ungrateful. They will consider nothing sacred. They will be unloving and unforgiving; they will slander others and have no self-control. They will be cruel and hate what is good. They will betray their friends, be reckless, be puffed up with pride, and love pleasure rather than God" (2 Timothy 3:2–4). What will it look like for us to stand in the opposite spirit? We, by God's grace and the empowering work of the Holy Spirit, will be lovers of God, generous givers, humbly gracious, God-fearing, parent-honoring, and continually grateful. We'll cherish the sacred and see the holy amid the common. We'll catch glimpses of heaven impacting the earth. We'll love and forgive. We'll generously bless others and be models of self-restraint. We'll be humble, kind, and cherish what is good. We'll be faithful to our family and friends. We'll forsake momentary pleasures for the greater glory that comes with deeply knowing God. "Religious imposters will steadily denigrate."* But we who fear God's name will shine ever brighter till the full light of day.

ALIGN YOUR MIND Read 2 Timothy 3.

ALIGN YOUR ACTIONS Look at the lists above. Which one do your heart and actions align with more? Repent of where you've wandered and ask God to make you more like Him.

ALIGN YOUR HEART

Lord, I fear Your name. Purify and empower me. Amen.

* *New Spirit-Filled Life Bible*, 1714.

Pure Heart, Pure Perspective

Everything is pure to those whose hearts are pure. But nothing is pure to those who are corrupt and unbelieving, because their minds and consciences are corrupted.

Titus 1:15

Brain science has proven what the Bible's always said: What you look for, you will find; where your thoughts go, your life goes. When you rehearse certain thoughts, even if they're not true, your brain will look for evidence to back up your mindset, even if it's all a farce. If you're convinced no one likes you, your brain becomes hypersensitive, picking up on any nuance to confirm your bias. When someone fills their mind with vile images, sexual exploitation, and depravity, they impair their perspective and actually damage their brain. Conversely, a pure heart and mind brings peace to the soul and life to the body.* When you renew your mind by reading and memorizing Scripture and guarding against toxic thoughts, when you guard against bitterness, unforgiveness, and offense, and when you believe the best about others and refuse to read between the lines, your whole life will be transformed. Your heart and mind are treasured gifts. Guard them with diligence. Life flows from those places. In due time, it'll be almost instinctive for you to think right thoughts, to believe the best about others, to see with redeemed eyes, and to enjoy freedoms that don't corrupt.

ALIGN YOUR MIND Read Titus 1.

ALIGN YOUR ACTIONS Some of the most important things you can do right now are to keep your heart pure and your mind renewed. List ways you can do these—then do them.

ALIGN YOUR HEART

Lord, reveal the hidden places within me that muddy the waters of my perspective. Help me think rightly and see redemptively. Amen.

* See Proverbs 14:30.

Minister from Mercy

When God our Savior revealed his kindness and love, he saved us, not because of the righteous things we had done, but because of his mercy.

Titus 3:4–5

My younger sister has the spiritual gift helping. I don't know anyone who has more capacity to help others in a variety of ways than she does. One minute she's cleaning out someone's gutter, and the next, mowing their lawn or cleaning their house or taking pictures for their family Christmas card. I have different gifts that I seek to steward well, but I constantly feel like a substandard Christian when, in my weakness, I measure my life against hers. Of course, it's not a competition, and we should never compare gifts with another. Paul reminds us here that we don't work our way into salvation. Praise God! I'd be in trouble otherwise. By His mercy He saved us. But out of the overflow of God's grace, Paul also charges us to help those in need, do excellent work, and steward well the call set before us. We get nowhere when we compare our service to another's. But we do well when we spur one another on to love and do good deeds.* When we strive to prove, we've forgotten mercy. When we serve for love, we remember it again. Life in the Spirit leaves us clean, fresh, redeemed, and restored. We have nothing to prove, but much good work to do.

 ALIGN YOUR MIND Read Titus 3.

 ALIGN YOUR ACTIONS Move out of your comfort zone this week and help someone in need.

 ALIGN YOUR HEART

> *Lord, I want to grow in good deeds because You've done so much for me. Increase my capacity to love and serve. Amen.*

* See Hebrews 10:24.

How to Energize Your Faith

[I pray] that the sharing of your faith may become effective by the acknowledgment of every good thing which is in you in Christ Jesus.

Philemon 1:6 NKJV

When I became a Christian, I understood that I was saved but didn't grasp that I was *loved*. It would take years for that truth to sink down into my soul. One day in college, two identical twin sisters approached me and asked about the twinkle in my eye. I told them about Jesus and His love for us. They were so filled with wide-eyed wonder, they grabbed other girls from their floor and brought them to me as well. The more I shared what I'd learned from God's Word, the more my faith quickened within me. I felt my spirit come alive. The word *effective* in the passage above is *enereges*, where we get the word *energy*. Paul prayed that Philemon would be increasingly activated and energized in his faith as he acknowledged the riches Christ had deposited within him. I eventually grew to understand that I was not only saved, I was loved and called and equipped and grafted into a royal family line. The more I learned, the more I had to share with others. This is why it matters that we not only share our faith, but that we understand what we possess. The deeper your well, the more you'll have to draw from, and the more energized you'll be as you share with others.

 ALIGN YOUR MIND Read Philemon 1:1–7.

 ALIGN YOUR ACTIONS Consider all God has done in you and your life—and share accordingly.

 ALIGN YOUR HEART

> Lord, give me courage to share who You are and what You've done. Activate and energize my faith! Amen.

When God Calls You to Return

It seems you lost Onesimus for a little while so that you could have him back forever.

Philemon 1:15

Philemon's slave, Onesimus, ran away, but then he met Paul, who introduced him to Jesus, who radically transformed his life. Paul discipled Onesimus, and he became a dear friend and brother in the faith. Because Paul was such a man of integrity, he instructed Onesimus to return to Philemon. "When God finds runaways, he often sends them back to the very places and people from which they ran in the first place. As God has become real in your life, how has your past come into new perspective? Are there still situations from your past that need to be resolved? In what ways has your relationship with Christ given you new opportunities and resources to face what you used to run away from?"* What might this look like in today's world? Maybe you ditched a relationship at the first sign of conflict. Or left an activity, team, group, or job when you didn't experience the affirmation you were looking for. Or abandoned serving others when it started to cost you. God offers grace, redemption, and forgiveness for all of these. Sometimes you can't go back and pick up where you left off. But you can go back and rebuild some bridges. Sometimes God calls us back for a short season so He can launch us out into the next season.

 ALIGN YOUR MIND Read Philemon 1:8–25.

 ALIGN YOUR ACTIONS Consider the questions above. Ask the Lord if you need to go back so you can go forward.

 ALIGN YOUR HEART

> *Jesus, forgive me for looking for the easy way out. Lead me to life and life abundant. Amen.*

* *Life Application Study Bible*, 2725.

He Cleansed Us, Then Sat Down

When he had cleansed us from our sins, he sat down in the place of honor at the right hand of the majestic God in heaven.

Hebrews 1:3

After He defeated death and cleansed us from sin's power to destroy us, Jesus sat down in the place of honor at God's right hand. If we could peel back the sky, we'd see the angels singing *Holy, holy, holy is the Lord!* We'd see power and light emanating from the throne. We'd be so undone by God's power and majesty that our knees would buckle right underneath us. Oh, to get a glimpse of the reality of heaven! We'd stop our striving and posturing, and we'd worship instead. We'd see the power of our prayers and the sacredness of our obedience. Jesus finished the work necessary to set us free. It's finished. Imagine if you started each day by telling yourself, *It is finished. Jesus already sat down. He's at His Father's right hand, ruling with power and majesty and authority. I am cleansed, forgiven, and free.* How do we so often miss what God offers us? We forget about the finished work of Christ. We strive to validate ourselves, to manage outcomes, and to control circumstances. If there is a glory spout, it's the place where we surrender our circumstances, entrust outcomes, and rest in the finished work of Christ. We're in good hands. The best hands.

ALIGN YOUR MIND ▶ Read Hebrews 1.

ALIGN YOUR ACTIONS ▶ This week, start each day telling yourself the truth above. See how it transforms your perspective.

ALIGN YOUR HEART ▶

> *Jesus, I want to live the powerful life You've made available to me. Lead me, Lord. Amen.*

Be Careful Not to Drift

So we must listen very carefully to the truth we have heard, or we may drift away from it.

Hebrews 2:1

My brother was spiraling, addicted to alcohol and drugs, thoroughly depressed. My brother-in-law asked him several times, "Are you ready to trust Jesus yet?" He never was. Rich gave him a piece of paper with his number and a Bible verse. He said, "Call me before you decide to take your life." Then Jeff hit bottom. With a weapon in hand, ready to end it all, he saw that piece of paper he'd tacked to the wall. Romans 8:28 stared back at him. He called Rich, who came right away, wrapped him in an embrace, and led him to the Lord. Jeff was radically, beautifully saved that day. He was miraculously delivered from his addiction too. Years later, the enemy taunted, depression surfaced, and shame put a chokehold on him. He began to wander back into his old ways. He was drifting because he'd stopped listening to the truth that sets us free. Thankfully, he didn't drift far before he came back to faith again. Some drift doctrinally; they lose their way. Others drift from their sense of identity, looking for love in all the wrong places. Still others drift into trying to earn their way because grace seems too good to be true. We're drifters by nature. We need to inhale truth and exhale lies every single moment of our lives. Truth sets us free. Truth keeps us grounded.

 ALIGN YOUR MIND Read Hebrews 2.

 ALIGN YOUR ACTIONS Are you drifting? Repent, course-correct, and open your Bible to discover the truths your soul needs.

 ALIGN YOUR HEART

> *Lord, show me where I'm vulnerable to drift. Impart the truth that I need.*

Think Carefully about This Jesus

Think carefully about this Jesus whom we declare to be God's messenger and High Priest.

Hebrews 3:1

Some of the Israelites idolized Moses and yet completely missed Jesus. Whenever we drift from a deep and intimate walk with God, we construct a savior that fits our preferences. But the author of Hebrews charges us to think carefully about this Jesus, the One who actually came to save us. At every turn, He frustrated people. They expected one thing and He delivered another. His own disciples wanted Him to overthrow Rome, but He came to save the world. Religious camps wanted Him to pick sides, but He picked sinners instead, because they needed Him. He's not soft on sin, but He's full of compassion for the sinner. He says, "Follow me and live," and yet He also bids us come and die—die to our imagined rights, self-preservation, self-promoting ways. He wants us to live free, secure, and whole. He calls us to love ourselves *and* our enemies. He offers no leniency for grudges, un-forgiveness, or dishonor. He's not impressed with passionate worship if the life behind it is secretly living in sin. You can't earn His favor or bribe Him to look the other way. He sees all, knows all, and continually calls us higher, to be more like Him. Do you really want to follow Jesus? Because He'll ask for everything. But what He offers is beyond your wildest dreams.

ALIGN YOUR MIND Read Hebrews 3.

ALIGN YOUR ACTIONS Think about the aspects of Jesus' character that challenge you. Lean in and listen to Him.

ALIGN YOUR HEART

Jesus, forgive me for trying to fit You into my idea of what You should be. Reveal Yourself to me. Amen.

Rest Is an Act of Faith

God's promise of entering his rest still stands, so we ought to tremble with fear that some of you might fail to experience it.

Hebrews 4:1

My husband has this Calvin Miller quote on his desk: "Lord, help me to remember that I can make more bricks in six days than I can in seven." God created us to work, and He us created to rest. When the Israelites wandered in the wilderness, they groaned and complained when they should have persevered and believed. God provided for them, performed miracles for them, and made a way for them—many times in spite of them. We exhaust ourselves in similar ways. We commit to more than God asks and fall apart. We strive to prove our worth, and we're left with either pride or humiliation, neither of which comes from God's heart. We forget about the sacred, eternal rest that awaits us, instead living like this life is all there is, forfeiting an eternal reward.* Rest is an act of faith. It can even be an act of war on the enemy of your soul. When the devil tries to bait you into striving, take your place under the shadow of God's wing and rest awhile. The enemy will hate it, and you will be restored. True rest requires perseverance, vision, and faith. So rest from your labors, from your striving and performance. We cannot mature until we learn how to rest.

 ALIGN YOUR MIND Read Hebrews 4:1–11.

 ALIGN YOUR ACTIONS Prayerfully examine your life. Are you striving for identity? Restless about your future? Still your heart before God today.

 ALIGN YOUR HEART

> *Lord, lead me to deeper places of rest and assurance. I trust You. Amen.*

* See 2 Corinthians 5:10.

God's Word, Alive and Powerful

> For the word of God is alive and powerful. It is sharper than the sharpest two-edged sword, cutting between soul and spirit, between joint and marrow. It exposes our innermost thoughts and desires.
>
> Hebrews 4:12

knelt down, bowed my head, and rested my forearms on the couch, its fabric worn out from my many months on bedrest. I cried out to God, "O Lord, You promised to supply all of our needs. We're dying financially. I'm sick. But I'm holding on to Your promise." Moments later, I spoke my fears to my husband. "We'll never get out of this," I panicked. "We have more medical debt than income. I don't see a way out." Instantly I felt pierced by the Holy Spirit. *You don't "see" a way out? Do you need to see for there to be a way? Your own words defy the promises of God. Bring your words into agreement with the Word of God and then you'll pray with power.* I was praying one thing and saying another. "So why would the Bible refer to the Word of God repeatedly as a 'two-edged sword' or literally a 'two-mouthed sword'? The Word of God is like a sword that has two edges, cutting both ways and doing terrible damage to an aggressor."* We're like a divided kingdom when our words conflict with God's Word. Want to walk in power? Say *and* pray God's Word.

ALIGN YOUR MIND ▸ Read Hebrews 4.

ALIGN YOUR ACTIONS ▸ Check your words. Do they line up with God's Word?

ALIGN YOUR HEART

Father, show me the inconsistencies in my thoughts and words. Call me higher. I want to speak with precision and pray with power. Amen.

* *Sparkling Gems from the Greek*, 109.

Obedience through Suffering

Even though Jesus was God's Son, he learned obedience from the things he suffered.

Hebrews 5:8

My legs were tangled up in the bedsheets. My T-shirt soaked with sweat. Awash in fear and anxiety, I was too young to be so sick. "Heal me, Lord," I begged. "Please, heal me. *Please*, Lord." Every night my prayers seemed to bounce off the ceiling. Did God lose my address? *Where are You, God?* One night He broke His silence—forever changing the way I walk with Him. *"If I healed you,"* He whispered into the dark of my night, *Would you praise me?* "Oh, yes, Lord!" I replied. "I'll shout it from the mountaintops!" *Why is that?* He asked. *Would you praise Me because I'm God, the One who put the stars in place and sent My only Son to die for you? Or would you praise Me simply because you got your way?* I was undone. I literally tore my shirt in repentance and went facedown on the floor. My life flashed before my eyes and I realized how much of it was about me, not Him. He'd been my Savior. But that night He became my Lord. Even Jesus learned submission through the things He suffered. Don't waste your suffering. It'll purify your heart like nothing else can.

 ALIGN YOUR MIND ▸ Read Hebrews 5.

 ALIGN YOUR ACTIONS ▸ Do you only praise and obey God in the good times? Start modeling your life after Jesus—in the good times and bad.

 ALIGN YOUR HEART

> *Jesus, You modeled holy submission in a way that takes my breath away. I offer my whole self to You. Have Your way in me. Amen.*

An Anchor for Your Soul

This hope is a strong and trustworthy anchor for our souls. It leads us through the curtain into God's inner sanctuary.

Hebrews 6:19

You and I are anchored upward to God, where He sits on His throne in His inner sanctuary. Imagine! Though the storms rage and the winds knock us over, we're anchored to God Almighty. Picture your soul's anchor leading upward. Remember that God's hold on you is stronger than your hold on Him. He wants you to partner with Him to accomplish His purposes on earth. You'll have to fight for some of the things God has promised you. You'll have to stand on His Word even when it doesn't feel true. But the battle will be worth it. And when it's all over, you can be assured that Jesus will get you safely home because that's what He promised He'd do. Having to fight and contend for the things God puts on my heart—while the enemy works to steal my joy, kill my dreams, and destroy my sense of purpose—has made me a fiercer woman of prayer. Anything worth having is worth praying for. The thing about an anchor is that it's built to withstand the fiercest storms. An anchor that's worth its weight will hold no matter which way the wind is blowing.* God's got you. Live by faith. Pray with power. You're secure.

ALIGN YOUR MIND ▶ Read Hebrews 6.

ALIGN YOUR ACTIONS ▶ Remind your soul just how secure you are. Be bold in faith. Be confident in prayer.

ALIGN YOUR HEART

> *Lord, You are my anchor! Help me believe that I'm as secure as I truly am and live accordingly. Amen.*

* Adapted from my book *Your Powerful Prayers* (Minneapolis: Bethany House Publishers, 2016), 110.

Don't Throw Away Your Confidence

So do not throw away this confident trust in the Lord. Remember the great reward it brings you!

Hebrews 10:35

Two steps forward. Three steps back. I fought and fought to come back from my recent health relapse. One day I'd gain ground and the next I'd lose it. My options? Give up and throw away my confidence, or rise up, grab a firmer hold on God's promises, and keep marching. My health battle was nothing compared to what persecuted Christians endured in the first century, or what they endure today. The writer of Hebrews charged believers to remember God's promises. Remember His love. He's worth it. And our faith matters. The word *confidence* in the verse above translates "cheerful courage, boldness, and assurance."* This speaks of both a steadfast spirit and a bold confession of God's faithfulness. It's amazing to think that our faith is so precious to God that He actually stores up a reward for us when we hold on to His promises. He gives us faith, encourages our faith, and then rewards us for our faith. How do we persevere when we feel like giving up? Verse 36 tells us, "Patient endurance is what you need now." Consider a long-distance runner, focused, paced, purposeful. Don't lose heart when the way gets long, and definitely don't make big life decisions when you're running uphill. Stay the course. God *will* reward you.

ALIGN YOUR MIND Read Hebrews 10.

ALIGN YOUR ACTIONS Today, don't back down. Take a firmer grip on God's promise and stay your course. Ask God for perseverance.

ALIGN YOUR HEART

Lord, this journey isn't for sissies. Help me to stand strong, stay the course, and remember Your promises. Amen.

---

* Strong's Interlinear Bible Search, StudyLight.org, Hebrews 10:35.

What Is Faith, Anyway?

Faith shows the reality of what we hope for; it is the evidence of things we cannot see.

Hebrews 11:1

Miracles happen every day. The sick are healed. The lost are found. The barren have children. Prodigals come home. But what about those who pray and fast and stand on God's promises, and still their loved one dies? What did faith accomplish in that case? What is faith, anyway? Faith is the strong conviction that God is who He says He is and that He will do just as He promised. We get tangled up in doubt when we determine God's intended outcome before He even reveals it to us. We zero in on one possibility and miss all of the ways God is working in and around us. If God doesn't give us what we hope for in this life, it's because His answers to our desires are better than we ever imagined, meant to be ours throughout eternity. Furthermore, when we engage our faith and place our hope firmly in God (and not in our expected outcome), something changes within us. We're so deeply connected to the life-force that flows from God, it can't help but shore us up and change us from the inside out. Our faith is never wasted, nor is it ever tossed aside by God. It's wise, though, to discern God's voice before we decide on what we think our outcome should reveal. His peace always confirms His ways.

ALIGN YOUR MIND ▶ Read Hebrews 11.

ALIGN YOUR ACTIONS ▶ Is your hope in God or an outcome you want? Reengage your faith today.

ALIGN YOUR HEART

Father, forgive me for hoping in lesser things. Help me live in faith and hope in You. Amen.

When the Lord Disciplines

"Don't make light of the LORD's discipline,
and don't give up when he corrects you."
Hebrews 12:5

When our boys were young and made choices they shouldn't, we'd get down on their level, look them in the eyes, and say, "You are too important to be making decisions like that." They'd stand up straighter even while they received correction. We tend to fall to two extremes when God brings correction: insecurity or indifference. We berate ourselves for messing up, or we shrug our shoulders and dismiss what's meant to stop us in our tracks. We crumble like we're nothing, or we refuse to change like it's nothing. God is a good, good Father, and He disciplines those He deeply loves. So when you've stepped out of the bounds God intends for you, God will come for you. But you can humbly stand up straight, knowing His correction resets your course to the important things He's planned for you. I've heard far too many stories of folks who've either lost heart because they allowed God's correction to bring condemnation (which is not from Him), or tossed aside their convictions and walked straight into a trap that destroyed their reputation. That's why the writer of Hebrews tells us to get rid of anything that will trip us up and slow us down. God wants us to last long and finish strong.

 ALIGN YOUR MIND ▶ Read Hebrews 12.

 ALIGN YOUR ACTIONS ▶ Have you allowed anything to remain in your life that gives the devil opportunity to destroy your influence? Get rid of it.

 ALIGN YOUR HEART ▶

Lord, give me the desire to live a powerful and pure life. Help me to humbly stand tall yet quickly change course when Your discipline comes. Amen.

The Best-Kept Secret in the Bible

If you need wisdom, ask our generous God, and he will give it to you. He will not rebuke you for asking.

James 1:5

Suppose you received a letter from your local bank. There's an account with your name on it. An anonymous donor pledged to continually replenish the account as you withdraw funds. What will you do? Distrust it and leave it? Or draw from the generous provision offered you? I remember stumbling upon this passage in James, desperate for wisdom on how to navigate sickness, medical bills, and motherhood. God highlighted it before me, and I realized that I never have to go without the wisdom I need. From then on I stretched out my arms and unabashedly asked for more and more God-given insight. To this day, I shamelessly run into God's presence and draw from His heavenly promise of wisdom. Amazingly, He's promised to not only give wisdom, but lavish it upon us. The word *wisdom* translates this way: "knowledge of things human and divine; the act of interpreting dreams and always giving the sagest advice; supreme intelligence such as belongs to God."* Imagine—God wants to impart His supreme intelligence to you. God's wisdom will keep you out of trouble, help you to rightly interpret your trials, and keep God at the center of your life. Wisdom points others to Him. You have a wealthy, loving heavenly Father. Draw on the provision He's so freely offered you.

ALIGN YOUR MIND ▸ Read James 1.

ALIGN YOUR ACTIONS ▸ Boldly, humbly ask for more and more wisdom.

ALIGN YOUR HEART ▸

> Lord, pour out fresh wisdom on me today! Give sight to my eyes, clarity to my ears, and discernment to my heart. Amen.

* Strong's Interlinear Bible Search, StudyLight.org, James 1:5.

Favor, Not Favoritism

My dear brothers and sisters, how can you claim to have faith in our glorious
Lord Jesus Christ if you favor some people over others?

James 2:1

Favoritism creates inequality. It shows partiality toward one at the expense of the other. I've been on the receiving end of favoritism, and there's something insidious about it. You know you're in an unjust system; you just happen to be on the upside of it. You're set up to succeed, but you don't really thrive because it contradicts God's order of things. You have to posture to maintain favoritism and live in fear that you may lose it. Favoritism holds you captive to people's opinions and tempts you to overlook how others are treated. God hates favoritism. But He's all about *favor*. What's the difference? The word *favor* in the passage above speaks of showing preference due to outward circumstances. But look at the word *favor* in this passage: "Surely, Lord, you bless the righteous; you surround them with favor as with a shield" (Psalm 5:12 NIV). It translates this way: "pleasure, delight, good will."* God indiscriminately lavishes love on people. He's not impressed with wealth, status, or appearance. But He's deeply moved by faith, humility, and love. He'll never see a convicted felon as worth less than the head of a global ministry or business. He looks at the heart. And if the heart is humble and receptive, He moves in and moves mightily.

 ALIGN YOUR MIND ▶ Read James 2.

ALIGN YOUR ACTIONS ▶ Allow God to challenge your prejudices that you might see everyone as He does.

ALIGN YOUR HEART

> *Lord, forgive me for misjudging others. Give me Your heart so I can love the way You do. Amen.*

---

* Strong's Interlinear Bible Search, StudyLight.org, Psalm 5:12.

Gateway Sins

For wherever there is jealousy and selfish ambition, there you will find disorder and evil of every kind.

James 3:16

When God awakens a fresh sense of purpose in us, we feel excitement, hope, and anticipation for what He might do. Other motivations awaken within us as well: Envy, impatience, comparisons, and ambition. We're all piles of contradictions. God first ignites this sense in us, and then He takes us through a training process.* And as soon as this fresh feeling of purpose arises within us, we have a choice to make: We either trust God and lean in to His purifying, preparatory work in us, or we run ahead, try to manipulate outcomes, and posture for promotion. If you're tempted toward the latter, I pray that the passage above stops you in your tracks. Where jealousy and selfish ambition are left unchecked, the enemy is given legal access to drive a wedge between us and our God-given purpose. Note the progression described in this chapter. These sins go from being earthly, to unspiritual, to demonic. God wants to preserve His dream for you in its purest form. And the enemy wants to pervert that dream so he can dismantle your influence. Settle it in your heart that God makes you wait because He's making you ready. When the time is right, He'll put you into position in an instant, and no enemy or obstacle can stop him!

ALIGN YOUR MIND Read James 3.

ALIGN YOUR ACTIONS Ruthlessly shut down the sins of jealousy, comparison, and selfish ambition. When you're tempted to feel these things toward someone, pray for them instead.

ALIGN YOUR HEART

> *Lord, use me! Prepare me for promotion. I trust Your timing. Amen.*

* I write extensively about this in my book *Your Beautiful Purpose*.

Battle-Ready

Submit yourselves, then, to God. Resist the devil, and he will flee from you.

James 4:7 NIV

Sometimes the devil comes after you because you're about to break through. He sees your potential, is threatened by it, and aims to stop you. Other times he attacks because your progress in the faith obstructs his destructive schemes. Still other times he attacks because he sees an opening and he takes it. How do we give the devil permission to attack us? By our attitudes and sinful disobedience, such as when we undermine authority, refuse to forgive, or embrace pride. The word *submit* in the passage above is a military term and means to get back in rank. We'll never have authority until we're under authority. On our own, we're no match for the enemy. But when we stand in Christ's authority, the enemy is no match for us! If you're dealing with enemy opposition, first search your heart. Check your attitudes and get back in rank if you've stepped out from under God's protective authority. Now you're positioned to send the enemy packing. Resist the devil and he *has* to flee from you—he literally runs for his life! If we could see into the spiritual realm, we'd see some Christians cowering in fear because of enemy opposition. And in other cases, we'd see the enemy running for cover because of the Christians who've learned to stand in their authority. Stay in rank. Stand in faith. Send the enemy packing.

 ALIGN YOUR MIND Read James 4.

 ALIGN YOUR ACTIONS Keep a close watch on your heart and attitudes. Stay in rank. Pray with power.

 ALIGN YOUR HEART

> *Lord, quickly alert me the second I step out of rank. I want to live under Your authority. Amen.*

Confession, Healing, and Freedom

Confess your sins to each other and pray for each other so that you may be healed. The earnest prayer of a righteous person has great power and produces wonderful results.

James 5:16

Bob Merritt pastored one of the largest churches in America. He's one of the most humble, honest leaders I've ever met. In his book *Done with That*, he openly writes about his struggle with wielding his words in a sometimes-hurtful way. During an interview for the book, he asked me, in his relaxed, non-assuming way, "So what's your signature sin?" I paused. "I'm very present when I'm with others. I listen well," I replied, "But when I'm in task mode, I'm in a hurry. I'll rush right past people and miss them completely." And as soon as I admitted my need for more of Jesus, I felt something lift. The word *confess* in this passage means "to acknowledge openly and joyfully." Have you ever thought of confession that way? You would if you knew how loved and forgiven you already are. We all have signature sins. But you'll never be delivered from a sin that you refuse to acknowledge. Things kept in the dark keep us captive. Determine to be free. Be honest about your shortcomings. Be joyful. You have a Savior. Stay in community. Healing and freedom are yours for the taking.

ALIGN YOUR MIND ▶ Read James 5.

ALIGN YOUR ACTIONS ▶ Find a trusted friend or two—or adult—who will listen to and pray with you. Confess your sins. Pray for healing. Seek freedom.

ALIGN YOUR HEART ▶

> *Jesus, I keep forgetting how free I am! Forgive me for keeping secrets, denying sins, and hiding my needs. I want to walk confidently, fearlessly, and freely. Lead me on. Amen.*

Don't Waste Your Trials

These trials will show that your faith is genuine. It is being tested as fire tests and purifies gold—though your faith is far more precious than mere gold.

1 Peter 1:7

Every moment of our lives is packed with eternal potential. Hidden in every trial is an opportunity for faith. Every blessing comes with an invitation to be a generous steward. Every setback provides the chance to persevere and mature. We want relief. God wants to redeem. We want a break. God's after a breakthrough. Dudley Rutherford writes, "If there weren't a wall standing in your way today, how would you be able to give glory to God for the victory He wants to give you in the future? How would you be able to praise God in the sight of your friends and neighbors for providing for you, healing you, forgiving you, giving you grace, or coming through for you in the nick of time? . . . Unless we have trials and obstacles to defeat, what other opportunity would we have to cultivate our character and to increase our faith?"[*] The Bible says that when your faith remains strong through your trials, your amazing faith will be acknowledged and honored before the whole world when Jesus is revealed as the King of Kings. Don't waste your trials. God tempers the storms so they will not destroy you. He allows enough hardship to refine you. And He provides ample opportunity for your faith to reward you.

ALIGN YOUR MIND Read 1 Peter 1.

ALIGN YOUR ACTIONS By faith, look past your trial and see the eternal potential.

ALIGN YOUR HEART

> *Father, thank You for giving me everything I need to press on and overcome in Jesus' name. Amen.*

[*] Dudley Rutherford, *Walls Fall Down* (Nashville: Thomas Nelson, 2014), 25–26.

Be Tenderhearted and Humble

Finally, all of you should be of one mind. Sympathize with each other. Love each other as brothers and sisters. Be tenderhearted, and keep a humble attitude.

1 Peter 3:8

I saw an online poll asking if the media is fair to our current president. The media is *never* fair in any way. Whatever your opinion—on anything, not just politics—you'll find someone who justifies your side and villainizes the other. We fall into their trap when we believe everything they say. As Christians, we're called to maintain a heart of compassion and tenderness, of empathy and kindness, toward everyone. But that doesn't happen on its own. We must steward our perspective and be careful about which inputs we allow to shape our perspective. Since we belong to Jesus and He paid a high price for our freedom, we must identify more with Him than we do with our personal opinions. Not to say we don't have thoughts, convictions, and positions on important issues. But as I've said, if you have to let go of love to hang on to your cause, you've lost your way. Peter charges us to be tender and humble and full of empathy. He writes, "Don't retaliate with insults when people insult you. Instead, pay them back with a blessing" (v. 9). We don't have it in us to return a blessing when we're cursed, unless we allow Jesus to change us from the inside out.

ALIGN YOUR MIND ▸ Read 1 Peter 3.

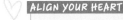 **ALIGN YOUR ACTIONS** ▸ Take a break from worldly inputs—news, social media, entertainment—and immerse yourself in the Word.

ALIGN YOUR HEART

Lord, I need a kingdom perspective. Show me what You see. Help me to live accordingly. Amen.

Use Your Gifts!

> God has given each of you a gift from his great variety of spiritual gifts. Use them well to serve one another.
>
> 1 Peter 4:10

When God gave me the desire to work in radio, a number of people told me that it would kill my "career" as a writer. They reasoned that if I spent all my time promoting others and their books, mine would never sell. But then one day a wise friend said, "Susie, you're not an author; that's something you *do*. You're a deeper-life woman and you thrive on rich, deep conversations. To me, you doing radio keeps you under the 'tent' of your calling; you're just holding a different pole." That made so much sense to me. Surprisingly, I became a better writer once I started my work in radio. It's important not to limit yourself by thinking only one way about your gifts. God is creative and loves to provide ample opportunity for you to thrive in your gifting—at any age. However, be sure to discern the difference between the opportunities before you and your God-given assignment. Seeing a need doesn't always mean you're called to it. Sometimes He'll call you to an assignment that seems small and insignificant, but hidden within is the chance for you to spread your wings and watch Him raise you up beyond your wildest dreams.

ALIGN YOUR MIND Read 1 Peter 4.

ALIGN YOUR ACTIONS No matter your age, you can embrace your gifts, grow them, and use them to bless and serve others right now. If you aren't sure what yours are, find out today!

ALIGN YOUR HEART

Lord, I love how You made me. Grow my gifts and my capacity to serve boldly and gladly! Amen.

Humble Yourself

So humble yourselves under the mighty power of God, and at the right time he will lift you up in honor. Give all your worries and cares to God, for he cares about you.

1 Peter 5:6–7

Charlotte Gambill wasn't a skier. Yet she found herself on a ski trip, taking lessons on the small hill. Thinking she was ready, she launched down a bigger hill, quickly picking up speed—and unable to slow down. As she hurtled toward a group of little children taking lessons, she noticed a tree close by. She thought, *I have to make a choice here: Personal pain or collateral damage.* So she hit the tree, got a bit banged up, but never hurt the children. There'll be times in our lives when we're faced with a similar choice. Absorb some pain or raise a ruckus because of how we're treated. We may have enough credibility to cause quite a bit of collateral damage. But what if we humbled ourselves instead? What if we entrusted our heartbreak to God, who misses nothing and deals meticulously with every situation? Scripture says that whenever we humble ourselves under God's mighty power, He'll lift us up in honor, which translates this way: "to exalt; to raise to dignity, honor and happiness."[*] God cares when you're mistreated, dismissed, or overlooked. It's beneath you to start a riot. Go to God with every bit of your angst. Watch Him intervene in ways that establish and vindicate you.

ALIGN YOUR MIND ▸ Read 1 Peter 5.

ALIGN YOUR ACTIONS ▸ Humble yourself before God today. Entrust every care to Him.

ALIGN YOUR HEART

> *Father, You don't miss a thing. I trust You. Intervene by Your power and authority. Amen.*

---

[*] Strong's Interlinear Bible Search, StudyLight.org, 1 Peter 5:6.

Power to Change

By his divine power, God has given us everything we need for living a godly life.

2 Peter 1:3

Pastor Jimmy Evans once shared how he started smoking as a young teen. Though he became a Christian in his early twenties, he continued to smoke. He'd page through his Bible and tap the ashes off his cigarette. One day the Lord spoke to him: "I want to use you in great ways, but you'll need to quit smoking." He tried and failed. Then one day he cried out to God, telling Him he didn't have the willpower to quit smoking. The Lord affirmed that he was right. He couldn't do it on his own. But by the power of the Holy Spirit, he could. The Lord said to him, "Next time you're tempted to light up, just say out loud, 'I'm a nonsmoker.' And trust me to help you." It seemed so simple, but it worked. He realized that the flesh cannot be whipped into shape. There will always be a war between the flesh and the spirit within us. But when we walk by the Spirit, we will not gratify the desires of the flesh.* The power to change comes from the power of the living, breathing, activating power of the Holy Spirit at work within us. If you're tired of striving, try abiding. Ask the Lord to give you godly desires. And He will.

 ALIGN YOUR MIND Read 2 Peter 1.

 ALIGN YOUR ACTIONS Where are your flesh and spirit at war? Ask the Holy Spirit to move in you—and trust He will.

 ALIGN YOUR HEART

Father, remove every desire that weakens me. Awaken righteous desires so that I may thrive and live free. Amen.

* See Galatians 5:16.

You Just Never Know

Yes, Lot was a righteous man who was tormented in his soul by the wickedness he saw and heard day after day.

2 Peter 2:8

I was so surprised to read that Lot was considered a righteous man—and that he was actually *tormented* in his soul over the wickedness he witnessed. He did, after all, choose to camp among the ungodly. And when he warned his family about the coming judgment, they didn't take him seriously at first. Which makes me think he'd lost some credibility with them. But I love how God sees through our circumstances and appearances, and knows intimately what's going on in the heart. Interestingly, Peter uses much of this chapter to describe false teachers. Yet he mentions Lot as one of the righteous ones. A truly false teacher willingly departs from Scripture and teaches that which is contrary to the basic cores of Christianity. Unfortunately, this accusation gets unfairly hurled around in Christian circles. We're all works in progress. I've interviewed many guests who shared how in their past, as new believers, they still actively sinned yet passionately loved God. They were in process. If someone grabbed a snapshot of that moment of their life, they'd notice the disconnect and write them off. But not God. His patience in our process is breathtaking. He sees what's true, and He will not abandon His own, no matter how messy the story or how long the process.

ALIGN YOUR MIND ▸ Read 2 Peter 2.

ALIGN YOUR ACTIONS ▸ Suspend all judgments and sincerely pray for those in whom you see a disconnect.

ALIGN YOUR HEART

Father, we live in a snap-judgment world. But I want to live and perceive differently. Open my eyes to see what You see. Amen.

A Thousand Years

> But you must not forget this one thing, dear friends: A day is like a thousand years to the Lord, and a thousand years is like a day.
>
> 2 Peter 3:8

Joni Eareckson Tada broke her neck in a diving accident as a teenager. During an interview, she shared how those days in the hospital were a blur. But once she left the hospital and moved in with her sister, the days slowed to a standstill. She felt depressed and hopeless. Then a friend came for a visit. He read her 2 Peter 3:8, and God met her in that moment. "We've all heard that a day is like a thousand years," she reflected. "But it never occurred to me that a thousand years is like a day. That means I can bear a thousand years' worth of fruit in a single day. Though I'm limited by my wheelchair, I'm not limited in prayer. How might we live differently if we truly understood the eternal potential in every day God gives us?"* What if we lived as if this was true? Would you pray with more passion? Speak with greater courage? Give generously with the assurance that God is storing up treasures in heaven just for you? Imagine if every kingdom investment you made today was multiplied a thousand times over. How might you live differently today?

 ALIGN YOUR MIND Read 2 Peter 3.

 ALIGN YOUR ACTIONS Reframe your day. Seek His kingdom first. Believe Him for great things.

 ALIGN YOUR HEART

Lord, show me my God-given assignment today. Help me to live by faith, give by faith, and walk by faith, not by sight. Multiply my offering. Amen.

* My paraphrase of my conversation with Joni.

Walking in the Light

But if we are living in the light, as God is in the light, then we have fellowship with each other, and the blood of Jesus, his Son, cleanses us from all sin.

1 John 1:7

A few days ago, we explored how the process to holiness and maturity can be messy, especially if there's a lot of heartache, brokenness, and dysfunction in someone's history. We need to be patient with the process of new believers because God has been patient with us. But here's the qualifier: Over time, there must be progress, evidence of fruit, growth in maturity. Some profess faith in Christ, then go their merry way, living no differently than before they said "the prayer." Jesus himself said that some who profess Him as Lord do not belong to Him. How do you know that you're saved? Did you sincerely repent of your sin when you first came to Christ? Are you bothered when you sin even now? Do you feel the conviction of the Holy Spirit when you step off God's path for you? Do you love God's Word? Are you drawn to the light of God's redeeming power, or do you prefer to keep things hidden in the darkness? Is there fruit coming from your life? Someone once said, "God's not after perfection. Just progress." We're saved by grace, yes. But if there's no transformation, there's no fellowship with other believers. Two people cannot walk together if they're headed in different directions.

ALIGN YOUR MIND Read 1 John 1.

ALIGN YOUR ACTIONS If you wonder about the salvation of another, ask God to overwhelm them with His saving power.

ALIGN YOUR HEART

> *Lord, bring radical, transformative salvation to every person I wonder about! Amen.*

Christians and Shame

And now, dear children, remain in fellowship with Christ so that when he returns, you will be full of courage and not shrink back from him in shame.

1 John 2:28

Shame chokes the life right out of us. Consider what's true about some of the mindsets we embrace without even thinking about it: It's not humility that compels us to shy away from God and ask little of Him—it's shame. It's not integrity that keeps us from asking for God's help when we need it—it's pride, independence, or shame. It's not kindness that keeps us from "bothering" God with our persistent requests—it's either spiritual laziness or shame.* Jesus wants to deliver us from all our shame. But here's a point we often miss. It's possible for genuine believers to shrink back in shame on that great day when we give account for our lives.† John's letter is to believers. He charges us to remain in Christ (abide, be held, kept continually) throughout our journey. God wants to reward a life lived in faith. Scripture charges us over and over to stay the course. Still, some will ignore all warnings and live solely for themselves. And when they see all God has prepared for those who took Him at His word, they will feel ashamed, sober, and regretful. Still, they'll enjoy heaven forever with Jesus. But that day of reckoning is real.

ALIGN YOUR MIND Read 1 John 2.

 ALIGN YOUR ACTIONS Ask God to remove every shred of shame from your life. Live ready with joyful expectancy.

 ALIGN YOUR HEART

> *Father, I don't want shame to rule me! Help me live a life that pleases You. Amen.*

---

* Adapted from my book *Your Powerful Prayers*, 172.
† See 2 Corinthians 5:10.

We Shall Be like Him

Dear friends, we are already God's children, but he has not yet shown us what we will be like when Christ appears. But we do know that we will be like him, for we will see him as he really is.

1 John 3:2

I've come so far in my faith journey. I don't at all resemble the person I once was. God has healed and delivered me from fear, anxiety, insecurity, and self-preservation. He's forgiven and delivered me from selfishness, striving, and jealousy. I cringe when I think of the person I used to be. But Jesus never cringes when He sees us. He pursues us with a heart full of compassion and love. I still have a long way to go in the ways of holiness. Yet I've noticed that when I focus on my frailties, that's all I see. John's letter reminds us that when we hope in the Lord, it actually purifies us. He's our life source. His oxygen energizes us. His blood cleanses us. His power redeems us. His life-giving power quickens our mortal bodies. Even though we're nowhere near the people we will one day be, Jesus treasures us just as we are. And when we finally see Jesus face to face, we'll become who we were always meant to be. Imagine! Your eyes will sparkle, your face will shine, and your heart will be healed and whole. That day is coming.

ALIGN YOUR MIND ▸ Read 1 John 3.

ALIGN YOUR ACTIONS ▸ Spend less time thinking about how you fall down, and more time thinking about how God continually holds you up.

ALIGN YOUR HEART

Father, my hope is in You! Thank You that one day I will be everything You dreamed I could be. Amen.

He Loved You First

This is real love—not that we loved God, but that he loved us and sent his Son as a sacrifice to take away our sins.

1 John 4:10

Before you were even born, God loved you first. Before you knew you were capable of sin, He sent His only Son to save you, forgive you, and totally redeem your story. Before you knew others would hurt or betray you, God promised to stay by your side. Before you knew you'd need divine direction during critical times in your life, God honored your story and spoke peace to your soul, so you'd know which way to go. Before you grasped the storms you'd have to endure, He offered His Holy Spirit to guard and guide, comfort and provide. When you decided to strive for appearance's sake, He watched and waited and loved you through it. When you got too big for your britches and thought too highly of yourself, He gently and lovingly showed you what's true. When you tripped up and fell down and friends scattered, He stayed close and loved you back to wholeness again. He loves how He made you. He loves to think about you. He loves to intervene on your behalf. And He loves what He's forming in you. He'll never look away or forget about you. He'll never lose your address. And He'll never be surprised by you. He knew who He was getting when He got you. He absolutely, unequivocally loved you first.

ALIGN YOUR MIND Read 1 John 4.

ALIGN YOUR ACTIONS Smile today as you ponder God's great, unfathomable love for you.

ALIGN YOUR HEART

Father, how can it be? Help me to grasp Your affection for me. I receive it and believe it. Amen.

Confident Prayer

And we are confident that he hears us whenever we ask for anything that pleases him. And since we know he hears us when we make our requests, we also know that he will give us what we ask for.

1 John 5:15

My husband was a workaholic. I missed him. And I wanted better for our family. He worked for a company that was life-draining, and it deeply impacted all of us. Still, he was a gentle giant of a man who loved God and his family. He just had this overdeveloped work ethic and couldn't seem to stop striving in a no-win situation. I believed with my whole heart that God had a better plan than the one we were living. So I went to the mat and prayed like I'd never prayed before. *Lord, I know You want more for our family. You said that if I pray Your will, I can know that I will have that which I ask for, so I'm thanking You now, ahead of time, for moving heaven and earth if You have to, to give my husband a new job and a new perspective on his work life. Do a mighty work in our family, Lord!* I prayed morning, noon, and night. God answered that prayer beyond anything I could have hoped for. God wants wholeness, redemption, and restoration in your story. If you don't have it, this promise gives you biblical grounds for passionate and confident prayer. What are you waiting for?

ALIGN YOUR MIND Read 1 John 5.

ALIGN YOUR ACTIONS Pray this promise with humble, bold confidence and see what God will do.

ALIGN YOUR HEART

Lord, You are a promise-maker and a promise-keeper. I trust You! Hear my prayer today. . . .

Your Full Reward

> Watch out that you do not lose what we have worked so hard to achieve. Be diligent so that you receive your full reward.
>
> 2 John 1:8

Scripture charges us time and again to guard what has been entrusted to us. John encourages us to be diligent about our faith journey so that we'll receive our full reward. Other translations of the verse above read, "what *you* have worked so hard to achieve." This passage shows how intermingled our lives really are. You've invested in other believers and they've invested in you. But what you do with what's been entrusted to you will determine your reward on Judgment Day. Eternity may seem far away, but your future rewards depend on what you do *now*—not just when you're older or further along in your faith journey. Every act of faith, prayer of intercession, and investment you make in others throughout your life is recorded. He rewards you for guarding all that He's sown into you for His kingdom's sake. Remember the parable of the soils?* Sometimes the Word lands on shallow, distracted, or unguarded hearts, and the enemy snatches it away before it has a chance to sprout. That's a loss for the kingdom, and that's on us. If the devil can't have your soul, he'll do everything he can to destroy your influence and rob you of your future reward—no matter your age. May your relationship with Jesus be your highest aim and top priority.

ALIGN YOUR MIND Read 2 John.

ALIGN YOUR ACTIONS Live as though what you do now matters in eternity. Spend some extra time with Jesus today.

ALIGN YOUR HEART

> *Lord, show me how to guard all You've entrusted to me so I can finish strong. Amen.*

* See Matthew 13.

Healthy in Body, Strong in Spirit

> Dear friend, I hope all is well with you and that you are as healthy in body as you are strong in spirit.
>
> 3 John 1:2

I spoke with a woman the other day who struggled with her weight. She shared about the judgmental, self-righteous atmosphere in which she was raised. "Of course the acceptable sin was gluttony," she said. "So we always ate too much, and all of the wrong things, but we sure were righteous and spotted sinners a mile away." This dear woman's soul shriveled under such influence. What happens in our soul, happens in our cells.* We will not flourish in mind, body, and spirit if we're out of whack in even one of these areas. Thankfully, Jesus stands before us with tender eyes and a kind heart and asks, "Do you want to be well?" If we answer yes, He will lead us into truth that sets us free. True flourishing comes when we care for our health, guard our mind, and feed our spirit on the things of God. He's wired us to thrive. Some of our wholeness we'll not know until we see Jesus, but far too many Christians settle for far less than they should because they don't want to make the necessary changes. Listen for Jesus' kind voice today and do what He says. He'll teach you how to flourish.

ALIGN YOUR MIND ▶ Read 3 John.

ALIGN YOUR ACTIONS ▶ Ask the Lord for wisdom, and then implement a new discipline so you can flourish.

ALIGN YOUR HEART

> Lord, I want to flourish! Give me a heart for all that's good for me! Heal me, restore me, and strengthen me! Amen.

---

* See my book *Fully Alive* for more on this teaching.

To the One Who Will Keep You

Now all glory to God, who is able to keep you from falling away and will bring you with great joy into his glorious presence without a single fault. All glory to him who alone is God, our Savior through Jesus Christ our Lord.

Jude 1:24–25

I've seen many key leaders fall away. Each time, I shiver in my bones and think, *But for the grace of God, that could be me.* One season I actually experienced visceral, unreasonable fear that I'd fall down and bring dishonor to my family. I wasn't secretly living in sin. I hadn't taken a doctrinal turn. And I wasn't all of a sudden breaking any laws. But the fear? Well, it made me constantly self-aware and insecure. But then I remembered this passage from Jude and my heart came alive. I began to pray it with boldness, thanksgiving, and conviction. The more I declared this promise, the more courage rose up within me. And interestingly, significant new doors of opportunity opened up after I prevailed through that battle. The devil doesn't know our future, but he sure sees our potential. If you're walking through a similar season and you second-guess yourself at every turn, remember who you are. Shut down the enemy's taunts and hang on to God's promises. God is likely getting you ready for a new place of promise. Your God-given purpose is a direct threat to the enemy's plan. God's got you. He'll keep you. Stay in step with Him.

 ALIGN YOUR MIND ▸ Read Jude.

 ALIGN YOUR ACTIONS ▸ Pray this passage several times (out loud) and allow God's power to strengthen you from within.

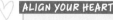 **ALIGN YOUR HEART** ▸

Jesus, I cling to You! Thank You for Your faithfulness to me. Amen.

Don't Be Afraid!

When I saw him, I fell at his feet as if I were dead. But he laid his right hand on me and said, "Don't be afraid! I am the First and the Last."

Revelation 1:17

John was worshiping in the Spirit when suddenly he heard a loud voice. He turned around and saw Jesus. He wore a long robe and a gold sash. His head and hair were white as snow. His eyes like flames of fire. His voice thundered like the ocean. John fell down like a dead man. We would too. We've grown so accustomed to a life without signs and wonders, to being present at church without a sense of God's tangible presence, that we cannot imagine anything else. But if Jesus came today in all of His glory, we'd be perfectly undone. While John's face was in the dirt, Jesus touched his shoulder and said, "Don't be afraid! I am the First and the Last." The word *first* translates: "first in rank, influence and honor." The word *last* translates: "last in rank, last man, lowest, last in time or place."* Jesus is the First. It all started with Him. And it'll end with Him. He's the Last. He humbled himself to the lowest place so we could reign with Him. He's at the front of the line leading us home, and at the back of the line, protecting us every step of the way. We have nothing to fear.

ALIGN YOUR MIND ▶ Read Revelation 1.

ALIGN YOUR ACTIONS ▶ Write out a prayer of wonder, awe, and thanksgiving for who Jesus is and all He's done.

ALIGN YOUR HEART

Jesus, I have nothing to fear in You! I worship You! Amen.

* Strong's Interlinear Bible Search, StudyLight.org, Revelation 1:17.

Your First Love

"However, I have this against you: you have abandoned your first love."
Revelation 2:4 VOICE

The large, established church of Ephesus got a lot of things right. They worked hard and served tirelessly. They guarded their doctrine and refused to normalize sexual sin. But they lost their pulse. God's love no longer tenderized their hearts. Their love for others waned. Plenty of Christians, churches, and ministries today have the same problem. They appear put together, but a closer look reveals that they're overworked and completely under-joyed. They're no longer moved by acts of God, no longer undone by a sunset, a baby's birth, or a life restored. They move so fast that they've forgotten why they do what they do. Hard work has replaced passionate, grateful worship. Dr. Warren Wiersbe writes, "The Ephesian believers were so busy maintaining their separation that they were neglecting adoration. Labor is no substitute for love; neither is purity a substitute for passion. The church must have both if it is to please Him. The church that loses its love will soon lose its light, no matter how doctrinally sound it may be."[*] What was the Spirit's response? Look how far you've fallen. Repent. Or you will lose your influence. Return to your First Love. We're nothing but noise without His love.[†]

 ALIGN YOUR MIND Read Revelation 2.

ALIGN YOUR ACTIONS Has hard work replaced passionate, grateful worship? Has doctrine become more important than love? Repent and reconnect with the One your soul loves.

 ALIGN YOUR HEART

> *Lord, I can so often lose my way. Keep me close to You. I love You, Lord. You're everything to me. Amen.*

---

[*] *Wiersbe Bible Commentary*, 1041.
[†] See 1 Corinthians 13.

The Dead Church

"I know all the things you do, and that you have a reputation for being alive—but you are dead. Wake up! Strengthen what little remains, for even what is left is almost dead."

Revelation 3:1–2

The church of Sardis was all show and no go. They *appeared* successful but they were dead. They no longer cared about the lost or the hurting or the broken. "The church was also told to wake up. Their wealth and comfort had lulled them to sleep. Their self-satisfaction caused them to die spiritually."* "Sardis was a church of lifeless profession. It had a reputation as a Christian assembly, but for the most part, it simply went through a formal, dull routine. It did not overflow with spiritual life. It did not sparkle with the supernatural."† It's interesting that the Spirit had nothing good to say about this church save for the small remnant of believers who kept themselves pure and alive and awake to the things of God. Most every church has a remnant of fiery believers who accomplish more from their hidden place of prayer than the world could ever know. If you're a part of a lifeless church or youth group, seek the Lord. He'll either call you to hold your ground and intercede, or He'll release you to find a life-giving body of believers.

ALIGN YOUR MIND Read Revelation 3:1–13.

ALIGN YOUR ACTIONS Have your blessings and comforts lulled you into complacency? How can you stay awake and engaged in your faith? Don't just go through the motions.

ALIGN YOUR HEART

Lord, awaken me! Keep my heart humble, tender, and vigilant. Help me cultivate gratitude so I don't drift into complacency. Amen.

* *Life Application Study Bible*, 2846.
† *Believer's Bible Commentary*, 2358.

The Lukewarm Church

"I know all the things you do, that you are neither hot nor cold. I wish that you were one or the other!"

Revelation 3:15

They say that anger is not the most destructive emotion in a relationship. Apathy is. I once knew a woman who "fell out of love" with her husband and children. She broke their hearts and didn't care. She didn't move out because she wanted the benefits of her husband's provision but not the responsibility of being his wife. Her husband wept bitter tears, begged and pleaded for some kind of response from her. She shrugged her shoulders and simply disengaged. The church of Laodicea had a similar problem. Self-absorbed and impotent, they simply didn't care. "By neglecting to do anything for Christ, the church had become hardened and self-satisfied, and it was destroying itself."* The worst thing about the church of Laodicea was how blind and naked they were. They were rich so they thought they were fine. They'd so blended with the world, they no longer influenced culture. Their gatherings lacked substance, power, and life change. They shrugged their shoulders over injustice, looked away from the lost, and enjoyed their wealth and comfort. Because of their spiritual impotence, nothing happened in the spiritual realm. Jesus gave everything to bring us into His family. He saved us from sin and death. He wants a bride that loves Him, serves Him, and enjoys life with Him. Why wouldn't we respond?

 ALIGN YOUR MIND ▸ Read Revelation 3:14–22.

 ALIGN YOUR ACTIONS ▸ Ask God if you've become lukewarm about anything that's important to Him.

 ALIGN YOUR HEART ▸

Father, ignite my heart once again! I am Yours and You are mine. Your banner over me is love. Amen.

* *Life Application Study Bible*, 2847.

The Throne of God

From the throne came flashes of lightning and the rumble of thunder. And in front of the throne were seven torches with burning flames. This is the sevenfold Spirit of God. In front of the throne was a shiny sea of glass, sparkling like crystal.

Revelation 4:5–6

God opened John's eyes to the heavenly realm and showed him the very throne of God. One day our eyes will behold Him and we'll be changed in an instant. We'll enter into the most powerful, pure worship we've ever experienced—worship that's in motion even now. No matter how vast our imagination, we're not at all prepared for what we will one day see and experience. Still, God invites us to worship Him now, by faith, because He is greater than our minds can conceive. He who spoke the galaxies into reality without lifting a finger delights in you. He loves you. He even likes you. Grasping His love will heal your soul. And yet some have become so chummy with God, they've forgotten about His holiness and the sheer power that emanates from His throne. Even now, today, whenever the living beings give glory and honor and thanks to the One on the throne, the twenty-four elders fall down and worship Him. They lay their crowns before Him and say, "You are worthy to receive glory and honor and power." Seek God daily. Run to Him gladly. But always remember who it is you're speaking to when you approach His throne.

ALIGN YOUR MIND Read Revelation 4.

ALIGN YOUR ACTIONS Look for some new worship music that ignites powerful, humble, heartfelt worship.

ALIGN YOUR HEART

God in heaven, You deserve all of the power, glory, and honor! You are God Most High! Amen.

The Lion of Judah

"Stop weeping! Look, the Lion of the tribe of Judah, the heir to David's throne, has won the victory. He is worthy to open the scroll and its seven seals."

Revelation 5:5

John saw a scroll that would reveal God's ultimate plan to destroy evil and to redeem those who trust in Christ Jesus. No one was worthy to open the scroll. John wept bitterly. He longed to see God's plan unfold and be put in motion. Imagine that jarring moment when the angel told John that the Lion of Judah, Jesus our Lord, was the only One worthy to open the scroll. He's the only One who left heaven and entered into humanity's plight. The only One who died our death. The only One who faced off with the devil himself and dismantled his power over us. He did all of this with a pure heart and a victorious spirit. He is King. He has no rival. And He'll finish what He started. Once the seals open up, terrible judgments will be unleashed on the earth. There are varying and equally respected views on whether or not the Church will be raptured (taken up) when all of this takes place. But one thing we know for sure: God's purposes will prevail. No one and nothing can snatch us out of His hand. What we suffer now is nothing compared to the glory that awaits us at the culmination of time. Our Lion roars a holy roar, and He is coming for His Church.

ALIGN YOUR MIND ▸ Read Revelation 5.

 ALIGN YOUR ACTIONS ▸ How can you, even now, live ready for Jesus' return?

 ALIGN YOUR HEART ▸

Lion of Judah, help me to live ready for Your soon return. My soul waits for You. Amen.

They Overcame

> "And they have defeated him by the blood of the Lamb
>   and by their testimony.
> And they did not love their lives so much
>   that they were afraid to die."
>
> Revelation 12:11

Jesus intends for us to overcome because He overcame. The blood of Jesus forgives and cleanses us and secures our eternity. The word of our testimony activates the spiritual realm and adds momentum to the kingdom story God is writing on the earth. The blood saves us. Our testimony activates us. And when we love Jesus more than our very lives, when we see our eternity as so precious that we'd give our earthly lives in whatever way He asks of us, there's nothing that the enemy can do to us. We render him powerless. We become overcomers. It's fear that keeps us under his thumb. It's self-preservation and love of comfort that render us powerless against him. But when we truly see that we're more spiritual than physical, more found than lost, more equipped than vulnerable, we'll dare to follow Jesus wherever He leads us. Amazingly, if you ask persecuted Christians how you might pray for them, you'll never hear them say, "Pray for an easier life. Pray I can move to a safer country." They say, "Pray I'll have the courage to endure for the cause of Christ." You may not have to die for your faith, but Jesus may ask you to stand up in a way that costs you. And He does ask us to pray regularly for our persecuted brothers and sisters.

ALIGN YOUR MIND ▶ Read Revelation 12.

ALIGN YOUR ACTIONS ▶ Add the persecuted church to your regular prayer list.

ALIGN YOUR HEART

> *Father, awaken courage and boldness within me! I will overcome when I fully trust You! Amen.*

The Great Divide
Has Already Begun

"Fear God," he shouted. "Give glory to him. For the time has come when he will sit as judge. Worship him who made the heavens, the earth, the sea, and all the springs of water."

Revelation 14:7

During the great tribulation, the enemy will seem to have free rein. God will give him authority to unleash evil for forty-two months. Sinfulness will abound. People will blaspheme our Lord in the most abhorrent ways. Those who love the world and reject God will be easily deceived when they see how the Beast's fatal head wound miraculously heals. God charges His own to endure persecution patiently and to remain faithful. Because suddenly, the tide will turn. John saw a vision of the Lamb standing on Mount Zion with the 144,000 who bear the Lord's name on their foreheads. Sounds from heaven will thunder over the earth. A great choir will sing a new song before the throne of God. John witnessed a glassy sea mixed with fire. Seven plagues will be unleashed upon the earth. This will bring to completion God's wrath against wickedness. Even now, the earth is shaking, and the divide is evident between those who fear God and those who revile Him. God is purifying His Bride, getting her ready for that great day. Know that every past trial has trained you to stand in this day as we speed toward that day.

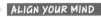 **ALIGN YOUR MIND** ▶ Read Revelation 14.

 ALIGN YOUR ACTIONS ▶ What distracts you from pursuing God and loving Him wholeheartedly? Rid your life of those things.

 ALIGN YOUR HEART

Father, I fear I'm not strong enough to stand in such days, but I know You are good and care deeply for me. Fill me with conviction, courage, and clarity. Amen.

No Middle Ground

> "Who will not fear you, Lord,
>   and glorify your name?
>   For you alone are holy.
> All nations will come and worship before you,
>   for your righteous deeds have been revealed."
>
> Revelation 15:4

In another vision, John saw that the temple in heaven was thrown wide open. The seven angels who were holding the seven plagues came out of the temple. They wore white, spotless linen with gold sashes across their chests. They were given authority to pour out God's final wrath on the earth. The temple was filled with smoke from God's glory and power. No one could enter the temple until the seven angels had completed pouring out the seven plagues. "The fact that no one can enter the temple till these seven plagues are completed may mean that no priestly intercession can now delay God's wrath."* Throughout history, God has made sure that anyone who truly wants to know Him will find Him. During the great tribulation, there will be no middle ground. All people will be marked, either with the Lord's name or with the mark of the Beast. Some will sacrifice all to follow Jesus. Others will sacrifice nothing and lose everything. God's been patient with mankind. He wants none to perish. Ultimately, everyone will get what they choose: life forever with Christ, or life forever without Him. Things may get worse before they get better for us as Christians. But a glorious eternity awaits us.

ALIGN YOUR MIND Read Revelation 15.

ALIGN YOUR ACTIONS You're totally secure in God. How can you send your roots down deeper into the soil of His marvelous love?

ALIGN YOUR HEART

Jesus, be glorified in my life. I need You every hour. Amen.

* Believer's Bible Commentary, 2373.

King of All Kings

On his robe at his thigh was written this title: King of all kings and Lord of all lords.

Revelation 19:16

Jesus stepped off His throne and entered our world by crawling into the womb of a teenage girl. He was born into poverty. Lived a humble life. He subjected himself to our trials, temptations, and troubles. He stayed out of the public eye but grew up under God's watchful eye. He first entered public ministry by going into the waters of baptism. Baptism was for sinners who longed to be forgiven and cleansed. He never sinned, yet in every way, entered into our plight with us. He put up with relentless harassment and disrespect. He didn't back down from religious bullies. He willingly associated with the lowliest of sinners. He noticed the ones the rest of the world missed. He died a criminal's death. It appeared as though the world shook Him like a ragdoll when He bled out on that cross. Yet in all of it, He was still God, still King, still the Savior of the world. People had, and still have, varying opinions about who He is. But a day is coming . . . He will ride His white horse with fire in His eyes and many crowns on His head. Everyone, dead and alive, will acknowledge Him as King of the world. Holy, holy, holy is the Lord Almighty, who was and is and is to come!

ALIGN YOUR MIND Read Revelation 19.

ALIGN YOUR ACTIONS In what areas do you still need to acknowledge Jesus as King? Do it today.

ALIGN YOUR HEART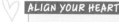

> *Jesus, You stayed the course, all the way to the cross, all for love. I give You my highest praise and heartfelt worship. Amen.*

The Books Will Open

I saw the dead, both great and small, standing before God's throne. And the books were opened, including the Book of Life. And the dead were judged according to what they had done, as recorded in the books.

Revelation 20:12

People hold God to a double standard. They blame Him for the evil in the world and dismiss Him for His wrath. People want a passive, gooey god that allows them to do anything they want, a god that deals with anyone who infringes upon their idea of what life should look like. God's ways are far higher than our ways. He is a God of love and a God of justice. His involvement is purposeful and His timing, meticulous. And He keeps good records. The murderer who rejected Christ will have more hell to pay than the guy who cheated his way through school. Just as there are levels of reward in heaven, there are levels of punishment in hell.* Those who have decided to live their lives the way they want will face the great white throne of judgment. They'll face God's wrath with no one to advocate for them. Eternal punishment awaits them. Christians will go before the judgment seat. God's forgiven our sin, but He's recorded our deeds, not for punishment but for reward. No one is exempt from Judgment Day. Don't waste a minute of your life. Steward your gifts with passion and purpose. God cares deeply about what you do and why you do it.

ALIGN YOUR MIND Read Revelation 20.

ALIGN YOUR ACTIONS Think eternity. Today. Tomorrow. And the next day.

ALIGN YOUR HEART

Lord, I want every minute of my life to count for You! Draw me closer still! Amen.

* See Matthew 11:20–24; Luke 12:47–48.

The New Jerusalem

And I saw the holy city, the new Jerusalem, coming down from God out of heaven like a bride beautifully dressed for her husband.

Revelation 21:2

After God deals a final death blow to the enemy of our souls, we'll behold the holy city, the new Jerusalem, as it descends from heaven, dressed like a glorious bride prepared for her husband. "The new Jerusalem is where God lives among His people. Instead of our going up to meet Him, He comes down to be with us, just as God became man in Jesus Christ and lived among us (John 1:14). Wherever God reigns, there is peace, security, and love."* In his vision, John witnessed the rise of Satan, the suffering of the saints, the wrath of God. Finally, he gets to see God's glorious plan for His people. God himself will wipe away every tear from our eyes. There'll be no more death or sorrow or crying or pain. Gone forever. God will make all things new. Brand new. We will drink freely from the springs of life. Every ounce of us will be satisfied. Our joy, uncontainable. Our hearts, healed. We'll experience a sensory explosion. We'll inhale scents that take our breath away. We cannot fathom the beautiful future that awaits us. But we can look forward to it with great expectation. God does not lie. Jesus is getting ready, preparing a place for us. Heaven awaits us.

ALIGN YOUR MIND Read Revelation 21.

ALIGN YOUR ACTIONS Try to imagine heaven. Jesus is right now preparing a place for you.

ALIGN YOUR HEART

> *Jesus, thank You for preparing a place for me. You have my heart forever. Amen.*

* *Life Application Study Bible*, 2881.

Jesus Is Coming Soon

"Look, I am coming soon, bringing my reward with me to repay all people according to their deeds. I am the Alpha and the Omega, the First and the Last, the Beginning and the End."

Revelation 22:12–13

He put the galaxies in place. Told the land where to stop and the water where to begin. Created birds to fly and fish to swim. Instituted the dawn of each day. He loves His creation. He especially loves us, for we bear His image. The Bible is God's grand love story to a sinful, wayward, broken people. All of the Old Testament points to the coming of the Messiah, our Savior. All of the New Testament testifies to His life, death, and resurrection. Jesus teaches us how to live—and love. God's love story culminates with this epic declaration: *I am coming soon.* Here's the beautiful truth: *You* are a part of this supernatural story. The living, breathing Word of God has a way of sinking deep into your soul and transforming your life. God's plans for you are found in the pages of His Book. We've walked through the Bible together and it's quite clear: God wants an intimate, thriving relationship with you. His Spirit is alive in you. So steward your story well. Love people but keep your hope in God. Keep your faith alive. Keep your heart engaged. Live for the One who gave it all for you. The King is coming again.

ALIGN YOUR MIND Read Revelation 22.

ALIGN YOUR ACTIONS Live for Jesus like He's coming back tomorrow.

ALIGN YOUR HEART

King of Kings, help me live as one who is spoken for. Give me boldness, courage, conviction, and love. Work miracles in and through me. I'm waiting for You. Amen.

Acknowledgments

To Andy McGuire and the Bethany House Team ~
Such an honor to serve with you.
Thank you for all you do for the kingdom.
Thanks for your help on this project.

To my friend Carra Carr ~
Thank you for sharing your brilliance
and lending your talents to this project.
We love and appreciate you so!

To my beloved sons, daughters-in-love, and grandchildren ~
You're ever and always on my heart and in my prayers.
Couldn't love you more if I tried.
May the love of Jesus become more tangible
to you with each new day.

To my amazing husband, Kev ~
Your love has made God's love so tangible to me.
Walking with you in life and partnering with you
in ministry is one of my greatest honors. Love you, honey.
Thank you for honoring God with your whole life.
It's for sure changed mine.

Susie Larson is a popular radio talk show host, national speaker, and bestselling author. Author of twenty-two books, Susie is also a veteran in the fitness field and has twice been voted top-ten finalist for the *John C. Maxwell Transformational Leadership Award*. Susie and her husband live near Minneapolis with their three sons, three daughters-in-law, a growing bunch of grandchildren, and a golden mountain doodle pup named Bella-Joy. Susie's passion is to see people everywhere awakened to the value of their souls, the depth of God's love, and the height of their calling in Christ Jesus. Learn more at SusieLarson.com.

Connect with Susie:

SusieLarson.com

 @susielarsonauthor

 @susielarsonauthor

 @SusieLarson